KEEPING UP

MICHAEL BATES: THE STORY OF A SPECIALIST WICKETKEEPER

MICHAEL BATES AND TOM HUELIN

Copyright © Michael Bates and Tom Huelin, 2019

All rights reserved

Independently published

ISBN-13: 9781090420169

Contents

	About the author	4
	Foreword by George Dobell	5
	Introduction: A history of wicketkeeping	7
	Acknowledgements	13
	Prologue: Wicketkeeping – a view from the middle	15
1.	The boy Bates	32
2.	England pathway	44
3.	Breaking into the Hampshire first team	63
4.	Skeg	77
5.	A wicketkeeping masterclass	86
6.	First-choice keeper	107
7.	Lords 2012	128
8.	Wheater	139
9.	Dealing with batting failure	149
10.	Fighting for my career	162
11.	Finding another county	176
12.	Life after cricket	189
13.	Adam Gilchrist	198
14.	Coaching	210
15.	Glory days are here again	222
	Epilogue	237

About the author

Tom Huelin was born in Jersey and now lives with his wife and two children in Southampton, a stone's throw away from the Ageas Bowl, the home of Hampshire CCC. Tom is a freelance writer and author with a passion for sport and music. In 2010 he started a cricket blog so good he can't even remember the name of it. Miraculously, the blog opened doors which would see his work appearing in the *Guardian*, *ESPNCricinfo* and *All Out Cricket*. From 2012, Tom was Hampshire correspondent for *Deep Extra Cover*, the county cricket website, where Tom penned – well, typed – match reports and news stories. His passion, though, was to interview players and tell their stories, a passion that led to him writing features on England internationals Chris Jordan and Moeen Ali, among others.

Foreword by George Dobell

If there was one moment that proved the value of a top-class wicketkeeper, it came from the final ball of the CB40 final at Lord's in September 2012. With Warwickshire needing one to win, Michael Bates' immaculate take – standing up to Kabir Ali – sealed the game. Where many keepers would have lacked the skill – and as a result, the confidence – to come up to the stumps to a bowler of Kabir's pace, Michael not only did so but made light of a tricky take (Kabir's attempt to deliver a yorker resulted in a low full-toss) to take the bails off in an instant. It was a classy moment that sealed a big match.

It was no freak, either. Only an over or so before, Michael had taken a leg-side wide standing up to Chris Wood's medium pace. He did it so neatly and unobtrusively that it gained little attention and few plaudits. But it was a brilliant piece of skill that was to prove vital in a match that finished with the scores level. Another keeper might easily have seen that single wide become five wides.

It was a similar story a couple of weeks earlier when Hampshire played Yorkshire in the T20 final in Cardiff. On this occasion, there was no moment that would necessarily have made a highlights package – no outrageous catch or lightning-fast stumping – but Michael's ability to stand up to the stumps throughout the Yorkshire innings would have played on the mind of the batsmen and made them less willing to come down the pitch to the bowlers. Even when he wasn't directly affecting the game with a dismissal, he was helping his bowlers by reducing the batsmen's options.

That skill – standing or keeping up to the stumps to the seamers in limited-overs cricket – used to be seen an essential part of the wicketkeeper's job. Think of the Gloucestershire and Warwickshire sides that enjoyed such limited-overs success from the mid-1990s to the early years of this century. It's no coincidence that their keepers (Jack Russell and Keith Piper respectively) were so proficient standing up to the stumps.

Now compare all this to the final over of the 2010 T20 final between Hampshire and Somerset. On that occasion, Somerset's keeper, Craig Kieswetter, only came up to the stumps for the final ball of the match. But by then, Hampshire had already stolen two byes in the final over. Again, in a match that finished with the scores level, those two byes proved vital and Hampshire went on to win. A keeper of Michael's ability would not have allowed them and might well have changed the result.

So, why are brilliant keepers not valued more highly? Well, keeping is only one part – a large part, admittedly – of the job. And, earlier in that 2010 final, Kieswetter had thumped 71 – the highest score of the game – to give his side a chance of victory. As a destructive batsman, he will also be remembered for winning the man of the match award in the 2010 World T20 final after making 63 that went a long way towards helping England claim their first global limited-overs trophy. The fact he dropped Shane Watson in the game's opening over is often overlooked: Graeme Swann caught the rebound and the error went unpunished. On such moments trophies and reputations are decided.

So there is no clear formula to ascertain when a player's poor keeping outweighs the strength of his batting or vice-versa. But, as you read this compelling book, you may well feel the balance has swung too far towards batting ability and that keepers are often the scapegoats for failings – particularly batting failings – elsewhere in the team. As Nic Pothas puts it so eloquently, if you can't fit your diamond into your jewellery fitting, you don't throw away the diamond. It remains a shame and a waste that a diamond like Michael is not currently enjoying a career as a professional cricketer.

There's another side to all this. Professional sport is a seductive beast. It lures in the young with whispered promises of glory and spits them out broken in body and mind. For every career that ends in an Alastair Cook-style fairytale, there are 10,000 more that end on a physio's bench or in an uncomfortable meeting in a director of cricket's office. If a cricketer as talented as Michael – and it's no exaggeration to suggest he was probably in the top 10 exponents of his art in the world at the time of his release from Hampshire – struggles to make a living from playing the sport, it should send warning signals to all young people considering pursuing a career in it. The MCCU scheme – whereby young people can further their cricketing ambitions while gaining more formal educational qualifications – remains immensely valuable.

Michael, at least, appears to have found another way. As a coach, all his experiences – the bad perhaps more than the good – can be harnessed to help the next generation along the way. He has a fascinating story and it's been very well told by Tom Huelin. But I can't help thinking that, aged only 28, he should still be out there as a player.

Introduction: A history of wicketkeeping

Your colleague's out. You're in. You pick up your bat and walk out of the dressing room, down the stairs and onto the lush green outfield. Adrenaline is pumping through your veins, "I have to deliver", you tell yourself.

A smattering of fans from the opposing team are scattered around the sparsely filled cricket ground. They're well oiled from an afternoon supping ale in the sun. They're giving you plenty of stick as you walk to the middle. "You're rubbish. You'll be out before tea time, mate!"

You pass your dismissed team mate, who's trudging off back to the pavilion you've just left. His head's facing the floor, his fist punching his bat. He played a loose shot, edged the ball behind and the wicketkeeper did the rest. Your team are in trouble. You're 154-7 having won the toss and decided to bat first. You talk to your batting partner down the other end. "The ball's moving around a bit, just try to see it through to tea. 15 minutes."

You head down to your end. You're on strike. Your face is as white as your clothes, or at least it feels that way. You ask the umpire for a middle-and-leg guard. You know the bowler's getting a bit of movement, so you stand a fraction outside your crease, so you can get closer to the pitch of the ball. The keeper, buzzing after his catch the ball before, is in your ear. The slips are chirping too. You look at the clock on the scoreboard down the Nursery Ground end – 14 minutes 'til tea.

You drag your foot down the middle-and-leg line the umpire's given you. You look out to see where the fielders are. There's a couple more slips than there were the previous ball, when you were still watching back on the balcony. They fancy this. They fancy you to edge it, the ball flying to the slips, to the keeper. "Watch the ball", you tell yourself. "Watch the ball".

***

You're coming on to bowl. The opposing team's openers have taken your two main bowlers apart. 57-0 off four overs. It's your first T20 game of the season – you only play white-ball cricket, so you've been playing in the seconds so far this summer. Now the TV cameras are here, the stands are a darn sight fuller and the pressure is on.

You set your field. You want a bit more protection on the leg side in case you stray a bit. Your skipper wants an off-side line. You've got to be accurate. You're not sure about your keeper. The previous one was rock solid behind the stumps – kept up to your medium-quick bowling, piling pressure onto the batters and mopping up anything loose you sent down.

But the club have brought a new guy in this season. He can bat a bit, but that doesn't help you right now. You need a keeper who's going to cling onto everything – is this guy going to cling onto everything? You're not sure.

Your field's set. you're at the top of your run. You look at the scoreboard. 57-0 – this has to be on the money – you have to claw this game back for your team.

* * *

It's the last over of the game. They need six runs to win the trophy. The skipper runs up to you. "We need you to keep up to the stumps." The bowler throws it down at a decent clip. Mid-80s mph or thereabouts. You're comfortable you can deal with that. You've trained all your life for this.

The skipper is running here, there and everywhere, fiddling with the field so that it's just right for the final six balls. The game could be over in one hit.

You look around – the crowd is buzzing. Your teammates, the batsmen, they're all tense. There's not a lot of chat. Everyone's focusing on what they've got to do.

You get the helmet on. The bowler's at the end of his run. You crouch down. A million things could happen, but your mind's blank. You want it that way. You want to react to what happens, not have any preconceptions of what might occur. You're set. You're ready to move any which way, depending on where the bowler puts it, or where the ball comes off the bat. The bowler runs in...

* * *

Cricket – a team game made up of a series of individual battles. Moments of complete isolation, interspersed with joyful moments as a team.

I'm Michael Bates, and I was a wicketkeeper at Hampshire between 2010 and 2014. I started playing cricket when I was seven and played all the way through the age groups with Hampshire's academy as well as England's age groups, before signing for my home county as a pro at the age of just 19.

I'm not an arrogant person, but it's fair to say I've had a fair bit of support from fans and in the media over the years. People have said, and written, that I was one of the best specialist wicketkeepers to play county cricket in modern times. Yet I retired in 2015 aged just 24 having been released from Hampshire, and then from Somerset.

Why was I released? Well that's a good question. My keeping was clearly rated, but my batting clearly wasn't. In *Keeping Up* I'll tell you about my progress through the youth cricket system, and how I was considered the best keeper in my age group in England for most of my teenage years. And how all of that, unfortunately, ultimately counted for nothing.

There are a variety of reason for that, which we'll explore in due course. First, it's important to recognise my place as a specialist wicketkeeper within the wider context of keeping. Wicketkeepers have such a pivotal role to play in a team, a bit like a goalkeeper in football. And the performance of a keeper can have a huge bearing on the success, or otherwise, of the team he or she is playing for.

At the time of writing, England have capped 67 wicketkeepers in Test cricket, the most recent of whom was Surrey gloveman Ben Foakes, who made his debut in the 2018 series against Sri Lanka. Ben is an out-and-out keeper, and a class act behind the stumps. That's nothing against Jonny Bairstow or Jos Buttler, who have both developed admirably as keepers. However, Foakes is a specialist, in the same mould as me I guess you could say.

The most successful English gloveman – purely in a wicketkeeping context, not including his batting at this stage – was Alan Knott, who finished his career having effected 269 dismissals. Alan played Test cricket between 1967 and 1981, an interesting time span as he played both before and after the advent of limited-overs cricket.

And that's a really important landmark in the history of wicketkeeping, as we'll discuss throughout this book. Limited-overs cricket changed the game. I mean, that statement's a bit of a misnomer; obviously it changed the game as it brought about a new format. But it changed players, teams, coaches and, ultimately, fans' expectations when it came to Test cricket. People got used to seeing more runs, scored quickly, and wanted that in Tests as well as one-dayers.

That first one-day international took place on 5 January 1971 at the Melbourne Cricket Ground between Australia and England. The teams were in the midst of a fiercely contested Ashes series when the first three days of the third Test were washed out by rain. So the sides agreed to play a one-off, one-day game consisting of 40 eight-ball overs a side.

"This was the point the wicketkeeping role significantly changed," Adam Gilchrist, widely considered the greatest wicketkeeper of modern times, told me when I spoke to him in 2017 for *Keeping Up*. "There's a limited amount of deliveries that a batting team can score runs from. Therefore, all of a sudden, the whole XI become accountable to contribute some runs."

And this is a really crucial point, which ultimately had a huge bearing on the careers of specialist wicketkeepers – myself included – and is a theme discussed throughout this book. Before limited-overs cricket, teams picked their best wicketkeeper – the person they felt would take more catches. It was as simple as that. Whoever could best keep wicket stood up to the stumps.[1]

The advent of limited-overs cricket really brought about a change in mindset, with captains and coaches feeling they needed everyone in the team to score runs if they wanted to compete at the highest level. This put more pressure on wicketkeepers and bowlers to score more runs, as well as doing their primary jobs really well, and thus the idea of the multi-dimensional cricketer was born. From that point, teams began to favour multi-dimensional cricketers – or all-rounders – over specialists, in order to get more bang for their buck.

Yet it wasn't until the 1996 Cricket World Cup, some 25 years after that first ODI at the MCG, that the idea of employing a "keeper-batter" really caught on. In that tournament, both New Zealand and Sri Lanka fielded keepers known just as much for their batting qualities as their abilities behind the stumps, if not more. It was an innovative move that, months later, led to Australia dropping the great Ian Healy from

---

[1] The term "keeping up" or "standing up" is one you will hear a lot through this book. It refers to a wicketkeeper standing right behind the stumps at the moment the bowler delivers the ball. This approach is primarily used when spinners are bowling. But with the growth in prominence of white-ball cricket – initially through one-day matches and now with T20s – keeping up to the stumps is employed more and more to quicker bowlers. This is because it applies pressure to the batsmen, who are uncertain about attacking the bowler by running down the wicket towards the ball in case they miss it, leaving the keeper with a stumping opportunity. Keeping up to 80mph+ is not for the faint hearted, therefore a keeper who can keep up to the stumps well, can add real value to his or her team.

their one-day side in favour of a swashbuckling wicketkeeper-batsman plying his trade in Western Australia – Adam Gilchrist.

Gilchrist was a freak, in the nicest possible sense. His batting was destructive and his keeping was exceptionally good too. Initially slotting in at seven, Gilly was quickly promoted to the top of the Australian batting order, such was the damage he could inflict. In the end, Australia's selectors couldn't resist including him in their Test team, putting to an end the glittering career of Healy, the last of the great specialist keepers in Australia.

And it was an inspired move as it turned out; Gilly finished his career with the second highest number of dismissals in the history of Test cricket, while his batting average of over 47 was ground-breaking for a keeper.

England's selectors were clearly watching on with interest. Jack Russell, a specialist gloveman in the Healy mould, had been England's keeper for a decade. However, when England named their squad for the 1997/98 tour of Zimbabwe and New Zealand, Russell was dropped in favour of Alec Stewart, a keeper who could bat. "When I replaced Jack, and Gilchrist replaced Healy – who was the best keeper I'd ever seen at the time – that changed everything," Alec says in *Keeping Up*.

Since Stewart and Gilchrist, we've seen the keeper-batter phenomenon go global. MS Dhoni, Kumar Sangakkara, Brendan McCullum, AB De Villiers, Jos Buttler and Jonny Bairstow: players with phenomenal, ferocious batting ability, who have developed their glove-work for the good of their team. Dhoni is probably the exception to this list, as he is a quality keeper in his own right. But the rest have definitely developed their keeping skills to be stronger all-round players who can offer more to the team as a whole.

So, is it the right move to select a keeper-batter who is perhaps not so strong behind the stumps in your strongest XI? It's the million-dollar question which captains, coaches and selectors have been agonising over for 20 years now.

Good wicketkeeping is a rare talent and a highly skilled, specialist keeper can have as much of a bearing on a game of cricket – in particular, limited-overs cricket – as a keeper-batter. Maybe more, in some scenarios.

That Sangakkara, de Villiers and McCullum all gave up the gloves part of the way through their careers – and indeed Bairstow doesn't keep for England in white-ball cricket all the time any more – suggests that, in actual fact, the specialist keeper may not be a dying breed after all.

This book charts my progress through the game of cricket, from a young boy playing regional cricket, then playing for various England age groups, through to being a professional cricketer at Hampshire. All the time, I will refer my cricket development back to this wider context of wicketkeeping in the modern-day game, the ever-growing trend to field multi-dimensional wicketkeepers as opposed to a specialist, and how that trend ultimately affected my career, which in the end meant I was forced to retire from the game I loved aged just 24.

I hope you enjoy the book!

Acknowledgements

Tom Huelin

Firstly I'd like to thank the man whose story we tell in this book, Michael Bates. I first met Batesy in 2012 when I was a fledgling cricket writer. I asked to interview him for *Deep Extra Cover* as I felt he was a player with awesome potential. Since that first meeting, sitting in an empty Ageas Bowl after a Championship game against Gloucestershire, Batesy and I have become friends, and I've interviewed him on several occasions since as his career progressed. I was at Lord's in 2012 when he won the CB40 final for Hampshire off the final ball of the match. We spoke when he was replaced by Adam Wheater, and then released by Hampshire in 2014. The highs and lows of a professional cricketer, but Batesy was always high class to talk to. When I floated the idea of writing a book together, I thought he might think I was crazy. But together, we've written something that, I think, we'll both be proud of for the rest of our lives.

I'd like to thank my wife, Maria, and my kids, Liam and Ella, who have had to put up with me tirelessly and endlessly transcribing interviews, researching Hampshire matches over the past 10 years, and generally writing away, trying to bring *Keeping Up* to fruition. Having said that, Liam did get to speak to Jos Buttler when he called for his interview, so he's pretty chuffed about that. Your unswerving faith and love drove me on when I didn't think I could get to the end – I love you so much.

Speaking of Jos, I'd like to thank him, and our other contributors; Adam Gilchrist, Joe Root, Sam Billings, Alec Stewart, Bruce French, Dimi Mascarenhas, Simon Katich, Jimmy Adams, Liam Dawson, Chris Wood, David Balcombe and Nic Pothas. You were all so eager to help us with *Keeping Up*, which is testament to you as blokes, but also to the regard in which you hold Batesy. Big thanks also to Glenn Beavis, Danny Reuben and George Bailey for helping us to secure those interviews, and to Dave Vokes (whose photos are on the cover), Rebecca Smeeth (cover designer), Michelle Tilling (editor) and George Dobell (foreword). The book would be the poorer without your help.

Finally I'd like to thank Mum, Dad and Lian, my sister, for always having faith in me, and for always being right behind me, whatever my little plan or scheme. My grandparents too, who inspire me daily, and who gave me the confidence to follow my dreams. My beloved Grandad passed away in early 2019, so he didn't get to see my first book – this one's for you, Gramps! x

Michael Bates
In writing this book I've been really touched by the number of players, past and present, who have been willing to help us out, sharing their knowledge and thoughts on wicketkeeping, and the game in general. Their kind words and reflections on my own career have been truly humbling, albeit hard to hear at times, with the continued question as to why I'm no longer playing being at the heart of most conversations.

While I've now moved on into my coaching career, I still look back on my playing days with fond memories and will always cherish the chance I got to live my boyhood dream of being a professional cricketer.

Many people along the way made that possible, especially my family, so I'd like to thank them for all their endless and unwavering support; for guiding me through all the ups and downs. I'm so grateful for all that I achieved as a cricketer, and to have been able to enjoy every moment with them made it all the more special!

Prologue: Wicketkeeping – a view from the middle

"He might well be one of the best wicketkeepers in the world, yet there is every chance he won't play first-class cricket again."

Jarrod Kimber, Writer at ESPN Cricinfo

"In my opinion, there's still not a better keeper in the county game than Batesy. He saved me millions of runs. I think he had a massive effect on us winning both one-day trophies."

Chris Wood, Hampshire bowler

"People ask me about Batesy all the time. It hits a lot of emotional buttons with people because of Batesy being the bloke he was – and that's dead set. We were genuinely trying to find ways to get him in. Four-day cricket, you need that heartbeat – and he was that. There is something about seeing a keeper excel at his skill. And that moment at Lord's, in a way, that was almost the perfect summation of him really. Not just the skill, but the reaction to it. It was a seminal moment for all of us, but for Batesy ..."

Jimmy Adams, Hampshire captain (2012–15)

Which keeper do you pick?

It's a debate that rages on and on in cricket circles. Do you pick a specialist keeper, one who can take unbelievable catches, one who can affect the game in the field, who can put pressure onto the batsmen every single delivery, just by being there behind the stumps as they bat. Or do you pick a multi-dimensional keeper, a modern-day keeper whose batting is as good as – if not better than – their keeping?

As long as players like me are still knocking about, this debate will run and run.

You won't be surprised to hear my view: that if you pick a strong keeper, your team will be strengthened, even if they have to come in to bat down the order, like I used to at Hampshire.

There are many moments I could point to, to back up my argument. People who know about my career will recall the stumping I pulled off at Lord's in 2012, to win the CB40 cup for Hampshire with the final ball of the match. I look back on that moment with fondness, of course. But there were plenty of other great moments, like a one-handed catch off Kent's Darren Stevens in 2011. Or a take off Sussex's Luke Wright in 2010, on my first team debut for Hampshire. To my mind, a specialist wicketkeeper can add so much to a team, especially in T20 cricket where your batters coming in at nine to eleven don't tend to bat much anyway.

I'm retired now, but at 28 years old, I still think I should be playing; I still think I could do a job for a county behind the stumps. That great Hampshire team of the early 2010s, which I was part of, we were so good in white-ball cricket. We suffocated batting teams, we had bowlers who took pace off the ball; spinners who were hard for batsmen to hit to the boundaries, or seamers bowling lots of slower balls, varying their pace so the batsmen didn't know what was coming next.

A key part of that approach was having me keeping up to the stumps to all our bowlers. Batsmen were in two minds whether to bat aggressively by skipping down the wicket, knowing that anything they missed, I wouldn't, and they'd be marching back to the pavilion. I could put pressure onto the batsmen; they could hear me breathing behind them, they could probably smell me, almost feel my presence about them. They could definitely hear me. It was all part of the game plan and that's part of what made us such a successful team.

But we'll discuss my career, and my approach to wicketkeeping, later. In this prologue, I want to share with you the thoughts of some of my peers on wicketkeeping; people I've played with or been coached by during my career, legends of the game, all of whom have spoken to myself and Tom – the co-writer of *Keeping Up* – exclusively for this book. But first, a little expert opinion from the press box. Back in 2013, cricket writer Jon Hotten wrote in his blog, "The Old Batsman", about how a specialist keeper should still be favoured by teams, particularly in T20 cricket. Jon's theory was that actually, due to the fact lower-order batsmen are less likely to bat in a game of T20, statistically teams should pick their best keeper, because they will have a more profound impact on the game. I'll let Jon explain his point fully:

The maths goes something like this: at the start of each game, the wicketkeeper is the only specialist position guaranteed to be able to affect a minimum of 50% of the match while using their primary skill (the 20 overs for which they keep). A bowler has 10% (four of 40 overs), the two opening batsmen an unlikely maximum of 50%, the other batters a sliding downward scale from there.

Accepting that almost everyone can field well, and that all-rounders increase their overall percentages by batting and bowling, it's easy to see that the most valuable player in these simple terms of opportunity would be an opening bat that can bowl (Chris Gayle, perhaps, although the occasions on which even the transcendent Jamaican carries his bat occur infrequently.)

If only Jon was a Director of Cricket on the county circuit! Seriously though, this nails my point. I've spoken to so many ex-colleagues while writing this book, many of whom I played with in that successful Hampshire side. All of them have said that Hampshire benefited from having me – a specialist keeper – in the team, between 2010 and 2012 when I was the first-choice keeper, and then sporadically until I left in 2014. It wasn't rocket science, but it worked for us.

One of the things that comes up time and again, is the fact you can't prove how important the contribution of a wicketkeeper – or a fielder in general – is to a team. How many runs saved, or conversely how many runs the team concedes, should a fielder or keeper put down a catching opportunity. Another excellent cricket writer, Tim Wigmore, explored this point in an article he wrote for the *Guardian* in 2017.

While Test cricket has always fetishised numbers, the paradox is that the shorter the format, the more useful they are. In Test and even one-day international cricket there are relatively few matches, a paucity of useful individual player data and so many variables from game to game that team analysts believe old data on a player becomes redundant after two years. But T20 is ideally suited to data analysis. There are fewer variables from match-to-match – pitches tend to be similar, and match scenarios far more repetitive – and leading players can play 50 T20s a year, providing a proper sample size for data-mining. And, unlike in international cricket, teams in T20 leagues need to be able to quantify a player's precise worth when assembling their squads.

The use of data is being accelerated by more outside voices, unshackled by cricket's rigid orthodoxies. They want to keep track of everything in pursuit of a competitive advantage, recognising how far behind baseball T20 remains in its use of numbers.

In the coming years that will change. Finally, the sport is gaining proper data on fielding – the runs fielders save, or cost, and the wickets they effect, or squander – which is increasingly influencing team selection. It is also impacting fielding positions; Richard Barker, the analyst for England's 2016 T20 Blast champions Northamptonshire, foresees that the long stop will return to being a legitimate fielding position, because of modern batsmen's propensity for ramps and scoops.[2] Data could also salvage one of cricket's most cherished lost species: the specialist wicketkeeper. Lower-order batsmen face so few balls – the average no. 7 faces seven balls an innings – that Barker believes picking the best keeper could be prudent.

This backs up my point, that picking your best keeper in your side is beneficial to the team, particularly in white-ball cricket, and especially T20.

But what do current cricketers think of all this? I decided to hit the road and head down to Bristol in May 2017, where England were training ahead of an ODI with Ireland. There, I sat down with two old friends – Joe Root and Sam Billings. I've known both since we were kids – we all came through the England age groups together – and in Sam's case we were direct rivals for the wicketkeeping position.

I was interested to hear their views on the role of the wicketkeeper in modern cricket, particularly Billings, who is now an excellent keeper playing for his country and in the Indian Premier League (IPL). The other, Root, is England's Test captain. So does Root envisage a time when he'll pick a specialist wicketkeeper in his England side?

"I mean, they would have to be absolutely flawless," Joe Root told us.

"But it's impossible to be flawless." Billings countered. "Everyone drops them."

"They'd have to come up with something," Root continued. "Cover three slips or something, or stand up to swing bowling or something outrageous. I can't see it to be honest. Nowadays you have to bat, and

---

[2] Modern-day cricket shots whereby the batsman essentially uses the pace of the ball to hit it over their own and the wicketkeeper's head.

then keep. But it's such a vital position, the amount of times a missed stumping or a little nick can cost you. Gilchrist is probably the one to blame. But he was such a good wicketkeeper as well."

Ah, Gilchrist. We'll come back to him in due course.

"Keeping is under so much scrutiny now," Billings added. "Even T20 now, the margins are so small. You miss one chance and you could lose the game. Someone gets dropped, and goes on to get 70, and that could be the game. Even a half-chance, a missed stumping opportunity."

And that's the counter argument. Do you go for a batter who could get you an extra 30 or 40 runs, or do you stick with a specialist keeper, one who could potentially turn a game with the gloves. Until you can quantify what a keeper can bring to a team with the gloves, as Tim mentioned, teams will always favour keepers who can bat instead.

As Sam, Joe and I chatted, on a selection of randomly assembled chairs in the hallway of the players' pavilion at Bristol's County Ground, Sam made the same point as Tim earlier, something that was undoubtedly a problem for me throughout my career: "There's no way of quantifying fielding or wicketkeeping," Sam said. "Obviously batting you can look at a bloke, if he's averaging over 50, it's clear. Similar with bowling. There's no way of quantifying that with keeping or fielding. And that's where the game goes wrong, because it can be down to opinion really."

I went back to Hampshire a lot when writing *Keeping Up*. However painful the end of my time there was, it's still the place where I grew up – as a man and as a cricketer. A lot of the lads there now are still friends of mine. I'm also close to Lewis McManus, the current keeper, and we've been working together on some technical aspects on a weekly basis for a while now, which is great for me and hopefully beneficial for him.

On one such visit to the Ageas Bowl in June 2017, I chatted to Jimmy Adams, Hampshire's skipper at the time I was playing, about the wider context of wicketkeeping in the modern game. "I think in an ideal world, people will look for multi-dimensionals," Jimmy said.

He continued:

> It means you get to have more all-rounders in your team. But, the beauty of having an all-rounder in your team is you can create space for a very specialist set of skills. And whether that's a keeper, in one-day cricket, certainly. I think in red-ball those days are numbered. But in white-ball I reckon that someone with exceptional keeping skills may be able to get in on the back of

what they can do. Standing up to guys, making a team tick. But it's going to rest on the make-up of the team. It's weird, because the specialist keeper is getting edged out by the multi-dimensional player, yet it might be that which leads to there being a spot for them.

So there seems to be a consensus, certainly among current (or, in Jimmy's case, recently retired) players, that wicketkeepers in the longest form of the game at least need to be multi-dimensional cricketers, with the ability to score runs ideally on a par with their keeping ability, if not slightly ahead. That's a view shared by England's Test captain, Joe Root.

> If you look at where Test cricket is now, compared to five or 10 years ago, the rate people are scoring – how many games go five days now? In one-day cricket now you're seeing scores of 400. I mean, we must have scored over 300, eight out of the last 10 matches when we've batted first, something ridiculous like that [as at May 2017]. There's just such a huge emphasis on batting and scoring runs, rather than being able to contain. It's all very aggressive and trying to be entertaining, because that's what brings the crowds in and that's what makes the money.

I really enjoyed talking to Joe and Sam. I grew up playing with those guys and we shared some great moments together, which I'll go into later. Plus these lads are at the forefront of the international game now. They're global superstars. As well as international duty, Billings has also excelled in the IPL over the last couple of years. So what other innovations, if you can allow me this brief segue, do they see coming into cricket down the line?

"Certainly in white-ball cricket I think you'll see people batting left- and right-handed," Billings suggested.

He continued:

> I think that's where the game can really go on. There's a young Sri Lankan bloke who can bowl left-armers to the right-handed batsman and then offies to left-handers. But why can't you coach kids like that? I don't understand what's stopping people doing that. If you can do it one way and you practice to do it the other way, that's great.

I digress, but it's fascinating to hear some of the ideas current players have for how the game can progress and develop further. I remember when Kevin Pietersen first did a switch-hit – now it's de rigueur.

* * *

In April 2017, I also caught up with my old T20 skipper at Hampshire, Dimi Mascarenhas. I wanted to talk to him about what his expectations were from me, as his wicketkeeper, during his time at the Ageas Bowl, Hampshire's home ground as it's known now (it used to be called the Rose Bowl, until it changed at the behest of the sponsors).

> In the modern game, a wicketkeeper has to be able to hold his place in a side as an out-and-out batter. Adam Gilchrist changed the landscape by the way he went about his batting and what he achieved. He came in, averaged 50 at seven and smashed the ball everywhere. He took the game away from you. Normally you get a team five down and you're well into the tail; Gilly didn't hang around, he took it to you.
>
> I think batting is a big part of the role of the wicketkeeper now in modern-day cricket. I'm not sure if there is *too much* emphasis, but my view is keepers need to be able to bat. In the T20 format you can get away with a keeper not being a top-order batter, but in Test cricket the keeper needs to average at least 35 with the bat.

A few people have said to me that, if I were playing in a different era, I might have played more cricket. Maybe even played for England. Before limited-overs cricket, before the likes of Gilchrist came along, when teams prioritised a specialist keeper over one who could bat, there might have been more of a chance for me. But isn't it also true that a good keeper can work on his skills with the bat, even if he's not a "natural" batsman?

"I put a lot of the success that wicketkeepers have with the bat these days down to the fact they're doing more ball skills training," Bruce French, England's current wicketkeeping coach, and the man who coached me during my time with the England age groups, told me. "The batters don't do as much fielding as they maybe should do, but the keepers will do an hour's keeper training every day. But I don't think there's any coincidence that, because keepers are doing lots of training; watching balls, picking length, hand–eye co-ordination, moving at speed, that it transfers to their batting, that it just adds something to the batting as well. It's all work, it's all ball skills. You're watching, you're moving, so I think that's got to help."

Gilchrist certainly changed expectations when it comes to what a wicketkeeper is expected to achieve with the bat these days. But in England, we had our own wicketkeeping trailblazer, in the shape of Alec Stewart.

Alec was my hero growing up, and I was fortunate enough to meet him several times through my career, and I also spoke to him specifically for *Keeping Up*. He pin-points the moment expectations for keepers in England changed – the moment he moved ahead of his wicketkeeping rival Jack Russell in England's pecking order.

> The turning point was when I was told I was England's first-choice keeper, despite Jack Russell being on the 1996/97 tour of Zimbabwe and New Zealand. Mike Atherton was the captain, and Bumble [David Lloyd] was the coach. That sparked a change in mindset, and under the new responsibility as the number-one keeper, I improved quickly. Although I was learning on the job, which in the Test arena was tough. But when I replaced Jack, and Gilchrist replaced Healy – who was the best keeper I'd ever seen at the time – that changed everything.

Alec told me he saw himself as a batter first, and a keeper second. In fact he kept more for England than he'd ever done previously for his county, Surrey. "I took the gloves because I didn't bowl in my last year at school," Alec continued. "I continued the job part time until I went away to Australia, and kept for a full season out there."

Stewart was England's answer to Gilchrist. He was strong and brave with the bat, taking the game to his opponents with consistent success, while his keeping developed as his career progressed.

By the time he'd retired, in 2003, Stewart had taken 263 Test catches and had a batting average just a fraction under 40. The modern-day wicketkeeper-batsman – in England at least – had been born.

So what was the key to keeping and batting well for England, in Alec's opinion?

> Concentration. And dealing with the scrutiny. Because you've got gloves on, people expect you to catch everything. Alan Knott told me "if you take nine out of 10 chances you're an exceptional

keeper", yet people will always scrutinise the one chance you don't take. It's dealing with being under the spotlight constantly that's the hardest part.

I knew if I did my job efficiently, took all the chances, held myself well, positive body language, collecting throws from fielders, running through overs, that would have an impact on the energy and performance of the team in the field.

I spoke to Alec a couple of times during my career, at times when things weren't going so well for me personally. As a bloke he's straight down the line; thoroughly professional and always looks in good physical shape, and always carries himself in a controlled manner. He was always really supportive when I spoke to him, encouraging me to keep practising hard, to keep working on my game.

I asked him what I could have done differently to have prolonged my career? "Consistency," he told me. "You showed glimpses of what you could do, but you weren't consistent enough in doing it. Don't over-try. Stay relaxed. Practise to achieve something. Not to overdo it."

Wise words. The whole "over-trying", "over-doing it" theme rings very true now when I look back and assess my career, certainly from a batting perspective at least. A captain or director of cricket is going to want a keeper who can score runs as well as keep wicket. I get that. But the problem I had was that my batting wasn't given the time to improve. Maybe if I'd stayed in the 2nd XI for longer at Hampshire, rather than being selected for the first team at 19, I could have nailed down a batting method that worked for me – one that allowed me to score runs even when I wasn't playing well. Maybe then I'd have had more success with the bat, which would have helped prolong my career. We'll return to these mental stumbling blocks – and how to deal with them – later in the book.

* * *

After my playing career finished at the end of the 2015 season, I started doing some one-on-one coaching at the Eversley Indoor Centre near Basingstoke. It was there that I got to know Neil Burns, another coach working there. Neil used to play for Somerset and Leicestershire, and since retiring from the game he's worked with players including Nick Compton.

Neil talks a lot about players like me slipping through the net. Players with potential who didn't make the most of their ability, and were then leapfrogged by others who just developed quicker. He told me about players like Compton, whom he worked with at Somerset, and how Nick had been thrust into the England team, only to be discarded in pretty brutal fashion once the powers that be within the England camp decided he wasn't up to the job.

Neil told me how Compton wasn't given much in the way of detail as to why he was dropped, and no advice on how he could win his place back. Compton's story wasn't an isolated case – I remember when my Hampshire colleague Michael Carberry was dropped by England following the 2013/14 Ashes series. He was dumped, again without any reason or advice on how to get back in.

Part of that is down to the fact that this is elite sport. In Compton and Carberry's case, this is international cricket – a level above the domestic game I was playing in. But Neil's take was that players need time to mature as people and as players before they can be judged – especially when they're coming into a new environment. Carbs and Nick were established players, so their situations were slightly different. But I was only young when I was being judged by Hampshire, so arguably I needed, or deserved, more time.

Neil also felt that the game is now so specialised, that teams would eventually return to having a mixture of batters who score big runs, bowlers who take lots of wickets, and a specialist keeper who is really strong behind the stumps.

Remember when England keeper Jonny Bairstow dropped a catch off Virat Kohli when England played India in a Test at Mumbai in 2016? Kohli was on 30 at the time, and went on to score a match-winning 235. Would a more specialised keeper have taken that catch, saving his team 200 runs? Would that be better for a team than a keeper who drops that chance, but is capable of scoring decent runs with the bat? That's slightly harsh on Bairstow as he's developed into a superb all-round cricketer and a proficient keeper, but you get my point.

When I met up with Joe Root, he'd not long taken on the England Test captaincy. So I was interested to find out what he had in mind for the all-important wicketkeeping position.

> I think you have to look at the balance of your side. You have to look at the other guys in the squad, what you expect from them. Are you going to have a keeper who bats in the top five? The top seven? Have you got all-rounders? Is your spinner going to bat? It all comes into consideration. And it's always a risk – it's a position you've got to be really confident in, and they've got to be very confident in themselves. If they're not, things can unravel very

> quickly, especially across a five-day game, the amount of deliveries he's going to be in contact with – he can come under a lot of pressure very quickly.

I also chatted to another ex-England age group colleague, and all-round superstar right now in world cricket, Jos Buttler. Jos and I played for West of England together from the age of 13, but it was me who got the nod as England's gloveman at 15. Jos only took up the gloves at 13, so he was still very much developing as a keeper, and was seen more as a specialist batsman at the time. Jos had realised that he needed to contribute more to the team than just his batting, so he took the wicketkeeping role on to strengthen his case for selection. A shrewd move, as it turned out. Given his reputation as one of the best keeper-batsmen in world cricket right now, what did Jos think of the multi-dimensional versus specialist keeper discussion?

> I definitely think the specialist wicketkeeper that can bat at number nine is not going to be involved in the game as much as they were. I don't think the skill level will differentiate as much anymore. At the start of this whole process, the wicketkeeping element would have been a lot poorer, whereas now I think the guys who can bat well can keep really well as well. It won't be as much of a drop-off as such.
> They need to give balance to the side, to give options to the captain or coach. And that's for everyone. A batsman who offers a few overs of off-spin, for example. When you're matching people up, who's going to be in the XI, if someone gives you something else, or even if you're a better fielder than someone else, it gives you a chance to get into the final XI. So I definitely think the multi-dimensional element will prevail.
> People have opened their eyes to how you can do both. Maybe in the past it was like: you can't do both. Whereas now, if you put the work in and you've got the talent, there's no reason why you can't do both to a really high standard. And that's probably where Gilchrist changed that for most people, and other guys like Sangakkara, someone who batted in the top order a lot of the time.

* * *

To me, keeping all day in red-ball cricket was something I thrived on, sometimes in the searing heat, other times on damp, windy, cold days where the ball is whooping round corners. I'll go into how I dealt with those mental and physical battles in my wicketkeeping masterclass chapter later on.

But my biggest strength was my ability to keep up in limited-overs cricket. Typically, keepers keep up when the spinners are bowling. But my strength was that I could keep up to the seamers as well. That's a bit of a game-changer, because it keeps the pressure on the batter all the time. Any slight mistake and I'm there to catch them out, quite literally.

Batsmen then try to put pressure onto the bowlers by skipping down the wicket, hitting the ball on the move rather than waiting for it to get to them. However, if you have a keeper up to the stumps, the pressure is back on the batter because if they miss the ball when running down the wicket, a keeper like me will invariably stump them. It's a game of cat and mouse, and it's a way a keeper can really influence a game. It was certainly an approach I liked to employ, and it became something of a calling card for me.

During my time at Hampshire, we didn't really have any 90mph-plus bowlers. Generally speaking, we had good, accurate medium pacers who could bowl slower balls really effectively, or spinners, meaning I was constantly standing up to the stumps. Jimmy Adams told us:

> With a guy that can stand up, they can create pressure. Jack Russell used to do it. That atmosphere around the batter, everything is happening quick no matter who is bowling. Batsmen can't use their feet, or if they do, they know there's a risk. There's just something about that, and that was part of what we had as a team back then.[3] We had this feeling that we were smothering teams. Batesy was a vital part of that. Nic did it well.[4] Nic was always keen to stand up. He was a good keeper. But Batesy was a more natural keeper.
>
> Batesy would just come up as part of our plan. People ask me about our success in white-ball cricket back then; it was purely because we didn't have to think about stuff. We knew where everyone fielded. We knew the plan. We knew Dimi would bowl then Batesy would come up. Everything was clockwork. And yet in a weird way it was loose, it wasn't like "this is what we always

---

[3] By "then", Jimmy means that period from 2010 to 2012 when we won three limited-overs trophies in as many seasons.
[4] Nic Pothas – my predecessor as Hampshire's wicketkeeper. A great man, who you will hear from a lot in my story.

do". It just happened. It got to a point where everything was almost second nature, and that's a pretty good place to be.

One thing people have asked me, is if perhaps I focused on my keeping too much during my career. Possibly, but then I wasn't the only one who valued the advantage of what a specialist keeper could bring to a team. Former Australia Test batsman, and my Hampshire team-mate in the 2012 season, Simon Katich, told us:

> I believe there still needs to be an emphasis on pure glovework. It is a specialist role that can have a big impact on other players' careers, particularly the quicks and the spinners. It is a tough role due to the physical nature of it, and the tough schedule of county cricket.
>
> But Batesy's fitness and professionalism was second to none and I also enjoyed how much pride he took in his glovework and footwork, to make sure he was always clean and tidy behind the stumps.

Me keeping up was part of the plan for us in white-ball cricket. And when I spoke to my England age group wicketkeeping coach, Bruce French, he accepted it was a skill few could perform well.

> Well, you did it, Jack Russell did it, both to medium pace. Certainly Ben Foakes is one who's got the talent in that area to maybe do it to the real quicks, sort of moving the bar up a bit more. He is a gifted keeper. And he's courageous, he's brave.
>
> So maybe that's one area we can start pushing the boundaries forward a little bit at the end of one-day games. It does restrict the batsman, it gets into his mind and restricts their movement. It just gets that little thought in their mind. It's something we don't use enough. It's sort of drifted out of the game a bit. It's time to get it back.

Clearly that line of thinking for a specialist keeper like me is spot on, but I get the need for keepers to deliver with the bat too. If you're calling a keeper an all-rounder though, because their batting should be at the level of their keeping, then I'm not sure I subscribe 100% to that view, because I think the impact a highly skilled keeper can have on a game can be far greater than that of a more multi-dimensional keeper-batter. In that sense, it's quite difficult to compare wicketkeeping all-rounders to their bowling all-rounder equivalents. Jimmy Adams expanded on this:

> Bowling all-rounders have the luxury that if they don't get runs, they might get wickets, and if they don't get wickets, they might get runs. With keeping, if you don't get runs, people don't look at the keeping like they do an all-rounder. We talk about keepers being an all-rounder, but they get the unfortunate task because it's not a 50/50 split. They're viewed as being 80% a batter. You almost need someone from baseball to come in with that moneyball approach – how you break it down would be the biggest challenge. And that's the challenge for coaches, you have to try to make a subjective call on something. I think in one-day cricket we may possibly see that, some sort of objective measure of what [a keeper brings to the game] because there's no doubt that standing up to the stumps is such an asset.

That takes us back to the data point raised by Tim Wigmore earlier. I also spoke to Liam Dawson, an all-rounder himself, ironically, at the Ageas Bowl in the summer of 2017. I played with Daws through the Hampshire academy and into the first team, and he had some words of support for having a more specialist keeper in the side:

> In one-day cricket I would rather have a wicketkeeper who was very good, like Batesy. Someone who can save a wide down the leg side, someone standing up to the stumps. That goes a long way. That keeps a batsman in his crease. As a bowler, you know that, if the batsman makes a mistake, the bloke behind the stumps will catch it, or stump him, or save you five runs. In a one-day game that's massive. Whereas in the long form of the game I think you do need a keeper who averages 40 with the bat. But in one-day cricket I think you should have your exceptional keeper.

Daws was speaking as a spinner. He was very much part of that success we were talking about at Hampshire. That game plan of taking pace off the ball and having a keeper – me – up to the stumps, making it very difficult for the batters to score runs freely, suffocating the run rate. (He's also a mate, so perhaps he's just biased!) I spoke to Bruce French, about which format, if any, he saw as being the optimum one for a specialist keeper. I didn't expect his response:

T20? Well no, actually I would say Test cricket. It's a longer game, there's more skills needed. You've got to get 20 wickets. In a T20 game you touch the ball, what, 20 times? Do you actually need a keeper in T20? Could you just have a fielder? I don't know. It'd be an interesting thing to look into, how many times on average does a wicketkeeper touch the ball in a T20 game. But, of those 20 times, there's a good chance those touches are going to be significant.

One person I was really interested in hearing from, who I probably didn't speak to enough when we were together in the Hampshire dressing room, was my predecessor behind the stumps at the Ageas Bowl, Nic Pothas. Nic was the senior keeper in 2010 when I first broke into the first team, covering for him when he was injured. In 2012 I took the gloves from him permanently following Nic's departure from the club at the end of the 2011 season.

Nic was a great pro – a top keeper but one who was probably renowned more for his batting, it's fair to say. As I came into the side his career was coming to an end, but unfortunately – for me at least – I never got the chance to be mentored by him as such, which would have been a really beneficial experience, I'm sure. When Nic was injured, he wasn't really around the group, and by the time I was given the gloves on a permanent basis, he'd left the club.

Tom had a good chat with Nic over the phone while Nic was in Colombo, working as Interim Head Coach with the Sri Lankan national team. Some of what he said was explosive, some of it was exactly what I wished I'd heard back in 2012. "When you transition a young keeper like Batesy into your team, you've got to be aware that it's going to affect the balance of your team," Nic (nicknamed Skeg) told Tom. "Effectively Batesy's an eight,[5] which means you've got to then play another all-rounder."

But what did Nic think I could've done differently, or what could the club have done differently, to help me develop my batting more? Nic continued to tell Tom:

> You've got to put a plan together and almost say, "we consider Michael Bates a lower-order batter in the mould of a bowler", certainly at the start of his career anyway. And then by the next year, we expect him to be at "this" level, and then into the third or

---

[5] By this, Nic means I should have been coming in at number eight in the batting line-up.

fourth year you expect him to be "this" kind of batter, which is the sort of level you're looking for. It needed long-term thinking.

If you look at keepers who have lost their careers like Batesy, or had their careers shortened because of their batting, you think of Ben Scott,[6] who was a really good keeper. James Foster, because he was a little bit older, he started in an era when wicketkeepers weren't needed to get as many runs or it wasn't as pressurised to get as many runs. So he got better and better just by playing and then when it did become pressurised to get more runs, he was more mature, more solid within his team, and then his batting obviously improved through work. Foster's a phenomenal cricketer, but he didn't have that pressure.

Michael Bates is a smart guy. He knows if he doesn't get runs he's going to be under pressure. He played for the 2012 season, and he knows that he has to score runs. He's 21 years of age. Senior players when they're under that pressure don't get runs, so how do you expect a guy, who to be fair is a young batter, to have that axe over his head and then go and try to perform. He was unfortunate in the era he entered the team.

But you can't just look at it from one angle. At the end of the day, it's your body, your career, your responsibility. Go and find ways of becoming better.

You can't only look at the club and say, they didn't handle the situation as well as they could have. We've also got to look at the individual, because we are ultimately responsible for our careers.

I couldn't begin to imagine what he's been through. He knows full well that he's good enough to play first-class cricket. As a keeper, he could pick up the gloves tomorrow, and he'd be the best keeper on the circuit. You have James Foster, you have Chris Read, but Batesy would be in that league and beyond.

At the end of the day, if you have a diamond, and it's not fitting in the setting in your ring, do you throw the diamond away? No, you just go and find another setting. You can't afford to throw away that value.

We spoke to many people for this book: ex-team mates of mine, ex-coaches, people who knew my game best. People who knew my strengths, my weaknesses. People who knew what it took to get to the very top of the game. And stay there.

---

[6] Ben Scott was a specialist keeper at Middlesex, who faced similar challenges to me in terms of his batting.

What was interesting was how many people could see the value in having a specialist keeper like me in a team. You can already see from the range of views in this prologue, how difficult it is to know whether a specialist keeper should be favoured over a multi-dimensional keeper, and if so in which format.

One of the key themes that came up from these conversations was how measuring the contribution of a keeper is still not being done effectively. And that's something that adversely affected my career, because while my batting stats were stark and, to be honest, pretty underwhelming (for all the potential I felt I still had to offer), there was no real data underlining my capability behind the stumps.

Everyone we spoke to agreed I should still be playing, which was bittersweet to hear; it was a nice compliment, but one that also made me feel gutted that I wasn't anymore. Writing this book has been a journey, recalling different moments throughout my career. But it has also been a journey exploring the art of wicketkeeping. How the role had changed over the last 30 years, and just why it had changed so much.

And so, with that in mind, there's no better place to start, than at the very beginning.

Chapter 1
The boy Bates

Wednesday 10 October 1990. The England cricket team were preparing to fly to Australia for a winter Ashes series down under. Elton John was in the charts with his hit single 'Sacrifice', and Martin Scorsese had just released the seminal gangster movie, *Goodfellas*. Oh, and I was born in Frimley Park Hospital.

I was born to Gordon, a teacher originally from Liverpool who'd moved south for work, and Janice, a barmaid-come-bank-clerk-come-teacher from nearby Camberley. They met in a local bar where she worked as a barmaid at the time and the rest, as they say, is history. I arrived in 1990 and three years later my sister Laura came along.

We lived in a leafy, sleepy suburb in north Hampshire called Yateley. Growing up there was great. We lived in a small, modest house at the end of a little cul-de-sac. As a kid I used to think the house was huge and the road that led to it was really long. But when I walk past there now I realise it was just my youthful, naïve eyes making me think that. It was small, but we were happy there.

I remember my childhood being really happy and fun. As a family we spent a lot of time with my cousins on my Mum's side. They all lived in nearby Camberley so we saw each other a lot. We'd have pool parties at my grandparents' house – my Mum's parents – who also lived close by.

I was really close to my grandparents – and I still am. They always believed in me – whatever I wanted to do, they'd say I could do it. Grandparents are great like that – they're so inspiring. Grandad had done pretty well for himself in his career as an accountant. He'd set up his own business which is still in the family today, and now run by my uncles. Grandad still goes in once a week to help out, even though he's in his 80s! I think it keeps him young.

My earliest memories are of starting at my local school; Yateley Manor pre-prep, which funnily enough was the school my Dad taught at. And, by the time I'd started there, my Mum had changed careers and was working there too.

In fact, there was a period a couple of years later when all four of us were at Yateley Manor at the same time, which was pretty surreal looking back, although it felt perfectly normal at the time. Laura and I were both taught by my Dad, but not my Mum. Dad was a popular teacher – all my mates liked him. He treated me and Laura the same way as he treated everyone else in our class, which was good, as if he'd given us any special treatment I think we'd have got plenty of stick for it.

Both my parents were relatively sporty. Dad was a rugby player when he was growing up, and Mum played netball and rounders at school. Mum's family were really into football; my Grandad supports West Ham – he was born a stone's throw away from the old Boleyn Ground in East London. My uncles didn't all follow suit – one's a Man United fan, another an Everton fan. Just one is a Hammer, like his old man.

Crucially, none of them were into cricket. So there was no natural route into the game for me from my family.

* * *

I was an active, athletic kid growing up. I was fit, but always pretty short. I was always running around the garden like a nutter, keeping my parents on their toes. I loved all sports but, even at the age of five or six, cricket was already my favourite. As I'd had no natural route into the game, my love for it must have come from watching it on the BBC. I started asking my parents if I could play cricket at home, so Dad made me a bat out of a flat piece of wood. We used chalk to draw some stumps on the garden wall, and we were away.

I used to talk Laura into playing with me in the garden at a young age; rather begrudgingly, she'd oblige. I used to get her to throw balls to me while I batted. It was always a battle getting her to play, but if I let her have a go with the bat, she'd throw me down a few overs' worth of balls at least.

One such game left an indelible mark on my memory – and my skull. I was about seven, Laura about four, and as usual I'd managed to blackmail her into bowling to me for a bit. It was a dull, chilly day, but it was dry so I was determined to get outside and play some cricket. It wasn't long, however, before she was moaning and whining, saying how it wasn't fair that I was batting and she was bowling, again, and that she wanted to have a go with the bat. Our neighbours must have loved us – we were always rowing in the garden!

Eventually I couldn't stand it any longer, so I handed her the bat. As is typical with sibling rivalries, there was a cunning plan behind my decision to hand her the bat; I was anticipating her to tire quickly of batting too, at which point I could get back in there.

Laura aimed a few lusty swings at the ball and missed miserably. "Ha!" I thought. Then finally she connected with one, the ball dribbling a few inches away from the bat. Still, she was happy with her efforts, shouting victoriously at the top of her squeaky little voice. Slightly annoyed, I walked towards her to retrieve the ball that had settled just a few inches from her. Thinking about what delivery I was going to bowl to her next, I bent down to retrieve the ball, when *THWACK*.

That was the sound of Laura's bat connecting with my forehead. My head flew back, my short, brown hair flaying in the air, a sharp, intense pain making its way around my green-blue left eye. The blow knocked me down for a bit, and there was a bit of blood spilt on Mum and Dad's lawn, a few tears shed and a few cries bellowed from my young lungs. I can't remember what Laura's reaction was, but I imagine she was laughing.

That little mishap wasn't going to deter me from playing cricket, though. By the age of seven I was obsessed with the game. Whether it was with my sister – after we'd moved on from that incident – with my Dad or my friends, I was always playing and practising. It was all I was interested in doing. And even at that stage, being a cricketer was the only thing I wanted to be when I was older.

Around that time Alec Stewart was England's first-choice keeper, and I'd often watch him on the TV and think what an amazing player he was. He always seemed to be putting in 100% effort, and gave so much to the team, not just his runs and his glovework too. I was aware, even at that young age, of the way he kept the team going behind the stumps, his energy, which is such an important trait to have for any good wicketkeeper. That attitude, not to mention his ability both with bat and gloves, definitely made an impression on me, even though I wasn't actually a wicketkeeper at that stage.

* * *

It was around the age of seven when I first started playing for the school cricket team. That was largely down to my games teacher, Mr Hetherington (Derek). Derek was the first person I can remember who had a real impact on me as a sportsman. He saw potential in me at an early age, and from that moment he guided me through my early years in cricket.

Derek was one of a kind. He was an ex-army man, old school and fit as a fiddle. I still see him now, in Waitrose from time to time, and he tells me he still gets to the gym twice a week and looks after himself. He's inspirational, and I dare say most of the kids I went to school with will remember him that way too.

Derek was a fairly unassuming bloke, he demanded respect but for subtle reasons. He went to war during his time with the army, and everyone knew that, so we automatically had a sense of respect towards him. He used to walk around the school grounds with a limp, clutching an A4 piece of paper which he'd folded over and over again into a small but thick piece, on which he wrote notes about all the kids playing sport. I imagine my name must have appeared on his little bit of paper at some point – I'd love to know what it was he wrote about me!

And it was Derek who helped me get my first real break in cricket, when he put my folks in touch with the local team, Yateley Cricket Club. He told the club I was a talent, and so they asked me along for a trial. I was just seven, which is really young to join a cricket team, and certainly Yateley didn't normally take kids on so young. But luckily enough they liked me, and asked me to join their under-9s.

That meant me playing up a year group, which was something I'd have to get used to in the years to come. 'Playing up' is all part of youth sport – it's usually a sign that you're a little bit ahead of where you're expected to be at your age, so you play with the year group above your own. Obviously it's great to be in that situation, although I wasn't really aware of that at seven years old! One downside was that, as a short lad already, me playing up meant I was conceding quite a margin in the height department. Swings and roundabouts, I suppose!

At that age I was a swing bowler. I was pretty accurate although not particularly rapid. I was also a handy batter, technically pretty strong for my age. Crucially, I was a confident lad. Whether I was speaking to coaches, meeting new team mates for the first time, or just going out to bat or bowl, I always felt confident in my ability and in myself as a person.

Being confident in my ability was certainly something I tried to maintain throughout my career, as I'll explain throughout the book. Once I took the gloves, there were two elements of my game which needed equal focus.

My keeping always took care of itself; it was always of a high standard, no matter what level I played at. But my batting was an area that I constantly needed to improve and, as a result, my confidence definitely took a hit at certain periods in my career. Those mental battles were often more pronounced, more difficult to overcome, than the technical issues I faced, and I'll explain how I dealt with those mental barriers later in the story.

Within a year I'd been picked for an under-9s district trial. Those district trials really give you a good idea of who was decent in your area in your age group, so it was a really big experience for me. The trial started with about 30 kids initially, we did a few sessions and from that they selected a regional team. Then the different regional teams in Hampshire played in a tournament, after which a group of 15 lads were selected to train with Hampshire County Cricket Club itself. Fortunately for me, I was one of the 15. Just imagine, nine years old and selected to train with Hampshire already! Unbelievable.

Training with Hampshire basically meant partaking in age group training sessions at Hampshire's ground once a week. Back then the first academy intake was at under-14s, so I still had a way to go before then. The age group sessions were every Sunday, so from the age of nine I was travelling down to Southampton from Yateley in north Hampshire once a week for training. That meant a lot of driving for Mum, Dad and my grandparents, but they were brilliant – they never complained once.

Straight away I loved it at Hampshire, and thankfully I soon hit my stride. Immediately I was put into the under-10s age group, playing up a year again. I don't remember thinking too much about that at the time. Looking back you think, "wow, I must have been good", but back then I was just getting on with it. It never fazed me.

When I started at Hampshire age group training, I was still bowling. But within a year I found my vocation in life – wicketkeeping. Our age group didn't have a keeper, so the coach asked if anyone would like to trial for the position. I put my hand up, and I got the gig.

It was around that time that I first met lads who'd become friends I'd keep throughout my time at Hampshire, and beyond, and with whom I'd share so many special moments in Hampshire's first team years later. Liam Dawson (Daws) and Chris Wood (Woody) were both 10 when we met. They were in the school year above me, but me and Danny Briggs (Briggsy) played alongside them in the under-10s as we were both playing up.

My early memories of those boys? Woody was a hyperactive nightmare growing up! He was hilarious – still is. But his cricket mind was always on point. He understood the game better than most, and was always very streetwise. Daws was a bit chubby at that age, but he was always massively talented; you could see he was going to go far. And Briggsy was incredibly consistent – he had so much control over his left-arm spin for his age.

I think all of us would agree that we were at Hampshire because of one man: Tony Middleton. Tony was in charge of the academy recruitment back then, and he's still at the club now as the senior team's batting coach. Tony had a unique eye for spotting talent, and he was also brilliant at bringing our games forward.

I remember one particular classroom session we had with Tony, where he went through what he saw as being the pathway to becoming the world's number-one cricketer, that is, the steps a young cricketer would need to take, and the milestones he'd need to achieve, to be the world's best. In Tony's opinion, that involved going through an academy to turning pro, dominating domestic cricket to earning an England call-up and then achieving world number-one status. I remember absorbing it like a sponge, transferring it to a piece of paper as soon I got home. That piece of paper stayed on my bedroom wall for a long time, and I would often chart my progress against it.

What Tony did with the academy, and how he built it up, was fairly revolutionary for those times. Pathway setups have come on massively in the last 15 years, but Tony was the man who implemented all that at Hampshire.

He also had a keen eye for spotting players, like Hampshire captain and England international, James Vince. Vincey was playing cricket for Wiltshire and was in Reading Football Club's academy when Hampshire came calling. Tony sniffed his talent out when Vincey was about 14. Daws was another one. He came to Hampshire from Wiltshire at the age of 10, working up through the age groups and into Hampshire's academy, and Tony definitely played a big role in his development. Daws recalls:

> We were having two or three intense academy sessions per week. That can only improve your game as a young player. Those years in the academy were great. You would learn not only about cricket but about nutrition, fitness, time-keeping, structuring your day in terms of when you were practising... That was all put in place by Tony, which for a young lad back then was brilliant for

me. I was being treated like a pro cricketer due to his professional attitude to the academy intake.

But Tony could only do so much; you'd have to have the talent, and the work ethic, to become a pro. Not every 15/16-year-old has the drive and the work ethic he wanted from players in the academy. Tony was very good at spotting those who weren't as committed, and leaving them out of games or not taking them into the academy, so he could concentrate on those of us who wanted to give 100% every session we attended.

That era was pretty exceptional for Hampshire's academy. With Vincey, Daws, Woody and Briggsy, as well as me, all coming through together. But to me it's no surprise that we had that purple patch, because Tony really knew how to spot and nurture talent. I don't think you'll get that many talented players coming through an academy and into the first team all at the same time, not for a long time anyway. And, in the case of Vincey, Briggsy and Daws, they all made it into the senior England team too.

With me, Tony acknowledged that my keeping was exceptional and stand-out, pretty early on. As a coach he was an interesting character. He definitely had that fear factor. He was a man of a few words, and everything he said was very calculated. You could tell he was very passionate. Without a doubt he wanted all of us academy players to do well. I have no doubt whatsoever that he cared immensely about us, and wanted us to succeed. However, at that stage I needed someone more communicative, more encouraging, more vocal than Tony. He was very introverted, reserved with his words and it was therefore really difficult to read him and understand what he really thought. So from that perspective there was always a bit of distance between us, and it wasn't the two-way relationship I wanted, or needed.

Although cricket was my first love, I was into other sports. I really enjoyed football, and when I was nine, I was scouted for QPR's academy as a goalkeeper. It's a similar skillset to wicketkeeping in some respects, which I'll explain in the wicketkeeping masterclass chapter later on. At that stage I was committing to both cricket and football equally, but I definitely enjoyed cricket more.

Eventually the decision was taken out of my hands, when I was released by QPR at the age of 12. They were selecting players they wanted to progress to the next stage of the academy, and unfortunately I didn't meet the level they were looking for. Basically, I was too small once we went into the bigger nine-a-side goals. In the smaller goals, my technical ability was good enough and I was a decent keeper, but once we went into the full-size goals it was clear I just wasn't going to be big enough. That's professional sport for you – it's brutal.

* * *

Yateley Manor went up to school year eight, and as I approached the end of my time there, my cricket was absolutely on fire. I'm told I still hold the record for my batting average at the school from my final year there, which is quite a nice personal landmark.

Some of the innings I played that season are still vivid memories in my mind. In one, against a strong team from Devon, I smashed 141 on a searing hot Wednesday afternoon in mid-summer. It was a big match for the school as it was part of the national knock-out competition. Gradually teachers inside the school caught wind of my knock, and started allowing their students to come out and watch. Then the teachers came out too. It was a great feeling, I was nailing the pull shot all day, and the better I played and the more runs I scored, the more people came out to watch.

We ended up going all the way to the semi-finals in that competition, where we hosted Millfield School from Somerset. That was a big game for our school. All the teachers were out watching from the start this time, even the headmaster. Again I was smashing it around everywhere with the bat, scoring 123 in the end. I was loving it. If you could bottle that feeling of how you played sport as a kid, and found a way of recreating that as an adult, you'd be laughing. You'd be so successful. I guess, in essence, that's what every cricketer – every sportsperson – is looking to capture, to play with that sheer enjoyment and complete freedom.

Ultimately we lost that semi-final against Millfield, but it had been a fantastic occasion playing in front of the whole school, and even at that young age it gave me a thirst to want to play cricket in front of big crowds again in the future on a regular basis.

At the end of that summer term, it was time to leave Yateley Manor. I'd joined the school as a little boy, one who loved playing cricket with his sister in the back garden. I'd progressed to playing for the local cricket side aged seven, breaking all sorts of records for my school team, before moving up to district and then age-group cricket with Hampshire. My education had been ticking away in the background, but my sport had really flourished during my time at the school, and that was largely down to one man, Derek Hetherington.

The day I left school was a poignant one, as Derek was also leaving, to begin his well-earned retirement. The school had arranged a special assembly for him, to acknowledge all the fantastic work he'd done with pupils past and present.

He took to the stage to receive a commemorative plaque and as he walked up the stairs to the stage, the hall erupted into applause. A few teachers, some of whom had been there almost as long as Derek had, took to their feet. Other teachers and then all the students soon followed. Before long the whole hall was standing, clapping and cheering in complete admiration for this great man. I'll never forget that moment, and I'll never forget Derek Hetherington: he was a hero, a teacher and a friend to me.

As is customary when you leave school, we all signed each other's shirts. Some teachers signed them too, and I'll always remember Derek taking a pen to my shirt and writing something which has stayed with me to this day. "Believe in your ability and you can live your dreams. I'll be watching you."

During that summer of 2003, I was asked to play a couple of trial matches for Hampshire's under-14s academy team, playing up a year once again. These matches were in the Southern Electric Premier League – the local men's league. Me, this short lad of 12, nearly 13, playing men's cricket already – I was buzzing!

After one of those games, as everyone else was packing up and leaving, Tony called me, Mum and Dad over to the side of the pitch. "What does he want?", I was thinking. I needn't have worried, as it was then that he officially invited me to join the academy for the winter, to train with the academy programme proper for the first time. Tony said it had been the way I'd handled myself with the bat that had impressed him the most. Without wanting to sound big-headed, I think it was always a given that my keeping was good enough.

As you can imagine, I was delighted. All that hard work – I'd started on this journey as a seven-year-old, so almost half of my young life had been devoted to cricket. I loved playing the game, clearly, but it had still been a hell of a commitment.

My journey was no different to the one taken by many young sportspeople. And for any kids reading this, my message to you would be that you can do it, but you have to be prepared to work hard and devote yourself to it. As Daws alluded to earlier, being a pro sportsperson is a lifestyle, and the quicker you can adjust to those on- and off-field requirements, the better off you'll be.

Once I was in the academy, unsurprisingly I was playing even more cricket. I was down at Hampshire's ground the Rose Bowl twice a week, either getting dropped off by my Mum or Grandad, or getting a train from Basingstoke and then a taxi from Southampton Airport Parkway to the ground in West End.

I was doing batting work with Tony, keeping work with Bob Parks and gym work with Iain Brunnschweiler. Even at that age there was a lot of emphasis on my batting, which was slightly behind where it should have been, although not miles away by any means.

On the batting side, with Tony, I was doing a lot of work on my positioning, making sure I was getting into strong, solid positions on the front and back foot. We used mini footballs quite a bit for this, putting them on the floor and lining them up in relation to where I wanted to make contact with the ball, then looking to hit them hard into the ground. I was also working on generating more power with the bat, which is partially down to gym work, but also down to technique, getting your hands through the ball quickly.

Keeping-wise Bob was getting me to follow the ball with my head, lining the ball up so that when I caught it, it was under my eyes, in line with my head. We also did a lot of work keeping up to the stumps, which would become my signature technique later on in life. In the gym with Iain, I was building up my basic strength, doing interval training and ensuring my cardiovascular fitness was maintained. So even as a 13-year-old, there was a huge amount of work being done.

And that work in the academy was in small groups, so it was intense – especially compared to the age group stuff I'd done previously. A lot of the drills were the same, but the academy work was a lot more intense, a lot harder, but you felt like your game was progressing that much quicker.

By this stage, at the age of 14, I was also playing matches every Saturday for my new school, Lord Wandsworth College. There, I was batting pretty well, dominating at times. But perhaps not as consistently as someone in the Hampshire academy should have been doing for his school team.

It always took a little longer for my batting to adapt to steps up in levels for some reason; whether that was a mental thing or more technical, it's hard to say. I always felt confident, and it definitely wasn't an inferiority complex as such, but my batting always took a bit more work to get used to the higher standard of bowlers I was facing. My keeping, on the other hand, was always flawless, no matter the size of the next step up.

At the time though, I was quite naïve about that disparity between both my keeping and batting. I never really thought about my game as much as I could have done, never really felt the need to impress my coaches – Tony in particular – as much as I maybe should have done, particularly with the bat. Identifying opportunities to impress your coaches as a youngster is an important skill, one which I never really grasped at the time. Now I'm a coach, I recognise the kids that get that, they are constantly on their game when I'm watching them, and I can see they are trying to impress me. And those kids tend to stand out compared to those who are just there for a laugh, and not really bothered about progressing either way.

And that's not to say that those kids will never get it. Some just need more time. I certainly did. But unfortunately sport at that level is constantly growing ever-more impatient, and time is a luxury young sportspeople don't have.

Still, that's me being ultra-critical, and also combining some of my thoughts as a coach now, and an adult, looking back on my teenage self. You can't change who you are at that age, but the kids who get that mentality just seem to be the ones who progress further and quicker.

That aside, my game was coming along well. By the age of 13, I was already playing for the men's team at Yateley Cricket Club. Even at that age, as a short, athletic lad with slightly scruffy brown hair and bright blue-green eyes, I was already keeping up to the stumps – even to the guys bowling quick. I loved it, and my performances were earning me praise from my team mates. After one game, when my keeping had been particularly strong, I sat on my bench in the small, archaic changing room at Yateley, while the blokes on my team went into the showers. Obviously I was a kid so I didn't go in. But I could hear them from around the corner, shouting, laughing and singing, while catching up on the game's events.

"Fuck me – Batesy – he's unbelievable!" I could hear them bellowing out, when talking about my keeping. I was buzzing.

When Tom spoke to Jimmy Adams, he recalled the promise I was showing at that age back at Hampshire:

> He was so far ahead with his keeping. I'd go to academy games, and he'd be doing stuff that the guys ahead of him weren't even doing yet. He was keeping up to the stumps at 14. I don't remember anyone else doing that, and the guys ahead of him certainly weren't doing that. It was clear how amazingly natural

he was behind the stumps. He'd always been a good mover, he was a whippet whether he was fielding or batting, but his hands were on another level. People talk about the moment at Lord's and in many ways that moment encapsulates everything that was good about Batesy's career. But in many respects he was doing that throughout his junior career.

It's like a Yorker. I'm not comparing Batesy to a yorker. But a keeper taking a leg-side catch – it gets a round of applause, like a yorker does. A leg-side stumping, something down the leg side or a bit of magic, still brings a feeling of, "this is cricket", which is what fans at the ground love to see. A bit like a cover drive, or a straight drive. As much as people like the reverse sweep, there's still something about watching James Vince slam the ball through the covers. While the game's moving on and that's great, there's still some things that don't change.

You stand next to some keepers, and there's just a lovely effortlessness to their keeping, and that's another thing that I'd associate with cricket. On a nice summer's day, that crisp sound, an almost effortless pouching of the ball in the wicketkeeper's gloves. And we see that less and less now, with manufactured keepers. I was lucky enough to play a lot of my junior cricket with Iain Brunnschweiler who was an outstanding mover and an outstanding keeper, and in some ways he was a bit of a template for Batesy. You always knew that potential was there. And on the flip side, you always knew that their batting would need a bit longer.

And in what Jimmy said, there was something that would dog my career forever, although I probably wasn't aware of it at that age – my batting. Clearly my keeping skills were progressing well, they were ahead of my age group, and then some. But my batting needed work and even at that age, in my early teens, it was something my coaches would acknowledge was a weakness, something I'd need to work on if I was going to progress in the future.

Chapter 2
England pathway

While things were progressing well at Hampshire, I was also starting to get noticed at a national level too.

When I was coming up through the age groups – although I believe it's changed slightly now – a young player's first opportunity to trial for their region was at the age of 13. Tony Middleton, the academy director at Hampshire, had put me forward for a trial for our region, which in Hampshire's case was the West of England. We were on the border really; the likes of Sussex, Kent and Essex fell into the South region, but Hampshire was grouped with Gloucestershire and Somerset, as well as minor counties like Devon, Dorset, Wiltshire and Cornwall.

As far as I can recall, I was the only lad from Hampshire to be put forward for a trial that year, Briggsy was a bit of a late developer and so wasn't selected, while Vincey wasn't quite on the scene at that stage.

The trials were held at weekends throughout the 2004/05 winter, in the indoor nets at Taunton, Somerset's home ground. Whenever I've gone back there since – as I've done from time to time throughout my career, for various reasons which I'll describe later – my mind always recalls those regional trials, all those years earlier. I remember turning up as a 14-year-old kid thinking, "this place is a bit dingy, a bit smelly". It smelled of damp, of sweat, of something not overly pleasant. They're not the fondest memories, I grant you. But that's how I remember the place, although having been back there since, I can assure you it's actually a very nice facility after all! It's funny the way your mind recalls things from your youth.

Still, that was the scene that greeted me, and about 20-or-so other lads, as we embarked on the next stage of our cricketing development. One lad I met at that first round of trials, whom I'd get to know quite well over the years as a rival in the wicketkeeping position, was a softly spoken local lad from Taunton named Jos Buttler. When Tom caught up with Jos during England's ODI series with Australia in the summer of 2018, he said:

I took up wicketkeeping when I was 13. For me I always felt I needed another string to my bow, so wicketkeeping was the obvious choice. I probably wasn't as natural to begin with, so I probably had to work harder at my wicketkeeping than my batting. Throughout the age groups Batesy was an outstanding wicketkeeper, and he was the benchmark in terms of, "that's what the best wicketkeeper is doing".

At those initial trials, Jos was a batter only, so he wasn't a direct rival as such at that stage. But what I will say about him is that, even at 13, Jos stood out. He seemed very aware of his own game, determined, driven definitely. He worked things out quicker than most, adapting to new scenarios quickly and thriving on a personal level as a result. The fact that, as he said, he took up keeping because he wanted more strings to his bow, wanted to be more involved in the game, says it all.

He was a nice guy, too. When it came to his cricket he worked hard, but away from it he was a good laugh – quite mischievous actually. He enjoyed a laugh and a joke, and as we got older he loved a night out. From the outside looking in, you could say he had that perfect blend of "work hard, play hard", and it certainly worked for him.

Those regional trials were a hard slog. It was an early start, getting up at the crack of dawn to make the long drive from Yateley to Somerset, with Dad at the wheel. When we arrived I already felt tired. Then I was faced with having to meet new people, adjust to new surroundings and then play cricket to the best of my ability. That was the most important thing, obviously!

Naturally, I was nervous going into a new environment and playing with a new group of lads, under a new coach. But in terms of being worried about the magnitude of what the trial represented, I'm not sure I'd really cottoned on to what it all meant. My parents were probably more worried about it than I was, more aware of what I stood to gain if I was successful, what I stood to miss out on if not.

But that's how you want it. As a sportsperson, particularly at that age, you don't want to be contemplating failure. You don't want to be thinking about the negatives, otherwise you'll be burdened by nerves and anxiety, and ultimately your performance will suffer. As you grow up, you become more aware of what you stand to win or lose when you play, both from a team perspective and individually, and that's when the pressure really builds. When you're older you train to perform in those pressured environments. At that age it just comes naturally.

Luckily for me at those regional trials, I did what I always did at that age – I went out and played good cricket. We did competitive nets, specific drills within your discipline – so keeping and batting drills in my case. The coaches really put us through our paces, I remember my keeping getting a really good working over, with lots of repetitions of drills trying to expose any deficiencies in my technique. Similarly with my batting, I faced a lot of balls, in different scenarios. We did a lot of work against spin bowling in particular, coming down the wicket, sweeping, trying to be aggressive. They were looking to explore as many facets of our game as they could.

Pete Bolland and Chris Twort were the guys putting us through the paces in those sessions, and they were the ones who would ultimately select lads who would make it into the West of England under-13s squad. So, as well as performing well as a cricketer, it was important to build relationships with the coaches. As a coach myself now, I can see how important that connection is. With certain players, even at that age, you get a feel for them. You know you can coach them, you know you can work with them, and that's a really important part of the process. As a 13-year-old back then, obviously I wasn't thinking about forming a relationship with a coach to benefit my game. But the fact I really got on well with Chris and Pete was a massive bonus.

Pete was in his 40s and from Cornwall, while Chris was in his 50s and was a long-standing teacher at Millfield School – the school I'd played against at Yateley Manor. Pete was really outgoing, and really encouraged me to be the best keeper I could be. Chris was a lot more understated. He didn't give praise out very often, so you knew that, when you received it, it was meant. Chris gave me a lot of reassurance at that stage, which I really appreciated.

Both of them made me feel like I was someone special, which I definitely needed back then. If I'd done something well, they'd tell me so. They'd come up to all of us individually, pat us on the back and say "good job". It was constant reinforcement, and for me that meant regular praise for my keeping in particular. Both of them were really complimentary about my glovework, and they just kept pumping me up and supporting me, and promoting the stuff I was doing well. Simple things, but it made a big difference. At that age, that's really important.

To be honest, I think everyone needs that sort of support at some stage in their career. I reckon I lacked that a little bit later on, when I was in the professional game. I mean you could say you shouldn't need that level of support when you're a professional sportsperson, but I don't really buy that. I think everyone needs to feel supported, to feel loved, to feel wanted even. We're all human.

Pete and Chris's approach certainly worked for me, as I was selected for the under-13's squad at the end of those regional trials. Another milestone reached in my pursuit of being a professional cricketer. Jos made it too, as a specialist batsman, although he was starting to turn his attention to his glovework by that stage.

My first appearance for the West of England was in an under-13s tournament at King's College in Taunton. I've got very good memories of that festival. I was playing with a great bunch of lads, and I can remember really shining with the gloves too. It was a great environment. Pete and Chris continued to be really supportive and encouraging, as they would throughout my time with them, between the ages of 13 and 15.

The next milestone was to play at the Bunbury Festival, a really prestigious tournament for young cricketers in the UK, where all the regional sides from around the country come together to play matches against each other. It's the first chance a young cricketer has to put himself in the shop window for the England setup, to test themselves against the best players across the country in their age group. At the end of the week, the coaches would select a squad of all the best players from the different regions, and that squad would essentially become England's under-15s squad for the following season.

That week was the first time I met a lad who would become something of a rival to me in the wicketkeeping position throughout the England age groups – Sam Billings. Sam and I were always very close to each other in terms of our keeping ability, from those under-15s days, right up until he broke into the senior side. Sam was a very competitive character, and we certainly had our fair share of clashes. I'm competitive when I need to be, but he was like that all the time. We were civil, but there was always an edge, a rivalry, between us. I guess it drove us both on to be better keepers, which is ultimately what elite sport is all about.

I was lucky enough to catch up with Sam in early 2017, just after he'd finished playing a blinder in the IPL. I wanted to understand how he'd approached his development through the England years, as clearly he isn't just a fine keeper, he's also a destructive batsman now, too.

"You very rarely see 'just a batsman' now," Billings told me. "You have to be either a gun fielder or bowl offies, or something, because when you come into a side, you have to offer something extra, because you're not established. If you're not offering something a little bit more than the other bloke, you won't get in."

"It can give you an extra two or three games," Joe Root interjects. I played with Joe throughout the England age groups too, and he dropped by to have a chat with Sam and I after he'd finished his media commitments ahead of an ODI with Ireland in Bristol. Joe had just been named England's new Test captain, so he was busy doing TV interviews, press conferences, not to mention film-shoots of "head-shots" – filming the footage of the players walking towards the camera, which you see on TV when each player comes out to bat.

"Those games can be all you need to turn your career," Joe continued. "If you get those extra couple of games because of an extra string to your bow, and you then get a hundred, you're off and away and you'll never look back."

That's certainly what Rooty did, when he burst into the senior side when England toured India in 2012. But that really does underline the freakish quality of the man. He was brilliant.

Back at Bunbury, and I can remember feeling like I'd had a pretty average week with the gloves, which was very unlike me. I was playing for West of England while Billings was keeping for the South, and there was plenty of chat flying around about who was going to get the nod at the end of the week for the under-15s squad. It was definitely between us two, but which of us it would be was still definitely up in the air, and the fact I wasn't at my best definitely made me doubt whether I'd be in luck.

At the end of the week, and to my great surprise, I was named as the top wicketkeeper there, winning a trophy which I possibly felt I didn't deserve, although I would never have told anyone that – certainly not Sam! The trophy was satisfying, but even better was getting the nod for the England under-15s squad.

And we were straight into action; just a week or two after Bunbury we were off to Loughborough to play a tri-series against Scotland and New Zealand. We played three games against Scotland one week, and then three games against the Kiwis the week after. Obviously the cricket was important, but so too was the life experience, as this was essentially our first opportunity to live away from home on tour. We stayed at Loughborough University in the ECB halls of residence. As a group we gelled seamlessly. There I was joined by Joe Root, Zafar Ansari, Azeem Rafiq and Jack Leach. It was just a brilliant experience for us all.

Our head coach was Richard Halsall, and I've got to say I really enjoyed working with him. He was great for me, and gave me a huge amount of confidence and motivation, which I took through the rest of my career. He got the best out of every single player in that squad, and taught us what was required if we wanted to go on and become professional cricketers.

The main thing he tried to get across to us was that being a pro sportsperson was a way of life. It was more than just playing the game. And those two weeks were a big part of that mental transition to a more professional mindset. He had really good advice on recovery from games, diet, hydration – the stuff away from the pitch which were massively important. If you weren't prepared to take that stuff on board, you were probably going to sell yourself short.

He used to ask us what we'd had for breakfast. We'd have a choice between a full English, and fruit and yogurt, and if you were abusing the former day after day, he'd let you know you needed to sharpen up. If we snacked at the hotel the day before a game, he'd point out if we were overdoing it. Some days we'd pop off campus to the local Sainsbury's. When we'd get back he'd ask what we'd bought, to make sure it was suitable. He was meticulous, but it made us realise how thorough our preparation needed to be for cricket at this level.

During that tournament, it was the first time I'd had access to video analysis. All the games were recorded, so we were able to go through our games, with Richard guiding us through that process. And he was really good at the little touches, all of which made a big difference. Like the day before the final match of the tournament, Richard put a note under each of our bedroom doors summarising how we'd done through the tournament. My note said "you've been fantastic all fortnight, now bring all that energy to the crease one final time". I think I batted pretty nicely in that last game, and Richard making the effort to individually communicate with each of us definitely helped me, as I'm sure it did the others.

As a team we bossed that fortnight. The opposition weren't particularly strong, but the way Richard got us to express ourselves was awesome. We did ourselves proud and we were all buzzing at the end of the two weeks.

It was such a great experience. We were 15-year-old lads, so just being away from our parents was an adventure in itself. There was a games room in the halls where we used to play a bit of table tennis, and from time to time we'd head down to the pool for a swim. We'd have food put on for us – it wasn't quite up there with some of the hotels we would be treated to later on in our careers, but it was still decent.

As much as anything, it was a good experience just being a group of guys together. We all got on well – there weren't cliques at all. We'd recover from games together, train together, basically we were with each other 24/7. When you think how much time cricketers spend away from home, it's no wonder the ECB wanted us to get used to that side of things from a young age.

On a personal level, I felt like I'd played a blinder that fortnight. I kept immaculately and I remember feeling that I'd proven why I'd been picked ahead of Billings back at Bunbury – to myself, as much as anything else.

After that tournament, Richard put me forward for a prestigious ECB Fielding Award, with the ceremony held up at the Savoy Hotel in London. I didn't realise it at the time, but the ceremony was a pretty big deal with lots of dignitaries present, while people like Stuart Broad and Ian Bell were previous winners of some of the awards up for grabs that night. I went there with Mum and Dad, and it was a totally surreal experience. When I went up to collect the award I had to give an acceptance speech. I didn't realise in advance that I'd need to do one, but when the other lads were going up to accept their awards they were all making speeches, so I realised pretty quickly I'd need to say a few words.

That's a pretty daunting experience to go through, realising you've got to go up and speak in front of a massive audience. Luckily I've never been too fazed by public speaking, and I got through it relatively unscathed. It was a pretty uninspiring collection of words. I remembered to thank my parents for their support and for always ferrying me around. But overall it was just overwhelming to think I'd won an award at England level. It was surreal, but I was getting a great deal of credit – being seen as one of the best keepers in the country at my age group, so I knew I was doing well. But I also knew that I needed to keep it up if my goal of becoming a professional cricketer was going to materialise.

I was still only 15, and there was a long way to go before I could call myself a professional cricketer, but I was starting to believe that, if I wanted to achieve it, I could.

As a kid you watch the England team playing cricket on TV, so to be involved in that setup, albeit at a young age, was fantastic. "One day", I would think, "that could be me keeping wicket for England, like I'd seen Alec Stewart do when I was a kid."

It felt like I was on course with Tony's "world's best cricketer" flowchart, which he'd described to me years earlier at Hampshire. That chart was still on the wall beside my bed at home, and I would often check it to see where I was in relation to it.

At that stage, I felt, I was very much on track.

* * *

After that ceremony, Richard put me forward for the so-called Skillsets sessions. These were ECB-run, high-intensity programmes, working on your particular discipline. Only Azeem Rafiq and me from the under-15s squad were given a place at the sessions, so I was delighted to be involved. To be given the nod ahead of the likes of Joe Root, Jos Buttler and co. was pretty amazing. But the coaches obviously saw Azeem and I as two leading lights from our age group at that time.

Obviously I was doing the wicketkeeping programme, and every time I attended them, I had a great time. It was the perfect setup, 10 young keepers away for a week with three or four wicketkeeping coaches, working on and talking about nothing but our glovework. I loved it. Our sessions were led by former England wicketkeeper Bruce French, or Frenchy, as everyone called him. "It was always clear that Batesy's keeping was going to be high quality," Frenchy told us. "Right from probably about 15, when he first came to the Skillsets sessions."

Frenchy was the first guy who really pushed my keeping along. Up until that point I'd been progressing well, but Frenchy really wanted to stretch me to see what I was capable of. He was very good at drilling the basics. He was a relaxed character, but the difficulty of the drills, and the speed and volume of the repetitions, were harder than anything I'd faced as a keeper up to that point. Sessions I'd had with Bob Parks back at Hampshire had always been 30 minutes to an hour here and there, whereas Bruce's job was to dedicate all his time to you, whenever you needed him. So we were able to smash it, day in and day out.

A lot of the drills we worked on involved these orange boards; plastic wedges, raised at one end and with grooves running across them. They look like a wedge, raised at one end. They're standard kit for keepers, and I still use them when coaching now. But with Bruce, I used them a hell of a lot, particularly in those Skillsets sessions.

Frenchy would be on his knees directly behind the board, which was about 8ft from the stumps – so, where the bowler would be looking to pitch the ball in a match. He'd skim the ball off the board, like you skim stones across the sea at the beach. The ball would kiss the surface of the ramp, deviate slightly off the grooves, giving me – keeping up to the stumps – a fraction of a second to adjust, move and take a clean catch.

Frenchy was an eccentric character – he loved his keeping but he also loved climbing, so after a few days hard work at one of the Skillset camps, which was based in Shrewsbury, Frenchy took us out on the surrounding hills to do some orienteering. It was great fun.

Obviously we worked on a lot of technical things on that trip. My posture was something that the coaches were focusing on, as they felt I was hinged a little bit too much on my back, rather than having my weight more on my knees. Frenchy was really into posture, and getting it right at that age would obviously help me as I progressed through the age groups. That would all come from those sessions with the orange board, where my reflexes and my speed were constantly being tested, getting my body into the right position to move efficiently, moving as late as possible so that I could take the ball cleanly, as regularly as possible.

On that trip, we talked about the mental side of the game a lot too. It's probably the most important aspect of a wicketkeeper's game, having the ability to clear your mind, ball after ball, so that you can be ready for whatever's going to happen next ball. It could seam off the pitch, take the outside edge of the bat, inside edge, come off the batsman's leg, a footmark on the pitch, anything. Frenchy continued:

> Technique you can mess about with, but the mental side, the strength of concentration, expecting the ball to come, is a gift. When I talk about gifted keepers, it always comes down to what the mind is like. To me, it was pretty obvious back as far as those Skillset sessions that Batesy had that. That's been his strength throughout. His technique has adapted, and he's turned himself into a quality keeper. It's a shame he stopped playing so young. He could have played for England years ago.

What Bruce was talking about was a keeper's mentality, which I had. It's very difficult to teach someone that. There's a level of anticipation to it, a sixth sense of knowing when the batter is going to miss it, and that only comes with an out-and-out keeper's mindset. You see a lot of keeper-batters, because they've got more of a batter's instinct than I did, they see balls that they imagine batters should hit. So they switch off, thinking the ball is not coming their way. But the batter misses those sometimes, leaving the keeper out of position. A keeper's instinct, though, will tell them that the batter is going to miss every ball.

Interestingly, when we spoke to Jos Buttler, he admitted that the keeper's mentality had come late for him. "It's only really the last couple of years where I feel like that wicketkeeping mentality is where I want it to be," Jos told us. "I definitely felt like I had all the attributes to be a wicketkeeper before that, but it's the training of the brain into that wicketkeeping mentality; you're expecting every ball, not having a batsman's eye thinking, 'oh this is a bad ball that's been bowled, he's going to hit this', and then they miss it and you've completely switched off."

Those Skillset sessions were great for my keeping, and I felt like I was on top of my game with the gloves as a result. But at the same time I had this nagging sense of dread, that my batting just wasn't progressing at the same rate. I mean, how could it? It wasn't getting anywhere near the same attention that my keeping was.

That said, after those wicketkeeping sessions, I was encouraged by the ECB – along with Ben Scott, one of my Skillsets colleagues – to go and work with England's batting coaches, to help bring our batting levels up a bit. Ben was another decent keeper, a bit older than me, but with the same need to try to bring his batting level up to a standard similar to that of his keeping.

I was acutely aware that my batting needed to improve – of course I was. In fact it was starting to become a bit of a complex for me. "Great keeper, but can he bat?", people were saying of me. Even at that age, I was being pigeonholed. And it wasn't a lack of effort either. I worked tirelessly on my batting, but it just never quite clicked.

I was always trying to find similarities with my keeping. How could I be such a good keeper, and just lack something with the bat? How was that possible? A similar sort of co-ordination is required, similar principles. At that sort of age, of 14, 15, I was good at batting. At school, and for my club, I was always the best at batting, or one of the best at least. I was always at the top of the order, my team mates would rely on me to perform, I guess it's only once you start getting into an elite environment, like the England age groups for example, that you start to see what your capabilities are in comparison with the best guys in your age group.

A year earlier at Yateley Manor as a 13-year-old, when I was scoring hundreds and fifties for fun, I'd enjoyed my batting so much. Who wouldn't? In general, I loved the idea of batting, but only when it was going well. Which is what I think most players would say.

So even at that age, coming into that time with England, and even though I'd been picked as one of only two players from my age group to go to these Skillset sessions, I think I was still aware that, even then, I had a couple of technical flaws and perhaps wasn't as capable with the bat as my peers.

When I caught up with Frenchy in spring 2017 I asked him, looking back, what he thought was going wrong with my batting. "From what I can think, and I'm not a batting coach, I just thought you were a little bit too intense with your batting," he told me. He was always straight to the point, was Frenchy, which I liked from a coach.

> I thought you were trying too hard if anything, rather than just relaxing a bit, and that's just looking from afar really. You just looked a bit tight, because you knew that you had to deliver.
>
> Obviously you would have played a lot more cricket at my age. It's a generational thing, but it's always been there. There's always been this thing of batting over keeping, even when I played, so it has always been around, but it seems to be more the trend now. Everyone says it's the Gilchrist effect, and they're probably right. You see someone come in and do what he did. Everyone wants one. And I don't think anyone's found one since he played. Maybe it's the wrong way to be looking at things. When I'm scouting for keepers now, in county cricket, they need to be batting at six at least.

Even then I was comparing my batting with my keeping, and wanting it to be at the same level, rather than perhaps thinking, more like Billings, "what can I add to the team as a batter, how can score enough runs to benefit the team?" Perhaps I was too focused on my batting technique being as close to perfect as my keeping was, instead of just learning to produce, as Billings talked about earlier. This awkward juxtaposition of my keeping versus my batting would continue throughout my career – developing as a keeper in the shadows of Gilchrist and Stewart was always going to be tough.

Despite the concerns over my batting, I continued to be involved in the England setup. I was so proud to be representing my country at that age. There's the knowledge that you're one of the best players in your age group in England, and you're playing with some fantastic players, and working with some excellent coaches, which is only going to help your game. We were so lucky to be involved and we all knew it. We got to go to some fantastic places, too. One year, I went to

Barbados on a training camp with the England boys, with lads like Ben Stokes, Jos Buttler and Joe Root. Great lads, and even then you could see, great players in the making.

It's amazing to think how much cricket I was playing back then. I was only in my mid-teens, and was working hard at my secondary school, Lord Wandsworth College. Looking back, it must've been a massive strain and sacrifice for my parents. Ferrying me around everywhere, to training, games and tournaments, all over the south of England.

Of course, they're my parents, and they'd do anything for me. They were massively supportive, and I owe them so much. They hadn't been particularly into cricket when I first started playing. But the more I played the more they enjoyed it, and by the time I was professional my whole family was turning out to see me play. Even my grandparents. They loved the buzz of the matches. Their support really drove me on, and it always gave me extra motivation when I was playing, knowing they were all there.

* * *

By the time you get to 16, 17, 18, if you're going to progress at your county you'll be playing in the seconds. I was about 16 when I made my debut for Hampshire's 2nd XI. Tom Burrows was the backup to first-team keeper Nic Pothas at that stage, and when he got injured the day before a match, I got a call saying I was playing. Last-minute call-ups are part and parcel of being a professional sportsperson, as I would find out.

It was an away game, so my parents had to drop me off at the team hotel the night before the game, because the rest of the squad were already there. I was used to going away for cricket because of all the trips I'd done with England, so I wasn't fazed about going into that environment, although the prospect of making my 2nd XI debut was obviously giving me plenty of nervous excitement.

Daws was already in the seconds, so he was there at the hotel, as was Vincey. Daws was a bit older, and had broken into the team earlier than me, while Vincey had developed quickly having moved from Wiltshire, and had been playing 2nd XI cricket from the age of 14 or 15. Both of them were very, very good, even then.

That match was a big moment for me. We were staying in a nice hotel for a few nights, and away from the cricket ground it was dawning on me that this was what my future could be like. It was great, and I definitely felt like I could get used to it. It beat having to pay to stay in that sort of a hotel, which would probably cost a fortune if Joe Bloggs were to rock up for an evening's stay. So it was a privileged position and I was well aware of that.

After that match I just wanted to get straight back to the nets and keep working, keep training and wait for the next opportunity to come along. But it's a long, hard slog when you're not getting 2nd XI opportunities on a regular basis.

Away from cricket I was facing the same regular challenges other 16-year-olds face. I was growing up physically and emotionally, I had exams going on, and the lure of going out and partying with my mates seemed to grow by the week. Pretty much every weekend friends would be going out, and most of the time I wouldn't be able to join them, or if I did go, I'd have to be picked up early, because I'd have to be up early the next morning for cricket. You constantly feel like you're missing out on all the fun, but at the same time I knew I had to be disciplined and dedicate myself to the cricket.

There were times when my parents would ask me, "are you sure you want to carry on with cricket?" And there were definitely times when I found it hard and it became a bit of a ball ache, and I wondered whether I should carry on. But I knew deep down I had to keep going.

Having wrestled with the lure of a normal teenage life, I took the decision to properly pursue my dream of playing professional cricket. It's one of those where, at the age of 16, you could easily decide to keep the cricket going almost as a hobby in the background, and put your studies first. I was going to do A-levels, no doubt, but I also knew it was time to put most of my eggs in one basket and devote the vast majority of my time and effort into becoming a professional cricketer. I needed to work harder and be even more focused than I'd ever been before.

* * *

At 18 I received my first development contract at Hampshire. It was a great feeling and another key milestone for me personally. The next phase, obviously, was getting a senior contract, but the development contract was a step in the right direction.

Then, towards the end of 2009, I went to Bangladesh with the England squad – the under-19s by this stage. Representing England was an amazing feeling. Everything you experience, even as an under-19 player, is just that little bit grander than you'd experience with your county. When we arrived at our hotel in Bangladesh, the staff put on a big welcome ceremony for us, dishing out free drinks in the reception area. We were all in our England suits, which had been tailored for us back in the UK, with the ECB badge on the blazer. And our helmets had the England badge on too, I've still got mine at home.

On the cricket field I had a really good tour. I did really well with the gloves and ultimately edged back ahead of my old nemesis, Sam Billings, once again. Sam was ultra-competitive, everything he did was to be better than the next person. So when you felt like you'd got one over on him as it were, it was a really satisfying feeling.

I came back from Bangladesh feeling like I'd outperformed him. And my confidence was well-placed as soon after we got back I received a letter from John Abrahams, the Elite Player Development Manager at the ECB, saying I'd been named in the squad to go to the under-19s World Cup, which was taking place in New Zealand in January 2010.

What an honour. I was off to New Zealand to play in the biggest youth cricket competition in the world, representing my country. Amazing.

My parents were super proud, but one thing I've realised through the process of writing this book, is how all of these things, the milestones and the heartaches, they probably affected my parents more than they ever affected me. At the moments of tension, they were probably more nervous than me. And in these moments of joy, while I took them in my stride, my folks were probably on cloud nine! I wish I'd taken a moment to reflect and appreciate what I'd achieved a bit more, but to me it was all part of the journey.

So in early January 2010, I met up with my England under-19 teammates at a cold, damp Heathrow Airport all dressed in our "number ones" – a polo shirt and chinos, ECB branded of course, ready to fly out to New Zealand. We all looked the part, and we got to go into the first-class lounge, which I hadn't done before.

And looking around that lounge, it was obvious we had a formidable squad. We had Ben Stokes, Jos Buttler, Joe Root and my Hampshire teammate James Vince. You couldn't help but feel we were going to have a very good tournament. One man missing from the group was Sam Billings, who was left out in favour of me. He'd have his time soon enough. But what his omission and my selection shows is that different players mature at different speeds, and at different stages in their career. Instead, for now, it would be Jos Buttler and I who would be contesting the gloves in New Zealand.

At that World Cup we were playing under Mark Robinson, who went on to coach Sussex and, more recently, the England women's team. Mick Newell, who would become an England selector, was also part of the coaching team.

I asked Joe Root about that World Cup squad when we met up. "As a group we got on pretty well together," Joe recalled. "And I think you can see that in the senior squad now. I know only a few have gone on to that level, but you can see how tight we are now in the full side."

Pretty much every player in that World Cup squad went on to play first-class cricket, which is really exceptional, and testament to the quality and commitment of the boys I was playing with. Normally you have three or four guys that fall away, but everyone from that group went on to be contracted by a county.

New Zealand was amazing. It's a beautiful country, and the people were really hospitable. The tournament was a little over a fortnight long, and games came thick and fast – pretty much every other day – so unfortunately we didn't really get to have a good look round.

All our games were based on the South Island, but we did spend a little time in Wellington training at the Basin Reserve, which is a stunning ground. It's surrounded by giant, green hills, with houses dotted sporadically among the greenery. Just a few blocks away was Wellington Harbour, which we cycled around on a rare day off. It was really windy, so the cycle was rather more hard work than I'd bargained for, to be honest. But it was still nice to get out and about.

The format of the competition was four groups of four teams, with the top two of each group progressing to the quarter-finals. We had a pretty straightforward group, and we comfortably progressed having won all three matches. I played in the first game, against Hong Kong at the Bert Sutcliffe Oval in Lincoln, and took a couple of catches off David Payne, which was pleasing. I didn't get a chance to bat as our top three saw us home, with the familiar names of Joe Root and James Vince weighing in with 70-odd each.

I was then left out of the second game, with Jos taking the gloves in my place. In the first game Jos had played as a straight batter, but Robbo obviously felt he wanted to try something different in that second match, against Afghanistan. It didn't affect the result – again we won having bowled out the opposition, our top order doing the job again with ease.

Our final group game, against India back at the Bert Sutcliffe Oval, would provide a sterner test, although we'd already qualified for the quarter-finals by that stage. Unfortunately for Jos, he was injured for that one, so I was given the chance to stake a claim for the keeper's position, with a place in the starting line-up for the knockout stages very much up for grabs.

For the first time in the tournament we batted first, and set India a pretty decent target of 247 to win. In that innings I had the pleasure of batting with Ben Stokes, watching on as he smashed a blistering hundred. Together we put on 62 off 41 deliveries, with me playing a supporting role, turning over the strike so Ben could fill his boots. I ended up with 27 off 28 before being run out in the final over, which was frustrating, but I felt like I'd done a job for the team.

With the ball we did really well. We bowled India out for 215, beating the holders by 31 runs and with it, topping the group. On a personal note I felt I'd done well; I took five catches off the quicks in that innings, helping us win the game and secure top spot in our group.

Our quarter-final two days later was against a West Indies side containing Jason Holder and Kraigg Brathwaite – no relation to Carlos Brathwaite, who would take down Ben Stokes in that memorable last over of the ICC World T20 in 2016. They were no mugs, but we expected to win. Jos was fit for this one, and sadly for me Robbo decided to play him ahead of me, which was really disappointing as I felt I'd done enough in the game before.

But that's elite sport, and obviously I got right behind the boys. We were a close group and we all wanted to do well as a team.

"By then I think my keeping was at a level where it was good enough to warrant me to play as the wicketkeeper," Jos told us about him getting the nod over me in that match. "Batesy would've been the better out-and-out keeper, but I was more of that modern type of wicketkeeper offering that batting option as well, which is where I started to have a nice sort of niche. I knew I could offer with the gloves and with the bat, whereas – I'm not saying Batesy couldn't, but he was seen more as that skilled wicketkeeper. But those are the tactical decisions which the coach has to take."

The quarter-final itself was rain-affected, and our skipper Azeem Rafiq put the West Indies into bat first. We bowled them out for 166 from their 36 overs, which we felt was really gettable. But batting conditions were tough, it was damp and the wicket was doing a bit. Jason Holder took both our openers, Joe Root and Chris Dent from Gloucestershire, and we never really recovered. We ended up being bowled out for 148, 18 runs short of the total, a massive anti-climax and a really disappointing way to exit a tournament we'd gone there to win.

I was gutted. We all were. We really felt we were in with a shout of winning that tournament. And to make matters worse for me personally, to have been left out of the side for that game was really disappointing. I wanted to contribute, and I felt if I'd kept up to the stumps in that game it would have given us an extra dimension in the field, but it wasn't to be.

It was quite a despondent dressing room afterwards. John Abrahams stood up and talked, telling us we'd all learn a lot from this experience, which we undoubtedly would, and to go back to our counties and build on what we'd achieved here.

Before we left New Zealand we had a 5th-place play-off, against India. It was a token game and one we could've done without, to be honest. I played in that one and was pushed up the batting order to five. I think it was John and Robbo's way of giving me a chance to go out there and get some runs, and show everyone what I could do with the bat. Unfortunately I managed only four, and my rival on that tour, Jos Buttler, went and top-scored with 78 at the top of the order. He'd definitely taken his chance with the bat, but then we all knew he was a class act – it's no surprise to me he's such a superstar of world cricket right now. He was quality then, and he's got better and better over the years.

I spoke to Joe Root about our World Cup campaign, and he was really complimentary about my work behind the stumps during that tournament.

> It's always a difficult one because it's such a vital role. I think it's well known that you were the best gloveman, certainly in our age group. In terms of technique and from what I saw, you could just see the time you had. The way you moved, and especially standing up to the seamers, it was very impressive to watch. When you've got a keeper who can do that, it puts so much pressure on the opposition. Someone bowling 85mph, keeper up, you're very limited then to what you can do as a batter. Not only that, but it's one thing standing up, but to do it so well, at pace especially, is very difficult.

Then Joe turned interviewer. This was a chat between old friends after all, so the conversation ebbed and flowed like such conversations do. We were sat in the pavilion of Bristol's County Ground, as England's backroom staff, including Bruce French, who we'd spoken to earlier, Graham Thorpe and Mark Ramprakash filtered out of the ground, down the stairs beside us and out onto the green outfield in front. That's professional cricket – especially at England level – famous faces everywhere.

So Rooty said to me: "Did you almost buy into the idea that everyone was saying? That you were such a good keeper, a keeper that could bat a bit, when actually your batting was at a decent enough level? It almost worked against you, being such a good keeper."

It was an interesting question. From my point of view, I was a perfectionist. I knew I was a good keeper, but in a batting sense I knew I could be better. Be more solid. Score more runs. I wish I'd just embraced the technique I had and tried to make it work. Use that to score some runs for the side, rather than trying to be the best batter out there, because that was never going to happen.

But that's me thinking with the benefit of hindsight. At the time, I came away from New Zealand thinking what an amazing experience that tournament had been. It had been great to see where I was as a player, both in terms of my own country but also players from around the world. It was a great setup and I certainly learned a lot. Perhaps I didn't realise that at the time, but looking back it was a fantastic experience.

The only regret was, with such a talented group of players in our squad, we didn't achieve as much in that tournament as we perhaps should have. As we've seen, we got knocked out in the quarter-finals by the West Indies, with Australia the eventual winners. The general feeling in the camp was that we could, maybe should, have won it, which was disappointing. We were all downhearted in that respect.

But there was also an overwhelming sense that this was the end of a journey. This was the last time our squad would reunite as an England age group. There were under-19 fixtures to come a few months later in the English summer, but the nature of the situation was, if players broke into their county's first team, that would take precedence. So we knew this was the end of a journey that had begun four years earlier at the Bunbury Festival, when we'd been selected for that under-15s tournament at Loughborough.

Sitting on the plane back home to England, I remember feeling quite flat. Not because of the sense that the England age group stuff was over, as such. More the sense that we'd let a golden opportunity of being World Cup winners slip through our fingers. At that stage you don't know what the future holds, whether you'll get a chance to represent your country again at senior level. You look at players like Root, Stokes and Buttler and say they looked nailed on to win full international honours. But the reality is, everyone in that squad would've felt they had a chance of progressing into the senior squad – I know I certainly did.

Now I can appreciate what a fantastic experience that was. Touring New Zealand with your country, a squad full of mates, playing and training in top international facilities, testing yourself against the best in your age group from around the world, it was phenomenal.

Going back to Hampshire, I was happy with the experience I'd had with England, but I realised that it would count for nothing if I didn't carry on developing and improving as a player. My next goal? To get into the Hampshire first team, get a professional contract and put myself in the window for the senior England squad.

Chapter 3
Breaking into the Hampshire first team

It was a gradual process but, by the summer of 2010, I was finally in and around the first team squad. It was surreal. I was surrounded by all these legends: England's Ashes-winning bowler Simon Jones, ex-England all-rounder and IPL legend Dimi Mascarenhas, not to mention overseas stars like Imran Tahir and Neil McKenzie.

Our first-choice wicketkeeper at that time was a formidable character too – Nic Pothas, or "Skeg" as we called him. He'd had that nickname for years, long before I knew him. It's an affectionate name that everyone calls him, in fact he even refers to himself as Skeg.

Skeg was certainly someone I looked up to coming up through the academy, although I didn't really get to work with him as much as I'd have liked. Once I was around the first team, he was either playing ahead of me, or else out injured, and when he was out injured he was out of the group. But he always seemed to be a fan of me, and supported me when I was coming through the age groups. Nic was incredibly hard-working, and was very much a leader out on the field. He'd motivate the boys, shouting and geeing them up during those long spells in the field when not a lot is happening, running through overs quickly to keep the pressure on the batting teams and keep the run-rate honest. He was the heartbeat of our team out in the field, and I was keen to take some of those leadership qualities and incorporate them into my game.

Dimi was another great guy, and a superstar in our squad. He was a limited-overs specialist, which epitomised the club's focus at the time. We were a one-day team, first and foremost. In some respects, it's no surprise to me that guys like Daws and Vincey struggled in the England Test side, because we were brought up to specialise in one-day cricket. That was the most important thing to our club.

Dimi was our T20 skipper. He was the catalyst of that team, and the List A team too, and was someone I respected hugely in terms of his cricketing achievements, domestically and in the IPL, as well as with England. Most importantly, however, Dimi was a top bloke to have in the changing room and someone you could speak to. As a young player coming through, he was always happy to talk to me about anything to do with the game.

But despite the fact he'd achieved so much, playing for England and in the IPL, he wasn't one to wax lyrical about his own achievements. Instead he would talk about the games *we* had ahead of us, how *we* should approach them and what *we* could achieve, as a team and individually. He'd use his own experience and turn it into advice for us on how to approach our next match, or the next stage of our career. He's a lovely guy – funny, bubbly, confident – just a born leader of men really. He'd get around the young boys and bring them along with him. He was a young kid at heart himself, which helped. His energy was massive. He gave us all confidence, and maybe that was why he was so good for us younger players, as we weren't really getting that sort of encouragement from our coaches. Not enough, anyway. Dimi told Tom:

> I first heard about Michael when he was coming through the academy system at Hampshire. All the reports were that there was a brilliant wicketkeeper coming through and it wouldn't be long before he'd be knocking on the door of the first team. I remember thinking at the time, "I hope he can bat as well as he keeps". At the time we had a brilliant wicketkeeper-batsmen in Nic Pothas, and it was going to be a stretch for anyone to be able to bat better than Nic.
>
> My first impressions when I first lay eyes on him was that his work ethic was second to none, and I hadn't even seen him keep at that stage. He looked super-fit, strong and obviously spent a lot of time in the gym working on his physique. Behind the stumps all the reports were true, he was a natural, had great hands and moved particularly well for a shortish lad.

Neil McKenzie, the South African batsman, was another guy I really respected and learned a lot from. Macca was a legend at the club. He was so laid back, but he delivered for us big time, consistently over several years. I talked a lot to him about my batting – he had an incredible amount of wisdom and experience, which he was only too happy to pass onto a young lad like me. Sometimes he'd suggest something for me to work on from a batting perspective. He'd talk me through it, then take me off to the indoor nets to show me what he meant. He didn't have to do that. I mean, he wasn't a coach. But he was a great guy who wanted to help. He was a legend.

And then we had Jimmy Adams, who became Hampshire's captain after Dominic Cork retired in 2011. Jimmy was solid as a rock. He was respected by everyone at the club and was the perfect bloke to lead us at that time as well. Jimmy told Tom:

> At the time, you didn't really have a good view of academies. Within the space of about 18 months I and probably some of the other senior guys went from being aware there were some talented young cricketers in the academy, to thinking "Wow – not only are these very good players, they're playing" [in the first team]. That was the difference from previous years and previous players. Previously you'd wait for that progression, you'd wait for them to take the opportunity. With Briggs, Bates, Wood – Daws had already trodden that path a bit, and Vincey too – they went from, you knew they could play and you were quite excited about them, to actually playing in trophy-winning teams and performing, actually carrying us in certain games.

Having the experience of all those guys in the squad was great to tap into. To be able to ask them about the different things they'd experienced in their careers; the highs, the lows, the successes, the failures, it really helped me, and gave me a lot of confidence.

But the best thing about the side, which developed over the years and arguably peaked in 2012, was the blend of youth and experience. Vincey and Daws had been regulars in the first team for a year or so by 2010, while Woody and Briggs broke through around the same time as me, although I was the last of the group to make my debut. Daws recalled:

> It was a good atmosphere in that team. It was good fun, and that makes a massive difference. If your mate does well, you think "quality". There's no jealousy. There's no thinking, "oh I want him to fail". We had a great energy – that's what happens when you've played a lot of cricket together before getting into the first team. If you've played since you were 14, 15, playing in the academy, the 2nd XI, it makes a big difference.

It was a big achievement from the coaches' perspective, too. Head coach Giles White ("Chalks" as he was known to everyone), Tony Middleton and all the backroom staff were praised at the time for bringing through so many players from the academy into the first team. We were like Yorkshire really, who are renowned for bringing through younger players together, and building their first team around local talent. Hampshire definitely had that sort of approach back then.

Now they're getting stick for doing the complete opposite; spending big money on international superstars like Kyle Abbott on a Kolpak deal. A Kolpak deal allows cricketers from countries with Freedom of Jobs and Movement Agreements in place with the EU, to come and play over here as non-overseas players. This is nothing against Kyle, who is a fantastic player and a top bloke. But it just seems Hampshire have deviated quite drastically away from their mantra in just a few short years.

I guess the demands on Chalks and the coaches to deliver trophies must be huge, and that does impact on the decisions they take regarding recruitment. But still, it's sad to see a move away from that academy focus, particularly as a graduate of the club's own programme myself.

* * *

18 July 2010. That was the day it finally happened; my first team debut. It's strange recalling all the circumstances that led to me playing that day. It's so long ago now and so much has happened since then. But the memories are still pretty vivid.

That morning I was at Loughborough training with the England under-19s, when I started getting peppered with calls from Chalks back at Hampshire. When I spoke to him, he sounded flustered, "you've got to get back to the Rose Bowl ASAP for the game today," he said. Skeg's knee had gone in the warm up, and the message was that I should get back as soon as I could to take his place. It was a T20 group game against a strong Sussex side, a game we had to win to make it through our group and into the quarter-finals.

My emotions were all over the place. It was a combination of panic at trying to get back in time for the start of the game, and shock at the prospect of playing for the first team. I ragged it back to Southampton from Loughborough and made good time. The boys were batting first and I wasn't even at the ground when our innings started! I went into the changing room and got my kit on, and pretty much went straight out onto the field for the second innings. I don't think I even caught a ball before we went out!

I didn't have any time to mentally prepare for the game, either. And perhaps that was a good thing, because it couldn't have been a harder game to make my debut in. It was one we had to win, against a strong

Sussex outfit which included England internationals Matt Prior, Mike Yardy and Luke Wright, and the game was also live on TV. Call it the ignorance of youth, or maybe because I hadn't been there all day to take in the build-up, but I just took it all in my stride.

In terms of the game itself, we won, and I felt I had a blinder on a personal level with the gloves. I was standing up to the stumps pretty much all game – I mean, it was the only way I knew how, after all. I remember one particular dismissal, when I was standing up to Woody. Luke Wright was on strike, and he feathered one down the leg side and I took a really sharp catch. It was one of those catches that would become my calling card in the years ahead.

At the end of the match I was interviewed by Sky Sports presenter, Charles Colville. It was like a whirlwind – one minute I was in Loughborough training with England under-19s, the next I'm being interviewed on TV! It was just great to have made my debut for the first team, and to think my friends and family could have tuned in to watch it, was really nice.

I was buzzing, and from then on just wanted to play in the first team as often as I could. I was training hard, but then I always did. Not because I was planning to take Skeg's place full-time as such, I just wanted to be the best I could be.

Looking back now I do wonder whether that first appearance, and the games that followed, just came a bit too soon. Because my keeping was at such a level I could cope with it all, straight away. But my batting was nowhere near ready to play at that standard. Having said that, I rarely got the chance to bat, as our batting was so strong and I was so far down the order, normally going in at nine or ten. That lack of time in the middle would have a knock-on effect on my batting, that's for sure.

Mind you, I wasn't really thinking about that at the time. I was in the side, and with Skeg's injury problems continuing, I was only going to play more cricket. The win against Sussex had earned us a trip to Edgbaston, to play Warwickshire in the quarter-finals. That game was close, but we got through it. They'd set us 153 to win and we reached it with a ball to spare, Vincey doing it when it mattered, again. We were on our way to Finals Day.

In county cricket, the T20 Finals Day is *the* showpiece occasion of the season. Everything goes up a gear; the TV cameras are there, the press box is heaving and the ground is packed. Your fans go crazy, desperate for you to win. It's massive to the players for all those reasons, but also because it is *the* competition we all want to win.

Championship cricket is where the tradition is, but T20 cricket is the format that most of us want to excel in. And as I said before, at Hampshire, white-ball cricket was definitely where the emphasis was, at that time at least.

And on Saturday 14 August 2010, winning Finals Day would be an even bigger deal for us because it was being staged at our home ground, the Rose Bowl. So we were desperate to get the result as much for our fans as for ourselves.

I was so nervous when I woke up that morning, the most nervous I'd ever been in my career in fact. Usually I knew my keeping was going to be on point, and I was pretty relaxed as a result. But on that day, with what was at stake, in front of the TV cameras and at our home ground, there were definitely a few nerves.

In 2010 I was living with Daws in Southampton, and on the morning of Finals Day he drove us to the game. We left our place in town first thing in the morning, about 7.30 or so, to beat the rush and get to the ground in good time. But when we got to the Rose Bowl, it was utter chaos.

We drove through the gates of the ground, just off Marshall Drive – named after the legendary West Indian seamer, Malcolm Marshall, who used to play for Hampshire. We headed up the hill, parking in the players' car park at the top of the hill, on the right. Already you could hear music blaring, as musicians sound-checked and DJs checked their equipment out over the PA system. We walked down the steep steps that take you down towards the Atrium, where the players' changing rooms are located. There were stalls setting up in front of us, with hundreds of people milling around in the Atrium getting everything ready. Daws turned to me and said "It doesn't get much better than this, mate." He was right, this was going to be a massive day.

People started pouring into the ground off Botley Road soon after, from 9.30 or so. The atmosphere started building and pretty soon there was a great buzz going around the ground. Plenty of other times that season we'd played at the Rose Bowl in front of one man and his dog, so the saying goes. Empty stands, only the die-hard members in attendance. Today was going to be a full house, and we couldn't wait to get out there and perform in front of a crowd like that.

We wanted to repeat the pre-match processes that had got us to Finals Day in the first place, so we were soon out on the pitch getting warmed up, having a pre-match game of football, as we always did. I enjoyed the warm up that day. The crowd were chattering away, there were a few chants going off already. Being out on the pitch for the warm-up allowed us to soak all that in. I found my parents in the crowd, clocked where they were sitting and gave them a wave, like I did every time they were at a game.

The weather was set fair all day, not too hot and sunny, more cloudy with the odd sunny spell. But crucially it was dry, and as a result got underway on time in the first semi-final, which was against Essex. They batted first and set us a target of 156 to win. It was a decent target to post, but we felt that if we got off to a good start, we could chase it down. But in these high-pressure knockout matches, you have to start well – it's so important. We always felt a score of 150–160 was about par, irrespective of the wicket. It was just the pressure of chasing that made it a competitive target. If we batted well, we'd expect to chase it down, but pressure can do funny things, and runs on the board was always a bonus.

On that day though, we made no mistakes. Jimmy and Abdul Razzaq set up victory with an opening partnership of 67 – in fact Jimmy had been absolutely bossing it all season, scoring two hundreds in the T20 competition alone. He was in the form of his life – form which got him an England Lions call-up for the following winter.

We won our semi-final with four balls to spare, and it must have been reasonably comfortable because I can't really remember a lot about it. Although that's probably only to be expected given what was to happen in the final.

The gap between the second semi and the final was massive. We'd experienced such a high beating Essex, the adrenaline was pumping and we were absolutely flying, but then we had to calm down again, relax and wait what felt like an age for the final. We went to the leisure centre across the road from the Rose Bowl, just to get away from the ground. We sat in the lounge and watched the second semi-final between Somerset and Nottinghamshire on the TV and I began to feel really, really tired. All the tension and emotion from our match against Essex had drained me of any energy, and I was now experiencing a major adrenaline crash! I'm sure some of the other lads felt the same but I wouldn't know – I was fast asleep.

When I woke, I found out that Somerset had edged out the Outlaws, meaning we were playing the men from Taunton in the final. Somerset were a very strong white-ball team at the time, and we seemed to come up against them quite a lot around then. Games between both sides were always close, so we knew the final was going to be a tough game.

We walked back across the road to the Rose Bowl, to start our pre-game preparations. That involved having a bit of food upstairs in the Atrium, before doing our warm-up back on the pitch. We felt good as a group, and having got the first game out of the way, my nerves were settled and I was ready to take on Somerset.

The men from Taunton batted first, Craig Kieswetter, their wicketkeeper-batsman, top-scoring with 71 as they reached 173-6. My England under-19s team mate, Jos Buttler, was in the Somerset side that day, as a batter only, but thankfully he managed just five.

We knew we were going to have to bat well to reach our target of 174 to win, but we still fancied our chances. In the changing room before we batted, Neil McKenzie said to the group, "Vincey, you got us through the quarter-final but don't worry, I've got the final." He was always saying stuff like that, which had a really calming influence on the rest of us in the changing room. Especially in those high-pressure moments, or when things weren't going so well up the order. He would always see us through. Always. And as long as he was at the crease, we always felt we were in the game.

Even when the run rate was creeping up and up, he was confident enough to block out the good balls, content to turn the strike over and deal in ones,[7] waiting for the bad balls to come along. We'd be in the changing room going, "What the hell is he doing?", but he'd always be in control of his innings and, more often than not, he'd see us home. He was a massive influence on all of us, especially us younger ones. Vincey got on really well with him, and would probably say he learned a huge amount from him.

In that final against Somerset, he did what he said he was going to do. As the sun was setting over the Rose Bowl, on a mild, late-August evening, Macca scored a brilliant half century which, we hoped, would put Somerset's chances of winning to bed. His knock really set us on our way, but he fell with us on 163-4, needing just 11 to win with 11 balls remaining.

He'd done a great job, as always. But losing such a senior batter, who was going along so nicely, at such a key stage of the innings, was a big blow, and his departure undoubtedly unsettled the ship. With him gone, someone else was going to have to step up.

---

[7] Macca's approach was old-school. Instead of trying to hit big shots for fours and sixes early in his innings, he'd instead try to get in, get used to the ball, all the while running the odd single to keep the scoreboard ticking over. Macca was supremely confident, and the longer he was out there, the more chance he felt he'd have of scoring the runs needed to win the match. Looking at his record, it's hard to argue with his approach!

When wickets fell in our middle order, I always started to panic that I might need to go out and bat. In the T20 competition that season, we'd tended to get off to good starts, and I therefore hadn't been needed. But on the odd occasion we'd struggled, I panicked that I might have to go in and get us over the line. In my three previous games in the senior side I'd not been required, so if I was needed in the final, I'd be going in completely cold. I didn't have the experience to bat in such a huge match, and as a result I was totally freaked out by the prospect.

But before I got anywhere near the crease, we still had a few batters left in the dugout. After Macca's departure, Michael Carberry joined Sean Ervine (Slug) at the crease, and at that stage we felt we should still win this game comfortably. But this was a final, and runs on the board always puts the team batting second under pressure. Added to that we were at home in front of a full house. It was a final. Funny things do happen.

A couple of balls later, Slug pulled one – he cracked it and we were thinking it was going for four. Instead, Somerset fielder Nick Compton almost caught it at square leg. It wasn't really a chance, in fact it was a fantastic stop of a certain four, but the risk was there. The pressure was mounting. Shortly afterwards, Carbs was out. Shit. And it wasn't just that a new batter would have to go to the crease – it was the fact he'd used up a couple of deliveries without scoring before getting out. Suddenly we were a little bit behind the eight ball – that's how quickly a T20 match can change.

Our overseas player, Australian all-rounder Dan Christian, was next in to bat. He joined Slug with us needing ten from eight balls, to win a game that had looked ours a couple of overs earlier. But further drama was to unfold; as we went into the final over, bowled by Somerset's quick, Zander de Bruyn, Christian had to call for a runner as he was suffering with cramp![8] Two games in a day, the pressure, the adrenaline, it can take its toll, even on a seasoned pro like Dan!

However, there was a problem with the wicket. The crease, which is painted on with white paint, didn't stretch to the next strip, which is where the runner would need to, well, run. So the runner wouldn't know where to run to, and the umpire wouldn't know whether he was in or not when completing a run.

---

[8] If a batsman gets injured, such that he can bat but can't run, then another member of the batting team can come to the wicket and run for the injured player. This is pretty unheard of in T20 cricket because the game is so short, hence the confusion that Dan's request for a runner caused in this scenario!

So the umpire had to call the groundsmen onto the pitch – in the last over of the final – to come and paint lines on the next pitch so the runner knew where to run to. Honestly, you couldn't make it up.

The groundsmen came on with their pot of paint and a long spirit level and set about painting the crease lines along from the wicket we were playing on, onto the next strip where the runner would run.

Finally we got going again. Christian and Slug – and the runner, Jimmy Adams – exchanged singles and twos throughout that final over, leaving us needing two runs off the final ball of the day to win the game outright. A single would tie the game which would suit us, as we'd lost fewer wickets, and we'd therefore win the game. Pure drama. A whole day's cricket coming down to one final delivery. That's why we all love T20 cricket so much, isn't it?

De Bruyn readied himself to bowl the final delivery. Interestingly, Somerset's wicketkeeper, Craig Kieswetter, came up to the stumps for that final ball. I say interesting, because I would have been up to the stumps all match, in fact I was pretty much up there for the whole innings we had bowled earlier. There's that difference again, between specialist keepers and batters who keep. Had I been on their side for that over, some of those ones and twos may have been avoided, and Somerset might have been further ahead at this stage. Minor differences. Marginal gains.

De Bruyn steamed in and bowled it full and straight. The ball crashed into Christian's pad and the Somerset team went up to appeal it. "How's that?!"

Meanwhile Christian's runner, Jimmy Adams, and Carbs, set off for the run. They completed the run, but by this stage Christian was in no man's land in the middle of the wicket, so Somerset could have run him out. Instead, Somerset threw to the bowler's end, where Carbs was already in, rather than going to the keeper's end and potentially running Dan out. They'd missed out on the run-out opportunity, and we'd won the game. Crazy.

After all the carnage of the last couple of overs, to win it, and in front of our home crowd, was a fantastic feeling. I just remember it being a frenzy at the end. Groups of players all over the pitch celebrating with each other, journalists running about like ants trying to get interviews, it was mayhem. It was a moment of pure ecstasy that we'd won, we were on such a high, absolutely buzzing and, ultimately, really relieved we'd got over the line having been in such a strong position just a couple of overs from the end. We almost threw it away, but we got over the line in the end.

"A few dodgy tickers in the dugout – just bonkers!" – Jimmy Adams told the media after the game, which as a quote just about sums up both the end of that game, and Jimmy as a person!

Then it all went quiet. Guys wandered around the pitch, some alone just quietly taking stock of what we'd achieved. Others having a chat with the opposition, offering a consoling word, while at the same time trying to conceal their own joy at what we'd achieved. I wandered over and found my folks in the crowd again. I gave them a thumbs up, before Mum and Dad ran down the stairs from their seats to the pitch side. Mum gave me a hug and Dad said "Well done, son." Those moments, they made all the years of hard work worthwhile.

Then, once the stage has been assembled on the pitch, the group came back together in time for the presentation. First up was the Man of the Match award, which unsurprisingly went to Neil McKenzie for his outstanding knock. Then we were invited onto the stage, one by one. I was buzzing. I couldn't wait to get onto that stage, get my medal, and then get my hands on the trophy!

Once we were all assembled, up came our captain, Dominic Cork, who lifted the trophy high into the dark Southampton sky, his face beaming from ear to ear. It was party time! Corks were flying through the night air – from the Champagne bottles, not the skipper. And then we all just sprayed each other with fizz. You've probably all seen it done on the TV, at the end of an F1 grand prix, or at the cricket itself. And I can assure you it is as much fun as it looks!

Then the fireworks went off all around us, with glitter spraying high into the night air. Some of the crowd, the majority of whom were our own fans, and our friends and family members, had stayed to see the ceremony, it was a fantastic atmosphere.

I was so overwhelmed by it all. I was 19, and to have been thrust into that team at the latter stages of the competition, and for everything to basically go my way from ball one, was just a dream come true. And I think that was the case for most of us young lads, we just got blown away by the occasion. As we got older there was always a bit more conscious thought about what we were achieving, a bit more effort to take it all in. In 2010, we were all like rabbits in the headlights! It's probably only looking back later that you realise what you've achieved.

After spending a fair bit of time out on the pitch, walking round with the trophy and posing for pictures, we eventually made our way back to the pavilion, and headed up to our changing room. As we went up the stairs from the pitch, I looked around the ground, and noticed it was now pretty empty. The stalls had closed up, the music switched off, the floodlights around the ground fading with every passing minute. It's strange to see the ground like that, the calm after the storm.

Once we got to our changing room, Macca said "Take it all in lads. These moments don't come around very often." At that stage I didn't think too much about what he said. But looking back now you realise he was right – especially now that I'm not playing any longer. Winning a domestic trophy, at 19 – what an experience that was!

Macca was definitely a leading figure in that dressing room. After those rousing words, he led a rendition of the team song. As you can imagine, after a win like that, we fairly belted that song out. Then we had some drinking fines. So if you'd scored a career best score in the match, or you'd got your best bowling figures, you'd do a fine, which meant downing a beer. It was normal stuff, all very positive and good fun. And then there was other light-hearted stuff, daft things you've said or done during the games which get called out, and you'd have to down a beer for that too. Macca had all these daft songs and chants he'd get going as we did all that, he was top-drawer.

The beers were flowing, blokes dancing and hugging each other all around the room. Then Rod Bransgrove, the Hampshire Chairman, came into the room. He was beaming. He went around the room and shook everyone's hand and congratulated us all. For it to have happened at the Rose Bowl, the ground he was so instrumental in developing for Hampshire, must have been a really proud moment for him.

Eventually it started to calm down a bit. Blokes headed off for a shower, while others would get into smaller groups and discuss the intricacies of the game; going over the key moments, "Remember when we nearly threw it away?", "Remember when Dan Christian needed a runner?" We could laugh about it all now.

The party continued late into the night. We got through a lot of alcohol, as you'd imagine with a group of lads who'd just won a trophy – it'd be the same up and down the country at any level of cricket. Our families were in the members' area, which is the room immediately next to the home dressing room at the Rose Bowl, so eventually players started drifting out of the changing room to have a beer with their loved ones, and the party basically became split between the two rooms.

But Finals Day is such a long day, that just the smell of alcohol was enough to get you drunk. I hadn't eaten much all day, and I'd burnt off so much nervous energy that by the time I was a couple of beers in, I was already ticking!

* * *

In the days that followed, after the hangover had subsided, I remember thinking what an amazing start it had been to my time in the first team. In the space of a month I'd gone from playing in the 2nd XI while training with the England under-19s, to playing at Finals Day, and lifting the trophy on my home ground. It was incredible, and I was desperate to build on that in the months ahead, in readiness for the next season.

As the season ended, I discussed with the coaches at Hampshire what I should do over the coming winter. They were really keen for me to go to Australia to attend Paul Terry's cricket academy in Perth. Paul was a big name at Hampshire, having played for, captained and managed the side in the past, so I was well up for going over there in the autumn.

And I wasn't disappointed with my decision to go; Perth was brilliant. It was a real coming of age for me personally, having to fend for myself for the first time in my life. It was the first winter I'd been abroad somewhere alone as such. I'd been away on tours before, when you're living in hotels and everything's provided for you, but here I was living with a group of lads in a house which Paul had arranged for all the academy lads. We had to cook and clean for ourselves and generally be responsible – well, as responsible as a newly turned 20-year-old could be.

I was sharing with guys like Matt Coles, the Kent all-rounder who came to play at Hampshire a few years later. Rob Newton from Northants, Chris Dent, the Gloucestershire batter who had been involved in all the England age group stuff with me a few years earlier. There were also a couple of other lads, a bit younger than the rest of us, who were staying with us too. It was a good craic; me and Denty got on really well, we'd cook together most nights while the other lads did their own thing.

The work I did with Paul and his team was excellent. It was a batting academy and we worked on lots of technical aspects, addressed a couple of flaws I felt I had in my technique, like being vulnerable to the straight ball. Paul and his team helped me develop some methods – physical and mental – to try to deal with that particular issue better. That work definitely helped, and I felt like I was timing the ball really nicely out there.

I also joined a local club called Bentley Blues. They were a level down from Grade cricket, known as Sub Turf. I kept wicket for them every Saturday, which was great as it allowed me to keep my glovework ticking over, while I was also able to put my improved batting technique into practice.

My housemates were all playing for teams they'd managed to join across Perth too. So every Saturday, we'd all go off across the city, playing for our respective teams. In the evening, we'd all reconvene back at the house, catch up on how everyone's games had gone over a few beers, then head out on the town to hit some bars.

It was a great winter, an awesome time during which I developed a lot as a person. I even shaved my hair off out there. I felt like I was shedding my kid hair and getting a man's cut. I was maturing, on and off the field. I was more focused on my cricket than ever, and I was loving every second of my journey.

I was due to be out in Oz for the whole winter, from October to March. But because we'd won the T20 cup, we qualified for the Caribbean T20 competition – the precursor to the Caribbean Premier League.

I flew from Perth directly to the Caribbean and met up with the boys out there. Macca wasn't there but we'd signed the experienced Johann Myburgh and he made a pretty big impact out there, in what was a young squad. Considering our average age, we did OK. We reached the final but lost to a strong Trinidad and Tobago side.

The tournament itself was brilliant. It was so rich in Caribbean culture. Locals turned out in their droves to watch, and they were singing and dancing all around the grounds. There were steel bands playing and a carnival atmosphere everywhere we went. When I looked into the crowd, all I could see was people dressed in every colour of the rainbow, all having a great time, with the beers and rum flowing and the vibe better than almost anywhere I've played in the world. When you see the quality of these domestic T20 competitions around the world – not just the playing quality but the atmosphere at the grounds – it's no wonder more players are signing white-ball-only deals these days.

As players we were treated really well too. We stayed at a stunning hotel in Antigua, which was right on the beach. It was times like that when I really felt like I was living the dream. I was a 20-year-old lad, travelling the world and being put up in all these stunning hotels, just because I played cricket. I had to pinch myself sometimes and think, "Wow, is this really happening?"

Chapter 4
Skeg

I wintered well in Perth and the Caribbean, and by the time the 2011 season got going, I was raring to go. Unfortunately for Nic, however, it was fairly obvious early on in the season, that he wasn't. The injury problems that had plagued the end of the previous season were going to continue into this.

As the season panned out, we pretty much shared the workload down the middle. We both played eight Championship games, in a disappointing season which ultimately ended with us being relegated to Division Two. Neither of us really shot the lights out with the bat, we both averaged around 20. From my perspective, it wasn't easy coming into a struggling team, and having to find some form with the bat when the pressure was very much on. In one-day cricket, I played 11 of our CB40 matches, while I also got the nod in six of the 17 Friends Life T20 matches.

I was getting good game time, and I really felt that I was making a mark on games from behind the stumps. There was a CB40 game against Kent, when I took a catch that was probably the best of my career. I was keeping up to the stumps, as usual, this time to Dominic Cork. Corky had a notoriously lively bumper, which he unleashed on Kent batsman Darren Stevens. It beat Stevens for pace as he attempted the pull shot, the ball flying high to my right.

Without thinking, my technique kicked in; my gloves moved to the right, my head followed. The ball rocketed straight into the middle of my gloves, much to my delight. I looked up and Corky's face was a picture – I don't think he could believe I'd clung onto it. After the game, he told me it was one of the best catches he'd seen, which was a massive compliment considering Corky's CV.

When you look at that catch against other key moments in my career – including that Lord's moment which we'll come to later – I'd say this one against Kent was a better piece of work. But no one outside the Canterbury ground that day ever saw it, because the game wasn't shown on TV. That's the thing with county cricket – not every game is televised. So that one's saved in the memory bank alone, although a cameraman did manage to capture a sequence of photos that illustrate the catch. The cameraman had been behind me, so you can see the look of disbelief on Corky's face as he ran down the wicket towards me in the background!

As an individual piece of work, it's a moment I look back on with the greatest fondness, because it demonstrated the difference I felt I could have on a game. Those kind of catches – the ones a keeper has no right to take in some respects – can change games massively in favour of the fielding team.

I felt as though I was contributing. Bear in mind I wasn't the full-time keeper yet, and was still adjusting to life in the first team. Plus I was in and out the side covering for Skeg. My keeping was earning plaudits, especially in white-ball cricket where I was keeping up to the stumps to most of our bowlers, and I was chipping in – when I could – with some runs. We batted deep, so I wasn't always required, and when I was, I didn't always get much time at the crease.

In spite of my successes, towards the end of the 2011 season and with Skeg clearly more and more susceptible to injury, I heard that Hampshire had been speaking to Essex's James Foster, about coming to the club for the following season to take over as our senior wicketkeeper.

I remember hearing that rumour while we were playing a Championship game up at Durham in mid-August. I was once again deputising for the injured Skeg, and given our perilous position in the league, it was a game we had to win. The first two days were written off due to rain, and I went out to bat on day three and scored 28 undefeated at close, as we tried to set up a match for the final day.

That night Chalks took me to one side for a chat and said "You might have heard rumours of us trying to sign James Foster from Essex. At this stage nothing is set in stone, but it is something we are considering."

Inwardly I was livid. But I wasn't really one to show my true feelings on the outside, so I pretty much just took it on the chin and said "OK, thanks for letting me know." I wasn't the kind of guy who would kick off when things didn't go his way. I've seen players do that when they're dropped, and sometimes you wonder whether acting like that makes you a bit harder to drop in the first place, because the coach doesn't want the hassle of having to deal with the fallout.

I'm not saying it was that cut and dried. But certain individuals I've played with, you'd instantly know in the dressing room when they've been told they weren't playing the next game, for example. And that creates an atmosphere that can filter through the whole squad. If the guy is then on 12th man duty, he can carry the mood for the rest of the day, and that can rub off on everyone.

Obviously the coach should be stronger than to care about what the players think of such decisions. But at the end of the day we're all human, and sometimes you'll do anything for an easy life. My reaction definitely made it easy for Chalks to persevere with the Foster deal, knowing he wasn't going to get a bad reaction from me. Perhaps he thought that, by me taking it so well, I didn't want to take over the gloves yet. Or didn't feel like I was ready.

Great man-managers, like Sir Alex Ferguson, can actually make a player feel good about tough decisions like that. You hear stories about Manchester United players actually being pleased they weren't playing a particular game, because Ferguson would tell them, "I need you next week, so be ready for that one and sit this next game out."

Not many managers and coaches have the ability to deliver bad news to a player like that, and almost turn it into a positive. The way Chalks told me about Foster, I certainly didn't take it as a positive, or a way of getting me to raise my game, to prove myself so they'd forget about Foster and back me. I don't know, maybe that's what he was trying to do, but it certainly didn't feel like it at the time.

Instead, I accepted the decision and moved on. In hindsight, that was probably a moment when I should have kicked off, and fought my corner a bit more. I'd played a lot that season, done well, and felt I'd earned the right to at least continue playing alongside Skeg into the next season, even if he was only going to play a bit-part role again.

Plus, with my coaching hat on, I find that I actually respect a player who comes back at a decision to drop them with legitimate reasons why they should stay in the team. "Hey, I can do the job – look at my numbers from the last six games," for example. Having the confidence to back yourself like that can impress a coach, as long as the player isn't just moaning for the sake of it.

On the other hand, I was only 20 at the time, and although I felt like I'd been playing well and contributing to the team, I didn't feel I had the right to complain. And maybe I was a little worried subconsciously, that my batting wasn't quite ready for the first team on a full-time basis yet. Having come up through the academy and through the 2nd XI, it was normal for trialists and new players to come into the group on a regular basis. So in a way, I think I kind of expected someone like Foster to come in.

Irrespective of that conversation, when I woke up the next morning I knew I had a job to do with the bat. It was a horrible day, especially considering it was the middle of August. The pitch was grassy and greasy and the weather was cold, grey and miserable; ideal conditions for bowling, a nightmare to bat in. But going out on that final morning of the match, I felt good. We were looking to score runs quickly to set up a match. I played nicely on a wicket that was doing a bit against the likes of Graham Onions and Chris Rushworth, hitting a career-best 58 not out which involved a 72-run partnership with Dimi.

That day I proved I could bat at that level, in testing conditions on a green, seaming wicket at Durham, on a cold and cloudy day. It wasn't all pretty, but it was an important knock, and I was delighted to have shown Chalks that perhaps he was wrong to be looking for another keeper.

Because we'd lost so much time in the game to weather, we agreed with Durham to make it a one-innings-a-side match. We needed to push for victory to stave off the threat of relegation, and it was worth risking defeat by pushing for the win. We set Durham 276 to win on the final day and we won by 50 runs, much to the delight of all of us, but especially me on a personal level as I really felt I'd contributed as a batter, probably for the first time in the first team, actually.

BBC Radio Solent commentator Kevan James interviewed me after the game, and asked me if the Foster rumours had played on my mind. That just gives you an insight into how rife the rumours were – everyone was talking about it. Had the situation given me an extra incentive when I went out to bat?, Kevan asked. No, I don't think they did really. Maybe subconsciously, but I definitely wasn't thinking about that conversation with Chalks when I went out to bat. I just went out, kept it simple and timed the ball nicely.

After that game the Foster rumours died down; he signed a new contract with Essex, and I played the rest of that season for Hampshire. I don't know whether that knock at Durham impressed Chalks and the guys enough to restore their faith in me. I kind of hope not, as one knock shouldn't make or break a player. But perhaps it showed I had the temperament to deal with situations like that, and the technique to deliver with the bat, even in challenging conditions.

It may sound like a struggle, that season. Obviously we were fighting relegation in the longer form of the game, but our T20 form was once again strong.

That year we'd absolutely flown through our group. We had Imran Tahir and Shahid Afridi as our overseas players, and the ground staff at the Rose Bowl were preparing really slow, turning and – if were being honest – shit-heaps of wickets from a batting perspective, to play to the strengths of those bowlers. And with those two, as well as Briggs, Woody and Dimi, we were turning teams over quite comfortably on those kind of decks.

As we'd get used to during my time at the club, we reached another Finals Day in 2011, which that year was held at Edgbaston in Birmingham. So off we went up to the Midlands on Saturday 27 August, hoping to retain the trophy we'd won 12 months earlier at our home ground in Southampton.

Skeg was declared fit to play that weekend, so he and I were both in the squad that travelled up to Birmingham. As well as I'd done in the competition up to that point, I was fully expecting the senior man to take the gloves for our semi-final against Somerset, the team we'd beaten in the final the previous year. But I was wrong. Chalks took me to one side at the hotel the night before the game and told me, "You'll be aware that Skeg is fit, but we'd like you to play the semi-final tomorrow. We feel that you are in superior form with the gloves right now, particularly to bowlers like Tahir and Afridi. And that's what we need for tomorrow."

I was happy to be playing in the semi, but not as happy as I should have been. Actually I felt under more pressure, because I'd been chosen on merit, as opposed to out of necessity. But I don't think I realised that. I still didn't really value my contribution to the team, even at that stage. I'd been chosen because I was seen as the superior gloveman, but I definitely didn't look at it like that. I was thrilled to be playing, but nervous too, definitely.

That decision can't have been an easy one for Chalks to make, or for Dimi – our T20 captain at the time – who was good mates with Skeg. Dimi recalled:

> One of the things Hampshire did well was leaving Skeg out and giving you a go. Skeg was a mate of mine but Hampshire were on a progression, and they wanted to give you every opportunity to progress. Although it was hard to leave my very good mate Nic out, I prided myself on doing what was best for the team, and having your best wicketkeeper in the side was just that.
>
> As Captain I had a huge say in selection and if I didn't want you in my team, you more than likely wouldn't have been in. In saying that, the brand of cricket and the make-up of the team also played its part in having you behind the stumps. Playing three gun

spinners in most cases and medium-pace bowlers with you up to the stumps was a big draw card in your favour. Your ability to keep up to both pace and spin, and do amazingly well at both, was paramount to our success.

Because Finals Day was in Birmingham that year, we had to stay in a hotel the night before, so our prep was already different from our successful campaign the year before. The Friday night had been pretty chilled out, we went out for dinner and got an early night. But then the morning of the game was a bit of a nightmare. There was a debate among the players and coaching staff, about whether we should go to the ground early and watch the first semi-final, to get used to the atmosphere and the surroundings, or whether we should stay in the hotel and just chill.

We decided to stay at the hotel, which was probably a mistake in hindsight. The young ones – me included – were all congregating in different bedrooms, chatting and getting overexcited. We just didn't know what to do with ourselves. Chris Wood was flitting from room to room like a buzzing bee, burning off more nervous energy than you'd imagine is humanly possible! It was like when you're waiting for a flight – you know you've got somewhere to be, so you can't really go off and do anything else. You've got to just sit tight and wait, and watch the clock tick over, minute after minute after minute.

You could tell the seasoned pros from us youngsters. The likes of Neil McKenzie got up early, went to the pool just to take his mind off the game, relax and ease into the day. The younger ones like us got up late, mucked about, didn't know what to do with ourselves.

Macca was brilliant. He was very chilled, and was trying to keep everyone relaxed too. He'd been in so many pressurised situations like this before, so he knew how to approach them. That's when it was great having a combination of youth and experience in your team. The kids like us had the energy and enthusiasm to drive us on, while Macca, Dimi and the senior guys were seasoned pros, they knew how to get the job done in these big games.

Eventually we went to the ground and got into our dressing room, and finally started to get our minds on the job at hand. But it just never really worked out that day, and we lost the semi-final in pretty miserable circumstances. It was one of those games which just didn't go to plan at all.

We batted first and had three rain delays during our innings, before posting 138-4 from 15.5 overs, which wasn't too bad a score in the end. Further rain meant Somerset's reply was revised to 95 from 10 overs using the Duckworth Lewis method, which they fell one run short of, Jos Buttler smashing 32 off 16 balls at the back end to earn Somerset a super-over play off. Somerset hit 16 off their six deliveries, and we could only manage 5-1 in reply.

It was so disappointing because we'd blitzed the group stages, but unfortunately the final just didn't go our way.

Putting the disappointment of the day to one side, there was a sense in and around the group that Nic Pothas was very frustrated at having been dropped for Finals Day – as you would be of course. I think he fell out with Hampshire pretty badly at that point, and he didn't play for the club again. It was bittersweet for me; obviously you never want a team mate to be annoyed, upset or struggling. Equally him being left out was my big chance to stake a claim for a first-team spot. Skeg was always as good as gold with me, and that's a massive credit to him as a bloke. He explained:

> I was coming towards the end. You've got to be realistic – I had 20 really good years. I was conscious that the next bloke was getting ready. At the time, personally, I thought the smarter move would have been for me to go into the second team, coached the second team, and you could have gone into the first team. And if you weren't successful I could have gone in and solidified the first team. You could have then come back down, got your confidence back up, and moved back up again. It would have been a really nice changeover, but I was never asked the question of what I wanted to do.

As well as coaching Sri Lanka in 2017, Skeg also worked with the West Indies in 2018, before being named Assistant Coach at Middlesex in 2019. Clearly his coaching is highly thought of. Just imagine if it had been Hampshire who'd first identified his talents. Not only that, but coaching the 2nd XI would have been a great way for Skeg to have cut his teeth as a coach, and I daresay the seconds would have benefited from his knowledge of the game too. And from my perspective, I would have benefited massively from him staying at the club. Mentoring me, giving me his insight, his experience into county cricket, helping me through inevitable dips in form. It would have been perfect.

As it was, Skeg was never asked to stay, and the idea was never even suggested, as far as I know.

* * *

As was customary at the close of each season, I had an end-of-season review meeting in late September. These meetings were the chance to sit down with your coaches and captain, and discuss how you'd done the previous season, and what you needed to work on for the next. They always took place in Chairman Rod Bransgrove's office, which was upstairs in the Atrium – the pavilion with the tent-style roof at the Rose Bowl. Rod's office was directly next to the home changing room, with a lovely view out across the ground.

Rod wasn't involved in the meeting, but Chalks, Tony and the skipper, which in 2011 was Dominic Cork, gathered in Rod's office to talk to me. Heading to the meeting that year, I was pretty relaxed. I felt I'd done pretty well when I'd been called upon. I was happy with my keeping, as tended to be the case all the way through my career, but I'd also shown glimpses that my batting could be good enough for professional cricket.

I walked up the white stairs at the Atrium, turned left and walked through into the members' lounge – the Robin Smith Suite. As I walked through the glass doors I saw the Rose Bowl ground ahead of me. It was a picture. Always was. I took another left and then entered Rod's office on the right.

I exchanged pleasantries with Chalks, Tony and Corky, all of whom were seated when I entered. We then discussed my form that season, but we moved pretty swiftly to the crux of the matter, which was that Nic was going to be moving on from Hampshire that winter, and I was being entrusted with the gloves for the first team the following year.

To be given that news, for Giles White and Dominic Cork to back me, it really meant a lot. It felt like the culmination of years of hard work, all being rewarded in one moment. All those dreams as a kid, training in the Hampshire and England age groups, the Hampshire Academy, the 2nd XI, getting the breakthrough in the first team, and now this. It really was a dream come true.

I was beaming from ear to ear in that meeting room, and obviously from Corky and Chalks' perspective, it was nice, I'm sure, to be able to give that sort of news too. Better than the conversation they'd have had with Nic, that's for sure.

It gave me the confidence that perhaps I needed. I could set myself up for the coming season, knowing I was going to play every game, no matter what. It was a big responsibility, but at the same time I was excited about that. I could start planning, getting myself mentally prepared to play all season. It was a brilliant opportunity and I was very thankful for it, especially considering those Foster rumours earlier in the summer. It felt like things had come full-circle pretty quickly, and I was intent on taking full advantage of that in 2012.

The meeting didn't last much longer. There was a discussion about what training I would do over the coming winter, again. What I needed to work on and where I should base myself. But I was just brimming with joy, and desperate to get out of there and tell my family and my girlfriend.

After the meeting, and once I'd digested the news a little more, I started thinking about the wider implications. Nic was leaving, and that in part was down to me coming onto the scene. When you're in elite sport, you understand there are ups and downs in any career. As a young player, you're reliant on a more established player either losing his form, getting an injury or moving on. If the player moving on is going on to something else, something better maybe, or just something different, then there's a feeling that you've both done OK out of the deal. But in this scenario Skeg had nothing immediate lined up, and that was upsetting.

At the same time I knew this was my big break, and I was determined to make the most of it. Throughout the T20 tournament that season I'd come into my own with the gloves, and it was the first moment that I'd been shown a bit of faith from the coaches.

To top it all off, before I went off on my holidays, I was given my first full contract, having still been on the development contract previously. It was another huge moment, and validation again that all the hard work and sacrifice I'd put in over the years had been totally worthwhile.

It sounds like a cliché, but I really felt like I was living the dream. It all just seemed to be falling into place. As a 10- or 11-year-old, you dream of one day playing professional cricket, playing for your county's first team. Here I was barely nine years later doing just that. A trophy already to my name, and now given the gloves permanently in the first team. With the ink still drying on my first pro-contract, I was on cloud nine.

Chapter 5
A wicketkeeping masterclass

Good wicketkeeping is an art form. That crisp sound of ball hitting glove, that sight of a keeper diving for a ball down the leg side, that run-out completed having taken a throw hurled in from short mid-wicket. Ping, the bails are off.

There's a lot of skill involved in keeping wicket, both mental and physical; strength, reaction, reflexes, concentration. Some keepers are natural catchers of a ball. Others have got immense powers of concentration that take them above and beyond. A "wicketkeeper's mentality", as Jos Buttler calls it.

In this chapter I'm going to give you my wicketkeeping masterclass. I'll explain how I went about it; my setup, my mental approach, the difference between keeping in red- and white-ball cricket, keeping up to the stumps versus standing back. I'll also give you an insight into why I feel a specialist wicketkeeper is so important to every cricket team, at every level of the game.

* * *

You hear a lot of cricket commentators saying that good keepers go unnoticed. That's true, to an extent. Poor keepers get noticed if they make a glaring mistake. But at the other end of the spectrum, if you're an exceptional keeper, you'll get noticed for all the right reasons.

To be an exceptional keeper you've got to be able to do the basics well; take each delivery cleanly when nothing's happening, keep the team motivated in the field with plenty of chat, running through overs nice and quickly to keep the over rate up, keeping the pressure on the batsmen. Then, when a chance does come along, or a half-chance even, you've got to be able to take the ball cleanly. Doing something out of the ordinary if necessary; taking a catch down the leg side, making a run out or a stumping you have no right to take. Basically, you've got to be able take everything behind the stumps; take every half-chance, stop as many byes as possible and generally make a major impact on the game. And then do something outstanding. Simple, right?

In games of cricket there's going to be those chances – those half-chances – which can change the course of a game. Without a doubt. In one-day cricket, if you're a part-time keeper, you can get away with hiding a little bit. Particularly in T20s. You can stand back a lot and only actually keep up to the stumps for the spinners, and probably do an OK job.

However, if you're willing to take that extra step, if you're good enough to get yourself up to the stumps to the seamers as well, all of a sudden you start creating chances out of nothing because of the extra pressure you're applying to the batter; you're keeping up to the stumps, the batsman can feel you breathing down his neck, he can hear your heart beating through your shirt.

When I was at Hampshire, our whole game plan in limited-overs cricket hinged on me keeping up to the stumps. We had seamers taking pace off the ball and plenty of spinners, all of which suited our strategy of stifling batting teams by restricting their run rate.

As the name suggests, the nature of limited-overs cricket is that there's a limited amount of deliveries to score runs from. Therefore batters have to score runs more quickly, play shots they might not otherwise contemplate – particularly in T20 cricket – and generally be more aggressive. You see batters running down the wicket, trying to take the bowler by surprise, change the angle of the delivery, get under a full ball from a seamer, get to the pitch of the ball off a spinner. If a batter shows aggression like this when I'm keeping up to the stumps, I'm loving it, because I'm massively in the game. If he makes any little mistake, I'll catch it and stump him and he'll be trudging off back to the pavilion.

What generally happened when I was keeping up in white-ball cricket, was that batters tended to stay back in their crease more. So me keeping up put the pressure back onto them; they wanted to be aggressive, but they knew one false move and they were toast. It was an aggressive approach to wicketkeeping, and it worked for me, and the team.

Aggression comes in different guises. We hear a lot these days about sledging, with the Aussies talking about a line of decency that sledging shouldn't cross. I was never that fussed about sledging per se; I felt my keeping would do the talking for me. Batters knew I was behind them. I'd be vocal by geeing up the bowler, keeping the fielders alert, "One more, lads", I was constantly trying to motivate my team, constantly buzzing around the batter like a wasp, very much in their face. But I never went into personal stuff. I only ever spoke to my team, encouraging them and giving them energy. By extension, the batter would feel the pressure, hopefully, just by my very presence.

In terms of my style, my method behind the stumps, I would say my technique actually changed and evolved quite a bit over the course of my career. Towards the end of my playing days I'd developed a hybrid technique between the traditional English style, and a more elaborate Aussie style. Let me explain…

There's a fundamental difference in the way Australian keepers keep wicket, to the way we do it in England. Keepers down under are often quite elaborate with their feet and hand movements. If you watched the 2017/18 Ashes series, you may have noticed the Australian bowlers tending to be a lot quicker than England's bowlers. It's generally accepted that Australia produce quicker bowlers than England do. When you think about it, it's no surprise. Wickets over there are harder and there's less movement through the air or off the pitch compared to in England, meaning bowlers need to rely more on raw pace than seam and swing.

Generally that makes keeping more straightforward. You have to deal with serious pace, but carry is generally very straight, very true. So keepers down under are able to stand a little further back than they do in England, giving them more time to get themselves into position. They can also allow themselves to make more elaborate movements when going for the ball, because the ball's behaviour on the way through is more predictable.

There's a benefit to those elaborate movements. It allows the keeper to create more rhythm. Keeping standing back is predominantly about rhythm. It's about getting everything working together; your feet, your head and your hands. If all those things are working in sync, it makes for a really smooth, flowing take. It starts to feel pretty good too. You feel good about the way you're taking the ball, you're moving into position well, there's plenty of energy about you, the ball's going in the middle of the gloves, you're buzzing. That's how you want it to be.

In England, you can only get away with the more elaborate style of keeping when the ball and pitch are unresponsive. When the ball's moving around more, you need smaller, more subtle, or later movements behind the stumps. The Dukes ball used in the UK tends to seam off the pitch and move through the air, particularly when the weather is damp or overcast, or the ball is new, making it harder for batters to hit, and thus we keepers are in the game a lot more, either because the batsman has missed the ball completely, or they've got an edge on it.

In Australia the main variation to contend with is the extra bounce and pace; here in England lateral movement is our nemesis. Combine that with slightly less carry and a lower trajectory and the job of the keeper becomes all the more challenging in the UK.

As a result, keepers in England will often need to make very subtle adjustments to his or her whole process of catching the ball. Less is more. If you're moving a lot, it's very difficult to adjust to a ball that's also moving, and coming towards you. Which is why keepers who have more elaborate movements sometimes struggle over here – South African keeper Mark Boucher when he first came over to England, being one example that springs to mind. Even Matt Prior when he first started out for England had similar issues. Both struggled because they used to move before the ball had actually deviated. They then had to make a second movement, which is always more difficult, because you're basically having to change direction, which is harder.

Think about a goalkeeper in football going one way for a shot, only for the ball to take a deflection. It's so much harder for the goalie to adjust to save the ball after that second movement, which is the same as keeping, particularly in red-ball cricket.

So what's a keeper's starting position? Well, a strong base or posture position is fundamental to allowing all other aspects of your wicketkeeping technique to work fluently. Much like the other disciplines in cricket, everything stems from a strong base that a player creates with their feet, knees bent, weight hinged between their ankles and knees.

The base is where the power comes from, and the ability to move powerfully is paramount to a keeper. It's that power which allows us to move quickly for the ball, and to dive if needed. A base position varies depending on the player. Some will have a wide base, some will have a narrower one. It evolves over time, and a fair amount of trial and error goes into it. If your base is too wide, yes it's going to be nice and solid, but moving is going to be more difficult. On the other hand, if you have a narrow base, you'll be able to move more freely, but you'll potentially be off balance.

But practice makes perfect, and eventually you'll develop a base position that works for you. If you're keeping all day, 90 overs a day sometimes, you're going to be getting into your base position a hell of a lot. So naturally your base strength is going to develop the more you do it. But I also supplemented my fitness with plenty of weights in the gym, just to make my posture as strong as possible.

It's often said that keepers love a squat. Picture your favourite keeper, and you'll imagine them squatting down, mitts on the grass, feet spread a comfortable distance, knees apart with their abdomen tucked in tight behind. It's like a coiled spring, waiting to launch itself. As the ball's bowled, they'll start moving up, but the trick is not to move too far from that base position too soon. If the ball looks like it's going into the batter's body and you start to straighten up thinking you're out of the game, only for the batter to get inside the line of the ball and edge it behind, you need to be able to move. Move late, that's what I always encourage the keepers I coach now to do; *move late*.

Some keepers might adopt what appears to be a very strong base position initially in their setup, but many will make the mistake of coming out of that position too early.

You always need to be able to adjust yourself, to change direction, particularly when dealing with a swinging or seaming ball. So your base position, even if you're moving from side to side – which you're going to have to do if you're standing back because you've got a bigger area to actually cover – must always remain solid, balanced and strong, adopting a powerful position ready to move again, maybe even dive.

Balance is also massive. Say you've taken a couple of steps to the side, to line a ball up as you're predicting it to come through to you, but it takes the edge of the bat. If you're unbalanced, you're not going to be able to dive sufficiently to get to the ball.

Powerful, explosive movements are very difficult to achieve without balance. While a degree of balance comes from the base, the head is also important to maintaining it. Whether I was keeping up to the stumps or keeping back, I always made sure I was lining up the ball with my head, with my hands out in front in my line of sight. The closer your head is to the ball at the point of catching, within reason, the safer and cleaner the catch will be. This is why keepers use their feet and dive, in order to shift their head as close to the line of the ball as possible, thus making the catch as secure as possible.

While a keeper's base and their head position is important, ultimately their primary job as a keeper is to catch the ball. It's not uncommon to see very successful keepers, with exceptional hands, make the job look easy. A natural catcher will triumph over a manufactured keeper all day long.

The art of catching is one that you're either born with, or you're not. Of course practice makes perfect and you can improve your catching, to a point. Drills using the orange board I mentioned earlier, with the coach skimming balls off it for the keeper to catch, will help to develop the reflexes needed to be a top catcher. But ultimately people either have that hand–eye co-ordination, that split-second speed from mind to hand to get your gloves in the right position to take a catch, or they don't.

But that's the same for all sports, for all disciplines in cricket, even. You look at Joe Root and, even as a kid, you knew he could play serious cricket. The practice then takes players like him to that stratospheric level. My advice, to any kid who has potential, is practice, practice, practice, as that's what you need to do to get to that elite level. It doesn't happen by luck. And the best players are usually the ones who work the hardest, too.

In terms of basic setup, mine would generally be the same, regardless of who was bowling. As far as alignment was concerned, whether you're stood up to the stumps or stood back, you want to get as tight to the line of off stump as you can, providing you can still see the ball. Alignment is massive. Vision, obviously, is also vital. If you're getting in tight to the stumps but you find yourself stuck behind the batter, that's useless because you can't see the thing.

So my setup would be strong and solid. I might have to tweak it slightly; if, say, a right-arm bowler was coming over the wicket to a left-handed batter, I might need to square myself up a little bit, just to make sure I was square on to where the ball was coming from. That might leave me a little bit skewed in relation to the stumps, but I always wanted to be square on to the bowler, whatever angle he was running in from.

That did evolve slightly towards the end of my career. When I went to Somerset in 2015, I worked with the fielding coach, Paul Tweddle. He suggested the idea of aligning my body towards mid-on, so I was essentially facing 1 o'clock looking towards the wicket from my position behind the stumps. That allowed me to set up for the ball going over the top of off stump. Ideally I wanted to get in nice and tight to the line of the stumps, almost anticipating the edge and moving that way.

In that scenario, if the ball's straight, your feet are already on the move in anticipation of the edge. If the ball doesn't catch the edge, you're still in line and you just take the catch on the inside. That approach gives you a bit of a head start every time, you're getting yourself going before the ball comes down, getting your feet moving, preparing for the chance. If it doesn't come, you end up getting a little bit ahead of it, but taking the catch instead on the inside, so to a right-handed batsman, you're taking it to your left.

A keeper facing mid-on like that tends to be more of a sub-continent trait of keeping, purely because it bounces more over there. It bounces more and it doesn't wobble as much as it does in England. So actually getting outside the line of the ball is easier, and less risky. If you think about it, it's a lot easier to take everything on the inside when its rising up at you, then it is to take the catch in front of you.

As well as setting yourself up, it's really important to set your slips up. The keeper should always be in charge of the slip cordon. That's paramount. And over time, if you end up playing with the same group of players, your first slip can become quite consistent. You both get a feel for where you want each other, and eventually it just takes care of itself.

From the first to the second slip, to third slip and beyond, the keeper would definitely have an influence in positioning those guys, but it's also important for the slips themselves to understand the distances they need between each other. Some catchers would like a big gap, others would like it a little bit smaller. Again, trial and error comes in to play here. That's why, when you see a few new faces in the slip cordon in the England Test team, it can sometimes wreak havoc, because the distances between each other might be all wrong, and catches go down as a result.

The stagger of the slips is just as important, particularly in English conditions where the ball doesn't carry as far as it might do in Australia. For this reason, having a steeper stagger is preferable. Sometimes the ball falls short of third slip or gully, so if the fielder can cope with being steeper – that is, standing closer to the stumps – that can increase their chances of successfully completing the catch.

It's important to get the slips as close to the bat as possible. You might have seen Joe Root donning a helmet and adopting an unusually aggressive gully position for England in the past. This is exactly the reason he chooses to get in so close, to ensure the ball carries.

The number of slip catchers is obviously a decision of equal importance. You'll see at the start of a match a slip cordon is brimming with slips in place, and a gully. Generally the number of fielders behind the bat reduces if the batting team start well, or if there's little or no swing or seam movement early on, and therefore the chances of the batters edging one behind are slim. Slips then come back into play as wickets fall, or as conditions – of the ball, the wicket or the overhead conditions which can also affect the ball's behaviour – change.

A keeper needs to feed into that decision, communicating his view to the skipper. I was young when I came into the Hampshire team; just 19 when I made my first-team debut, 21 during the 2012 season, which ended up being the pinnacle of my short career. My ability to impose my views from behind the stumps onto the skipper Dominic Cork, and then later Jimmy Adams, was perhaps not as high as it could have been, and that's just down to a lack of confidence and experience in the role.

But looking back now that's not really an excuse. It's absolutely vital that the keeper has that confidence to express his views to the captain, whatever his age or level of experience. It's part of the role, part of the job description. As a keeper you're behind the stumps, you have a unique view of the game – only the batsman has a better view of the ball and the pitch, and he's on the other team. The keeper is the one who can truly see the behaviour of the ball. Is it deviating through the air? Is it seaming off the pitch? Is the ball sticking in the wicket, or is it picking up speed?

These are all questions only the keeper can really answer – the bowler is going through his action and the slips are at a slight angle to the stumps. You, as the keeper, are gun-barrel straight. As the keeper, your view of proceedings is absolutely vital; you're the eyes of the team, so you need to say what you see to the captain, and influence decisions accordingly.

I was really young when Corky was captain, but once Jimmy took the reins in 2012, I was the senior keeper in the side. Jimmy would always ask me for my opinion though, to be fair to him, and quite often I was too timid to give it. He was normally stuck at mid-off, and had a million and one other things to think about. So having me there giving him a bit of an idea about what's going on from behind the stumps was obviously a help to him. Is it seaming? is it swinging? What do you reckon, do we need two slips? Are we too deep? Do we need to stagger the slips more aggressively?

Ultimately, I had the best view of what was happening, and while I did impart my view, my tender years meant perhaps I was a little more reserved to say, "Let's stick another slip in there, skipper", "Yeah let's go in closer", than I would've been had I been a more experienced keeper. After a while, Jimmy stopped asking for my opinion, or at least he didn't ask me as much as he probably wanted to, perhaps because I wasn't giving him enough back. That's not a criticism of him, it was my bad – I should have been more forthcoming.

Plus I don't think I had a real appreciation of the broader game when I was in the first team, even when I was first-choice keeper. I was constantly thinking about my role within the team, my technique and my processes, and perhaps didn't notice the wider contest of the match. Perhaps I was too insular, too obsessed with myself and what I was doing, to pick up on little chinks in the batter's technique. "He's wafting at the wide ones, let's get another slip in there" – I just don't think I picked up on that sort of stuff enough. Although, on the other hand, imagine if I had said "No we don't need another slip" and then, next over, a chance goes straight to that spot in the slip cordon where we were thinking of putting another catcher? I'd have been bollocked. Or at least that's what I felt would happen. As a result, I probably did sit on the fence a bit more, or erred on the side of caution at least, going with the majority rather than really committing to my convictions and saying what I felt, informed by what I was seeing from my unique position behind the stumps.

And that is a bit of a regret for me now. Yes, it was tough for me as a young keeper of 19, 20, coming into the side and immediately having to express my opinions behind the stumps, at times views that opposed those of the skipper, the bowler or other senior players involved in the on-field decision-making. But I think it's imperative that young keepers coming into a team are given the confidence to do just that, because it is an important facet of the job, and the sooner the keeper feels comfortable doing that, the better it is for the team.

As a coach now, I encourage the young lads I work with to be vocal, to back their judgement and to communicate those views to their skipper. They have the best view on the pitch of what's going on between bat and ball, and their insight could lead to a wicket. It won't always, and you won't always get it right. But we all learn from our mistakes, and part of blooding a young keeper into a team is appreciating that they won't be infallible. Just like any of us going into a new work environment wouldn't.

I just think young keepers need to be brave enough to make those decisions, be strong enough to deal with those mistakes, but also show that they're capable of making a call that could lead to an opportunity, or a field move that helps stem the flow of runs.

Plus, taking ownership like that is a great trait to have as a professional sportsperson in itself. Had I backed myself more to say to the skipper, "Put another slip in", even as a 19-year-old, that may have said more about me than just agreeing with his view not to put one in. "He's got an opinion, he's got a mind, I like that." These are little details, but they all add up, especially in elite sport, where all those marginal gains are so important.

Keeping up to the stumps

For me, keeping up to the stumps, particularly to seamers, was the easiest part of the role. For one, you don't have as much distance to cover as when you're standing back. It's mostly a case of seeing the ball and reacting. You're either quick enough to do it, or you're not. Fortunately for me, I was quick enough – I could do it. All those years flying after balls skimmed off the orange boards had improved my reflexes and my reaction time, my gym work giving me the strength I needed in my legs to move for the ball at speed, it all added up.

For me, keeping up – or standing up as it's also referred to as – is all about aggression. You can tell immediately when keepers don't fancy standing up. They're a little bit more stand-offish, a bit reluctant to get up to the stumps and into the game. These keepers are there to catch the ball, and throw it back to the bowler, not necessarily to apply pressure to the batters.

To be a top keeper, you need to completely avoid that. You need to believe you're there for a reason. You're there to influence a game, and being as aggressive as you can be behind the stumps is definitely a key component of that. Believing you can intimate the batsman, make him alter the way he bats, question himself, make him less sure of whether to come down the wicket and attack, or not, is absolutely key.

Aggression doesn't have to mean chirping away at the batter. Like I said before, I'm not a massive believer in sledging. I used to let the batter know I was there, of course. I'd tell the bowler he was doing well. I'd keep the fielders focused and interested. I'd bring an energy, an intensity, to our team in the field. I'd want the batter to know he was in a contest, that he was under pressure, big time. But actually insulting him or anything like that, I don't think that's the way. Plus, a lot of the guys on the county circuit, we'd known each other for years. coming up through the age groups, then playing in the first team, you play with and against these guys year in, year out. And on the whole they're all really good blokes, so there's no appetite to be rude or nasty to each other, on either side. Of course, you want the batter to feel nervous, anxious that you're there. But actually abusing them is only going to wind them up and, probably, have the opposite effect of what you're trying to achieve.

But it wasn't just about the words. I'd generally try to buzz around the pitch, being really enthusiastic towards everything, particularly in one-day cricket. Running through overs quickly, running to grab the helmet if someone was going to field in close, getting the ball back to the bowler quickly after each delivery.

Running through overs could be quite frustrating, actually. You could be running through nice and quickly, getting the fielders through too, only for the bowler to then take six minutes to bowl an over. Kabir Ali was the worst for doing that. That sort of stuff is totally out of your control, yet if we had a slow over rate, invariably the fingers would be pointed to me. Keeping the over rate up was a major part of my role, as was setting the right level of intensity in the field.

It's about adopting a positive, proactive mindset which in turn helps to make your physical movements more efficient. You move that little bit sharper and quicker. You're alert, you're concentrating on every ball, waiting for that chance. And that can shave a split second off your reaction time which in turn can lead to a stumping, or a catch, which can make all the difference in a game.

Obviously when you're keeping up, you have less time to react to a delivery, particularly to the seamers. So you need to take as much information from what you know about the bowler as you can. What do they like to do in certain situations? What is their stock delivery? What are they most likely to do at that moment? A yorker? A slower ball? A cutter?

I'll use my academy pal Chris Wood as an example. His stock delivery would be back of a good length, aiming for the top of off stump. His variations were predominantly slower balls – he'd bowl a bumper occasionally, but because I was stood up and he's not the quickest, that often wouldn't be the best option. But he'd bowl a variety of yorkers; slower-ball yorkers, normal yorkers, wide yorkers – he was and still is a very good yorker bowler. The wide yorker in particular was a big go-to for him, and we'd set the field accordingly. He had fairly simple plans, but he was so good at executing them, so much so that he very rarely missed. So my job would be to take a lead from Woody, the field placings, the game situation, to ascertain what delivery was coming down, and therefore where I should be expecting to take the ball if the batter missed.

Obviously if we've set up the field with lots of catchers on the off side, I know the ball is likely to be bowled on or wide of off stump. If we've heavily manned the leg side, I know the ball is going to be arrowing into a batsman's pads, so I could be in the game down the leg side. If an opponent needs boundaries from the last couple of overs to win the game, I know they're going to be swinging more aggressively than at the start of the innings, perhaps using their feet to get to the pitch of the ball. All of this information is running through my mind as I squat down ahead of each delivery.

Then, when that ball comes down, you need to maintain that strong base position, wait for the ball to pitch, while watching the ball at all times. As the batter plays his shot, you have to expect him to either miss it, or feather it through to you. And if he does miss, or he feathers it, then and only then do you move. You move quick, the alignment of your head and hands on point with the ball, and in the ball nestles into your gloves. Well, that's the dream, anyway.

Keeping up to spin is different. There's a timing aspect to it. You can't just see the ball, react and move, because the ball is travelling slower. So you've got to wait a little bit longer before you can actually move. You want to move as late as you can to spin. If you move too early, your movements can become a bit stop-start, a little bit lethargic. Once you've moved once, it becomes very difficult to then move again if the ball spins, takes an edge, or does something unexpected.

Again you need to take information on board prior to the delivery. As well as the match context and the field set – which of course you will have input into – you also need to know what sort of a spinner you're facing. Are they a big turner of the ball? Is the pitch conducive to spin? Does their slower ball turn?

You want to stay in a strong position for as long as possible, ideally. You're waiting for the ball to bounce, watching it rotate in the air, before it grips on the dry, dusty surface and spins. Very quickly you need to ascertain what it's done off the pitch, has it spun and if so, how much? Once the ball pitches, you learn if it's actually spun and, if so, in which direction it's headed. But still you have to wait, because the batter still has to do his best to get bat on ball. Again, you should be expecting the batter to edge or miss every ball, and if they do, then you move. You want to be moving as late as that, and if you do move that late, it forces your movement to be quicker, more efficient. And that keeps it to one smooth movement, as opposed to moving and then having to move again.

The best season I had keeping up to the stumps was in 2011. We had Imran Tahir, Shahid Afridi, Liam Dawson and Danny Briggs all bowling for Hampshire; four international-quality spinners.

They were all very different. Tahir could turn it big, and both ways. Afridi's variations were a little more subtle, apart from his quicker ball which was rapid, significantly quicker than his stock delivery. I absolutely loved keeping to those guys. I always, always felt like I was in the game. I felt the ball was going to pass the bat every single time, and that's exactly how you need to approach keeping. You always need to expect the ball to come your way – again, the wicketkeeper's mentality. If it is actually coming your way then obviously it makes your job far easier, and it becomes really enjoyable because you're constantly in the game.

Jos Buttler spoke about his own approach to that wicketkeeping mentality when we chatted, which I thought was really interesting because it showed how his own batting instincts potentially impacted his concentration powers when keeping.

> There are definitely times when you see a ball being bowled and you kind of switch off because your batting mindset tells you, "Oh no, they'll hit this." And that might invariably be the one that they edge, or they miss when they run down the wicket. You might be out in the field for 90 overs, and in the 89th over they nick one which goes low to your left, and you need to be in the mindset to take that one, so it's definitely a tough job mentally.

With Tahir, part of the skill of keeping to him was reading his different deliveries. I wouldn't say I could read them all straight away, but over time I learned. I used to keep to him as much as I could in training, and I'd get behind the stumps to him on the morning of a game, or when he was bowling through in practice. I'd just try to see as much of his bowling as I could. Over time, during the games, I'd then start reading his variations, and I'd get a natural instinct for what and where he was going to bowl.

I knew he was going to turn it big both ways. If I hadn't already picked the delivery and I wasn't sure which way it was going, I'd be keeping still, ready to move, ready to react. If I'd picked it, I knew how it was going to turn, I'd be thinking, "I know this is turning away from the bat, how much is it going to turn?" I know I'm going to have to move quickly – by anticipating it in my mind I'm giving myself a slight head start. I'm ahead of the game, and although my body is still, I'm poised and ready to move as quickly as required.

What I did exceptionally well that season was holding my position, staying strong and moving as late as I could. So that if I did get it slightly wrong, if I didn't read the flight of the ball quite right, I still had a chance to read it off the pitch, and still be able to move into a position to take it. The keeper has that extra metre or so than the batter does, so a bit more time to react allowing you to move that little bit later.

Take Danny Briggs as another example. He wasn't the biggest turner of the ball, and if we were on a pitch that wasn't conducive to spin, he wasn't going to turn it at all. So if he was pitching the ball on middle stump, I would be thinking, "there's every chance it's going to skid on, and I'll be in the action down the leg side". So in the back of my mind, I'd be preparing to move that way, even though I'm staying dead still until after the batter's had a go at the ball. And that's a really important point to make here. I've talked a lot about appreciating the game position, knowing what the bowler's stock delivery is, acknowledging the fielding positions, but it's important these bits of information don't force you into a premeditated decision.

The most important thing then for me is to not allow those thoughts to predetermine how I was going to move. So I was conscious of holding my shape, doing everything from a physical perspective I can, to prepare myself to react and move. I'd be thinking "Be aggressive, be aggressive, move late, move quick", but while you can have an idea of where you're going, you'll never truly know until the batter has gone through with his shot.

A lot of this stuff I did naturally. I probably didn't think too much about it until I'd stopped playing. Now I'm a coach, I've got to try to draw as much information from my playing days as I can, so that I can impart this knowledge to the guys I now coach, helping them to get those thought processes into their games.

And what I tell keepers now when I'm working with them, is to ensure their mindset is really sharp. Expect the ball to come to you every delivery. If you have a small lapse in concentration, if you can't sustain your concentration for a long period of time, then no matter how good you are at catching, it's not going to work. As keepers out there will know, the minute you think the batter's going to hit it, sod's law is he'll miss it and it'll catch you by surprise.

Standing back
The key difference between keeping up in white-ball cricket and then standing back in red-ball cricket basically boils down to mindset. Again.

Standing back in the red-ball game is all about rhythm, timing each catch, enjoying the process of trying to nail each catch, trying to take every ball in the middle of your gloves and then having the mental capacity and drive to repeat that process every single ball, often for 90 overs a day in the hot sunshine.

In red-ball cricket, when the wickets are conducive to swing and seam, the ball is going to be beating the bat a lot. There are going to be a lot of catches and chances coming your way, and the difference between the two teams will most probably be who can take ten wickets the quickest – as in, the team to take the first ten chances that come their way. If your opponent missed their first five chances, and you score 50 more runs, that could be the difference in a low-scoring game.

Personally, I loved coming in to keep on a green, seaming wicket in a Championship match in April. In that scenario, as a keeper, you're constantly in the game. The ball's constantly beating the bat, meaning a chance is always just around the corner. That's brilliant. That's what you want.

I suppose there are part-time keepers out there who would hate to be in the game constantly, because it would potentially expose them. They might prefer a flat wicket where batters are finding it reasonably comfortable to score and leave the ball. There's the odd play and miss, the odd leave, but on the whole there's not enough there for them to be in the game all that much. That's not how my mind worked behind the stumps, I wanted to be involved every ball.

When you're standing back, rhythm is so important. You want to be timing your movements towards the ball perfectly, so that as the ball arrives, you're there. You're ready for every catch and you're completely controlling the process.

That's something I'm big on when I work with keepers, young and old, amateur and professional alike. You don't want to be in a position where the ball is suddenly hitting you, your gloves not necessarily in the right place. You want to make sure, ideally, that you're in complete control of when you catch it. You're catching the ball when you want to catch the ball; you're dictating the precise point at which you want to make the catch, not just catching it because the ball's on you.

It's a "feel" thing. You've got to understand what sort of positions you need to be in. You need to understand what your perfect take looks like. In order for that to happen, in order for everything to click, for the ball to go right in the middle of the gloves, you need to know what that's going to look like, what it's going to feel like.

On the flip side, it's also important to acknowledge that it's not always going to happen. It's not always going to be possible to take every catch perfectly. Sometimes it's just not your day, you're physically fatigued from the day before perhaps. Or you might be doing everything you possibly could do on that day, but it's just not quite clicking. In that instance you've got to keep striving for that perfect take but accept it just might not happen. Dealing with that just comes from experience.

It's essential to get young keepers, established keepers, part-time keepers, whatever they might be, to try to appreciate that feeling of wanting to take the ball cleanly every single delivery. Because if you're out there, in the dirt for the whole day, potentially 180 overs in a game, you've got to learn to enjoy that process. You've got to want to take the perfect take, every ball.

If there's not a lot happening out there, if the ball's not doing much and the batter's dealing with everything pretty comfortably, you've not got a lot to feed off. The bowlers are running in over after over, and there's just nothing happening; no movement off the pitch or through the air, no chances, everyone in the field is feeling a bit flat. That's where a keeper can really earn his corn. If there's not a lot coming your way, somehow you've got to try to stay interested. If you're always striving for that perfect take, if you're always trying to create that energy, that rhythm, and if you're able to achieve it on a regular basis, there's a real enjoyment and satisfaction to come out of it.

It's almost a game within a game, within the match itself. And that focus on doing your own job well, the joy you can feel as catch after catch goes neatly into the middle of those big leather mitts on your hands, there's a real sense of enjoyment that comes from that. And that enjoyment can in turn rub off on your team mates, giving them a boost when seemingly there's not a lot else happening with the ball. A keeper's job is never done – it's so important that you keep the team going when things aren't happening – that's when the phrase "the heartbeat of the team" really becomes relevant. Geeing everyone up, "Come on lads, keep going. We're bowling well, a chance is going to come" – the keeper has got to provide that buzz.

And as a keeper, when you're in that moment, when you're enjoying it, that's when you play your best. Things will happen eventually, and if you're keeping nicely and you're spurring your team on, you're focused and executing your skills, delivery after delivery, eventually the chance will come and you'll take it, because you're on it.

So that's what I was trying to achieve when I was keeping in red-ball cricket. I was trying to enjoy the process. To take satisfaction from catching every ball neatly and tidily, from being at your best, enjoying the whole process, and just letting it flow.

A massive element of standing back is how good you are at diving, too. Diving is the difference between an average keeper and an exceptional one. When you're standing back, you've got so much more ground to cover. Keepers are able to cover a certain distance efficiently using their feet, shifting their body without diving. But there's going to be a point when you're going to have to dive, and you've got to be competent at doing that. If you want to take half-chances standing back, the big edges, the thick edges, the ones that aren't quite carrying, diving well is key to taking those opportunities.

Improving your diving is all about volume and variety of training. The keepers I'm working with now, like Lewis McManus at Hampshire, he's reached a certain level with his keeping where, he's in Hampshire's first team and he's obviously a very proficient keeper. We've had discussions about how he can take his game to the next level, and diving is one of those elements which can help him achieve that step up. Being really efficient at diving, being really confident to take the ball one-handed, so that when those situations occur in a match, and he's pushed to the point where he can only use one hand, he has the confidence to take those catches at full stretch.

Like anything, you can develop your diving technique through training, experimenting slightly with how you want to dive. There are a few techniques to use, and making sure you can execute them well enough, so that they hold up under pressure, is really important.

The conventional technique is to dive and roll, as a way of softening the landing. That generally involves catching with two hands. So if the ball is in a range where you can get two hands to it, you'd be looking to do all the basics well; creating a strong, solid base from which you can properly push off from, then lining your head up with the ball. Then using all that power, push off into a maximal dive, pushing straight to the ball, catch it with two hands, and then come out of it with a roll. All of the momentum that you've generated by pushing up from your feet, through your knees, will help you roll and land smoothly.

Then you can start looking at one-handed catches, a full-on maximal dive with one hand, which looks to me very much like a goalkeeper's dive in football. That's what a proper, one-handed dive looks like in cricket: a goalkeeper tipping the ball round the post from a low, raking shot arrowing straight into the far corner of the goal.

There's a lot of parallels we can draw from goalkeepers in the way a wicketkeeper should dive. The two-handed, more comfortable dive for wicketkeepers would look slightly different from a goalkeeper in football, because ultimately we've got to catch the ball. Goalkeepers these days are predominantly shot-stoppers, and will mostly parry the ball out wide, so it's subtly different. But when goalkeepers are at full stretch at a comfortable height, saving the ball with a one-handed dive, then I think the techniques look very similar.

Speaking of diving around all day, I can remember keeping to a particularly rapid spell from ex-England bowler Simon Jones back in 2010. He was at Hampshire at the time, trying to rediscover his best form after returning from injury. I kept to him during a 2nd XI game on the main pitch at the Ageas Bowl. We were trialing the new pink Dukes balls in that match and I can tell you, they move! They seem to misbehave more than the red balls do, and definitely more than a white ball does. I didn't like them at all, I just didn't get on with them.

Jonah was bowling quick that day, up there at 90mph, if not more. And me and my slip cordon were standing so far back, almost on the 30-yard fielding circle. And for whatever reason, these pink balls were just doing everything. It was probably the quickest spell I'd kept to – you don't find many bowlers in county cricket bowling that sort of heat. And the pink ball, once it pitched, was just seaming all over the place. I didn't feel like I could pick it up as well as I could normally the red balls. Maybe it was because I wasn't used to it, but I found that spell really challenging.

In a situation like that, it becomes purely about instinct. Catch the ball. So all that stuff I spoke about earlier; forming a strong base, lining your hands up with your head, exuding a good energy with good rhythm, everything flowing – suddenly that had to come purely from instinct, because I didn't have that time to think about it. I couldn't set myself up properly, because I didn't know when or where the ball was going to move next. In that situation I had to rely on my years of training, hoping that my technique held up. I stayed as still and as solid as I could for as long as I could, and just backed my ability to catch the ball. It becomes as simple and as instinctive as that.

Compare that to the 2012 season, when I kept a lot to another seamer, David Balcombe. That season, we were a prolific combination. I effected more dismissals than any other keeper in either division of the County Championship that year, with 52 dismissals to my name, while Balcs took 59 wickets, meaning he was the leading wicket taker in Division Two.

Balcs was a joy to keep to, because what he did with the ball was very consistent. That season in particular he was very dependable with the line he was bowling, constantly hammering an off-stump, fourth-stump line, gently swinging it away from the right hander – the perfect delivery to bring the keeper into the game.

He was getting good bounce out of the pitch, with good carry through to me behind the stumps, meaning the slip cordon and I could stand a good way back. For a keeper that's all awesome. I could set myself for the ball swinging away, and because we were a good distance back, I had plenty of time to react and move towards the ball. And the ball was always beating the bat, so I felt like I was always in the game. That, as a keeper, as a purist, is probably the pinnacle. You can start achieving that rhythm, that flow and you know you're never far from an edge coming your way.

And the stats don't lie – 15 of my catches that season were off his bowling. We just clicked.

Don't get me wrong, there are going to be deliveries where you switch off momentarily, and you don't think the ball is coming your way. That happened to me loads of times, and all you can do is hope you get away with it. There'll be a ball where the batter's hit it, and you'll think, "Actually, I wasn't even ready for that". It happens to all of us, and the skill is to minimise the balls where you're not 100% on it.

All the things I've spoken about in this chapter so far are skills, and you're not going to be able to do all of them as soon as you start keeping. So don't worry if you're a young keeper suddenly thinking, I've got a long way to go. I spent a long, long time when I was younger trying to learn all the different mental and physical aspects of keeping, and there were times when I wasn't able to achieve some of these elements regularly. It's something you've got to practice, commit to and stick with, and make a conscious effort to develop. That's the most important thing.

But that's the difference. I'm a purist keeper. I love keeping. I was good at it. That sort of environment when I was being tested constantly, I absolutely loved it. I loved that challenge and completely rose to it. If the ball was constantly beating the bat, if the batters were struggling and the odd edge was flying my way, I was massively in the game and I absolutely thrived on that. I just wanted to be in the centre of the action all the time. I think any specialist keeper would say that.

Young keepers
Young keepers, little kids, no matter how good they are at catching, you can always see the ones that want to be involved in the game. They want the ball, they're hungry to get into the game. Jos Buttler took up keeping at the age of 13 for that very reason – he wanted to be more involved in the game. He was a specialist batter until that time, but he wanted to contribute more to the team so he took up keeping. Look at where his career has taken him, he's now one of the most respected keeper-batters in world cricket.

That desire, to always want to be involved in the game, will always triumph over keepers who are perhaps better catchers, but who haven't quite got that appetite to be involved. Always. Particularly because you can teach the rest – you can't teach that hunger.

When I'm coaching young keepers now, that desire is the first thing I look for. *Then* I look at how they catch a ball. If a young keeper has got good hands, they're a good catcher of the ball, that's a great start. If their positions are horrible, but they're still managing to catch it, you can work on those other elements along the way.

For me, the art of catching – if we can call it that – a lot of it is down to natural instinct and talent. It's natural hand–eye co-ordination, consistently catching the ball cleanly. That crisp, clean sound of the ball landing in the gloves. It's about timing. As I said earlier, you can train that, to a point. You can do drills like the ramp, high volumes of deliveries, varying speeds, random deviations and so on. But like footballers who just have a knack of scoring goals, part of catching is just pure instinct.

In terms of physically catching the ball as a keeper, there are a couple of different approaches you can employ. Some keepers take the ball directly under their eyes, whereas I used to catch it with my hands out in front of me. In terms of my posture, I'd be in a squat position with my weight slightly forward, on the balls of my feet. My head position was really important; I had my head slightly ahead of where my knees were, allowing my hands to work freely without restraint. I was in a strong, balanced position ready to move, ready to catch.

There are a number of benefits to pushing your hands out slightly in front of your head. Your hands end up operating in this space that's completely free. You're not hampered by your knees, or your legs. Your hands are working out in front of you, in front of your eyes so when the ball's on its way you can see it clearly, you can also see your hands in the same line of vision. It becomes very easy to line the catch up, and you can watch the ball all the way into the gloves.

On the other hand, some keepers – like Jack Russell and Tim Ambrose – preferred to catch the ball closer to their body, more directly under their eyes. Generally their arms are quite "long" and their take would look subtly different.

It varies slightly, but essentially, we're all after the same feeling. It's about imagining what that feeling of catching the ball cleanly looks and feels like. You need to recreate it, try to achieve it, ball after ball, the end result being exactly the same every time. You get the ball going right into the middle of the gloves as crisp as anything, making a really clean thud that echoes around the cricket ground. It might look slightly different from keeper to keeper, but the end result will sound and feel exactly the same.

When I'm coaching young keepers now, I encourage them to catch the ball out in front of their eyes. That's the modern way, and it was hugely successful for me throughout my career. When you look at some of England's finest keepers today, like Jonny Bairstow and Jos Buttler, they're catching the same way, with a really strong, powerful base, pushing their hands out in front of them.

Bruce French, the current England keeping coach, is at the core of a lot of that. He coached me as a youngster, and he's working closely with these guys now. I think he's had a big influence on that. The ex-Notts keeper Chris Read mentioned something quite similar in an interview recently. He said he feels like he found a bit of a blend between the sub-continent style, the Aussie way of keeping with elaborate movements, plenty of footwork and flamboyant hands and the English technique. I reckon that's pretty similar to what I achieved by the end of my career – a combination.

And it was this hybrid method of keeping which would be tested to the full as I became Hampshire's new first-choice keeper at the start of the 2012 season.

Chapter 6
First-choice keeper

A county season can be a long and gruelling stretch. I mean, it's brilliant, but it's bloody hard work too. Your body is pushed to the limit – as is your mind – and by the time you reach September, you're done in and ready for a break.

2011 was the first season I'd ever played anything close to a full season of cricket, and I was definitely looking forward to a rest as the season drew to a close.

When the final game of our season was done, it was like a mad exodus away from the cricket ground. Players headed to airports in their droves, to jet out of the country for a well-earned holiday. It had been a busy end to the season for me personally, and with the excitement of taking over from Nic as the first-choice keeper in 2012, I was really looking forward to a break to prepare for the next season.

I went away to Tunisia with my girlfriend at the time for a couple of weeks, which was great and it really refreshed me. I definitely relaxed and forgot about cricket for a while, although by the time I got back to England I was desperate to start working again.

As an aside, a couple of years later, Dale Benkenstein – our coach at Hampshire in 2013 – would tell us younger players that rushing back into training was a bit of a mistake. "Lads, you're supposed to be off – I don't want to see you at the cricket ground!" he'd say. Looking back, I reckon he was spot on. That October period, a few weeks after the season has finished, but before pre-season has kicked off, is too early to be going back to the grind of training. You need a break, mentally and physically.

As a young bloke with no responsibilities, I just wanted to work on my game, and improve on what I'd done the season before. Obviously the older guys who had families, they wanted to spend time with their kids. Even the experienced guys without families, they just knew the value of recovering properly, completely getting away from it all for a good couple of months. They knew, once the new season came around, you would have to put your body back on the line for another six months, so that time off was absolutely vital.

Now I realise the importance of getting that rest in ahead of a season. We were playing 16 County Championship games back then, that's potentially 64 days of cricket. Then with all the one-day games we play, you're basically looking at – depending on the success of your team in those competitions – around 80 days of cricket a summer. That's a massive amount, particularly when you add in all the training days on top of that, and all the travelling you do up and down the country. Therefore, it's absolutely vital that you get your rest in during that period from the end of the season to late November.

Every winter a cricket squad is split up. Guys go on tour with England, either with the full squad, the Lions or a development squad, or they go to play in one of the many T20 franchises around the world. The younger ones meanwhile tend to go abroad – quite often down under – to work on their games in warmer climes.

In 2011, I was intending to stay at Hampshire for the whole winter. There were a couple of technical aspects I wanted to work on from a batting perspective. We reported back in late November, although the first few weeks back was generally made up only of gym work. I'd been maintaining my fitness during the down time, so it was pretty easy for me to get back into the groove.

In terms of actually getting back into the cricket, the typical routine tended to be for batters to pick up a bat again in December, while the bowlers wouldn't bowl until the new year. That winter was the first I'd had to myself in years. Previously I'd been away in Perth with Paul Terry's academy, and the year before that I was in New Zealand with England at the under-19s World Cup. I was really happy to be staying in England that winter and working at the Ageas Bowl. It was the first time I really felt in control of my cricket. All winter I was working with Tony Middleton, my old academy coach at Hampshire, on my batting, and I got it to a point where it was probably the best it had ever been. I've spoken to Chalks and Tony since, and they both said that I was absolutely smoking with the bat that winter.

In those cold, dark winter days, batting practice took place in the indoor nets at the Ageas Bowl, behind the Atrium. You climb the stairs next to the long bar along the back wall, turning right at the top. You walk around the balcony, on the opposite side of the Atrium to the players' changing rooms and the pitch itself, until you reach another set of stairs which take you to the indoor centre. It's a good-sized hall, nice and light – unlike the dingy one at Taunton – and it was there that I spent hours with Tony that winter, preparing for what was going to be a huge season for me personally.

I was working on my backlift, which was an ongoing thing for me really. Tony filmed me batting, and we'd analyse how I was lifting the bat when things were going well. It was about building a method, a repeatable process that I could trust throughout the season, even when things weren't going so well, which would invariably happen at some point.

I felt like the work I was doing with Tony that winter was a really good use of my time, and my confidence with the bat was soaring as a result. Batting's a fickle thing; when it's going well, you love it, but when it sucks, you hate it. That winter was probably the best I've ever batted in my professional career, and I just wanted to do more and more of what I was doing. It was like a drug – the more I connected with the ball, the more balls I wanted. It became self-perpetuating, natural – dare I say it? – easy.

But the coaches were really encouraging me to go and get some game time down under, and in the end that's what I did. So just after Christmas, in early 2012, off I went to Darren Lehmann's batting academy in Adelaide for a couple of months.

Despite my initial reservations, Adelaide was great, and I had a great time out there. I was staying with a brilliant bunch of lads including Ross Whiteley from Worcestershire, Jamie Porter from Essex and Tom Bailey from Lancashire. Sam Billings had been there before Christmas, but he'd picked up an injury and gone home, so our paths didn't cross that time. We lived in student accommodation right in the middle of Adelaide, close to everything that was going on. The weather was glorious and we spent a fair bit of our off time on the golden, sandy beaches. It was like a holiday, but I got a lot of work done too.

My batting was getting better and better the longer the winter went on. At Lehmann's academy I did a lot of work which really helped me iron out a couple of technical flaws, like my tendency to get out to the straight ball – I felt I really nailed that one in particular out there.

The coaches out there were really innovative in their approach. They were forward thinking, always trying to find new ways of keeping us interested. It wasn't just bog-standard net practice, or batting out in the middle. They threw a lot of different ideas into the mix. At the time I was pretty sceptical, but looking back I think we were doing some pretty clever stuff. We did one session, during which I was thinking, "What the hell is going on?" We had a bowling machine bowling tennis balls at us, which we had to hit with a baseball bat! We also did batting practice where we had to play with a middling bat, which is essentially a normal bat with the two edges chopped off. Any time we missed a ball, or we played a false shot, there would be consequences.

I also got my first taste of Grade cricket, playing for Sturt Cricket Club. The standard was good and they played hard, as you'd imagine down under, which was great for me and I learned a lot. It had been a long winter, but I loved it. I got the technical work in with Tony, and I'd then been able to go to Australia and freshen it up in a nice place, while also playing a really good standard of cricket for Sturt.

I felt as though I was in the form of my life with the bat. And while there was no doubt I was improving, I'm not sure my batting was quite ready for a whole season in the team as the senior keeper. You often find with young batters, they come in and out of the side at first. They tend to go in, do well for a bit, then struggle, at which point they drop out of the team again. They do a bit of work on any technical issues, refresh mentally, all away from the glare and pressure of the first team. Get some runs in the 2nd XI, then go again.

I wasn't going to have that luxury; I was first-choice keeper and would need to play every game. My new deputy, Adam Rouse, was a decent keeper and batter, but he was young too, so he wasn't the steadying influence they could throw in for a couple of weeks to allow me to reset, to get back to what I needed to do away from the stress of playing in the first team.

At the start of the 2012 season, that was a good thing. I was buzzing that I was the first-choice keeper for the following season, and the fact I was going to play every game gave me huge confidence. But at 21 years of age, I wasn't thinking about my long-term development, I was just dealing with the here and now.

Looking back at how my career panned out, I think it's pretty clear that I was going into a massively pressurised situation, without much backup if things went wrong. In that respect, it was a pretty risky strategy from the club's perspective.

Liam Dawson, a bloke I've known throughout my career, someone who knows my game better than most, shared that view when we spoke in June 2017.

> I always thought it was going to be hard for you to play [in 2012], because you were following Nic. Skeg was an out-and-out batter, and he was good with the gloves. Not great, like you. But with the runs he'd score, he'd win you a game with his runs at the end of an innings. People were always going to ask, "Can Batesy do what Skeg did?" When Skeg finished, I think everyone would've been

expecting you to pick up where Skeg left off. I don't think that really helped you.

I never really gave the idea of replacing Skeg much thought, I must admit. I focused on what I needed to do to be successful in the role, but as for how I'd be judged as Skeg's successor, that idea never really registered. But looking back now it's pretty obvious that people – coaches, team mates, fans – would immediately compare my performances to Skeg's. I mean, I had skills behind the stumps that Skeg didn't, but people were always going to expect my batting to be up to his standard. And at that stage, it just wasn't there.

But as if I was going to turn around to the coaches and say, "Hang on a minute guys, I'm not quite ready for this yet". I'd worked so hard, come through the academy and 2nds, through the England age groups. Now I'd been given my chance, there was no question I would take it. No question.

But looking back, I wasn't ready. My batting had improved that winter, but that process, that method for batting, I just hadn't been doing it long enough for it to be embedded in there – in my mind as much as anything. I spoke to Dimi Mascarenhas about this recently, and he agreed. "Honestly, probably not." Dimi said. "I thought keeping-wise you would be more than ready behind the stumps. But the batting was going to be the issue, especially after the person you were coming in for. There was a standard that had been set, and to match that would have been hard for anyone."

* * *

After Adelaide, I joined up with the rest of the Hampshire lads in late February, and soon after we headed off to Barbados for our annual pre-season tour.

Those trips were always good for a number of reasons. Firstly, it was a great way for the group to get back together after a winter spent apart. I'd been away in Adelaide and Jimmy had been with the England Lions, to mention just us two. So the trip was great for getting back into the Hampshire bubble, so to speak. By then, Jimmy had been named as our new captain having taken over from the retired Dominic Cork, so it had been a big winter for him on a personal level, and it was nice to celebrate his success on that trip, too.

The second reason those trips were so good was that it was basically a bit of a blow-out before the hard work of the new season begins. That was a genuine reason for the trip, and even the coaches would acknowledge that. It was also a bit of a reward for the guys who hadn't been away during the winter, who had instead worked hard for months in the gym and the indoor nets at the Ageas Bowl.

Finally, obviously, it was a great chance to get outside and play some competitive cricket. Clearly you can't get out and play in England in early March. Well, getting out and playing in early April, when the season tends to start these days, is hard enough, but that's another conversation.

I loved being back in the group. It was nice to re-bond with the lads over a few beers, while staying at the fabulous Coconut Court Hotel, which was right on the beach. Plus it was good to get some decent cricket in before returning home to the cold. And after spells in Adelaide and Barbados, those cold late-winter days back in Hampshire were a massive shock to the system, I can tell you.

By the time we got back to the UK, the start of the County Championship season was almost upon us. But first we had a final warm-up game against Loughborough University, where a familiar face would line up against me. Sam Billings was taking a break from Kent and was studying at Loughborough while keeping the cricket up by playing for the uni side.

At Kent, Sam had former England Test keeper Geraint Jones, and then Paul Dixie, ahead of him in the wicketkeeping pecking order, so he'd taken the decision to go and study, and get another career option under his belt in case the cricket didn't work out. As with his approach to cricket, he was determined to have multiple career options. Given the level of success he's enjoyed as a pro cricketer, it's pretty obvious he made the right choices for his career.

Instead, I'd decided to go down the professional cricketer route immediately, and had signed a pro contract with Hampshire just a few months earlier. It shows there's more than one route into the professional game, and everyone's route is always different.

When I caught up with Sam in 2017, he told me that while he was at uni he worked specifically on his batting.

> I was a keeper first as opposed to a batsman, and that probably changed when I went to university. It was then that I realised that I needed to be a top-order batsman in order to get into the Kent team, because I had two in front of me with the gloves.
>
> Initially I got picked ahead of Daniel Bell-Drummond. It was a toss-up [between us] but I was picked simply because my fielding was better than his. So it shows how the modern game has

evolved, in that you have to offer as much as you can to the side. It was that realisation, when I went to uni, that I had to work really hard on my batting, and take responsibility for myself to give the team something more than just my keeping.

Listening to Billings talk, what struck me was that steely determination to get to the top. He'd identified that he needed to strengthen his all-round game for him to be successful, and he took the best approach for his long-term career by going to Loughborough and spending some time developing his batting.

He had been my rival during our England age group days, but when I look back now, it's fantastic to say I was with him throughout his formative years with England. Ultimately Sam made a decision to take on more responsibility with the bat, so that he gave more than just his keeping to the team. Ultimately Sam was quite clever with his thinking, looking longer-term rather than just being eager to get into the first team.

That's not to say I was wrong to sign the professional contract, as I did at the end of 2011. Ultimately, if a professional side is offering you a full-time contract, and a place in the first team, you're probably going to jump at the chance. But equally I do think the comparison with how Sam's career started in professional cricket compared to mine, and looking at where we both are now, tells its own story. I always saw my keeping as an asset to the team and perhaps I thought that my keeping alone was enough to secure my place. Sam knew he needed more, and the rest is history.

As an aside, I did actually have a place lined up at Durham University. I was enrolled on some token degree in sports and business, but I had to keep deferring it and deferring it, because I didn't want to give up on my cricket career. The guys at Hampshire had encouraged me to think about higher education through the academy programme, but the decision as to whether I should actually go to uni instead of staying at the club and trying to break into the first team, was mine and mine alone.

Ultimately I had to make a decision on the degree, and decided not to go for it, instead devoting myself to my cricket. The fact that I got into the first team and won trophies means I'll always feel that I made the right decision, although there's no doubt I would have loved to have gone to uni.

If you're a young sportsperson reading this book, and you're wondering whether to devote your life to your sport or not, I'd just say, think long and hard before you decide. I know that football academies offer scholarships now where youngsters are educated as well as coached, so that if they fail to become a professional footballer, they still have qualifications such as coaching to fall back on. I think that's really sensible.

What Sam did, going to Loughborough and getting qualifications, was a really smart life choice, and it also worked wonders for his cricket because his batting clearly flourished there too. Did I make a mistake in signing for Hampshire too early? I would never say I made a mistake, and I'm proud of where my career took me, the successes I enjoyed – some of those moments I'll remember forever. But it's clear you have a choice to make, so make sure you give that decision the time and consideration it deserves. Life, like sport, is all about decisions; maybe Billings just made a better call than me at that point.

As it was, I had a good game against Loughborough, scoring 93 which I dare say had Billings thinking he'd made the wrong choice at the time. That's sport – full of ups and downs.

* * *

It was early April, and finally the season was upon us. The clocks had gone forwards, the days were lengthening ever so slightly, and the weather was thawing – or at least that's what the weather forecasters were telling us should happen.

I was feeling really good about life. I was going into the season as the number-one choice behind the stumps, my batting was probably in the best place it had ever been in my career, I was hitting the ball really well and I felt my coaches were really happy with where my batting was at.

One of our first games was against Gloucestershire at the Ageas Bowl. That year, our ground-staff were producing particularly green pitches, and our quick bowlers, Balcs in particular, was having an absolute field day as a result. The ball was seaming this way and that; it was really tough to bat on – for both sides I might add – while I was leaping around like a salmon behind the stumps, trying to get my hands on anything wayward.

Against Gloucestershire, Balcs was absolutely on fire. As I said in chapter 5, he was incredibly disciplined with his line and length that year, and that game was probably the high point. He ended up taking career-best-figures of 8-71 in the first innings, five of which were nicks I caught behind. I bagged another one off Chris Wood which gave me six catches in the innings, an Ageas Bowl record at the time.

Unsurprisingly it was a low-scoring game, and we ended up needing 290 to win in the fourth innings. As would become a bit of a pattern for us that season, our top order didn't get off to the best of starts. When I came in, after Michael Carberry got out, we were 72-6 and staring down the barrel. I joined Woody in the middle, and together we batted pretty nicely on what was a gorgeous sunny day in early spring. The wicket was still green and offering the bowlers some assistance, so it was going to be a tough examination of my batting acumen, but I was confident that I could do a job for the team.

I guess in some respects, coming in under those circumstances – the game looking lost from our perspective – it freed me up a bit. I could only improve the situation – if I failed, it was no worse than what anyone else had done, and if I went well it would be a bonus. So there was a fair bit to gain and nothing really to lose from that situation.

And that's definitely how we played. Together Woody and I put on 118, and while the win seemed a long way off still – we were running out of time on the last day of the match – a draw was becoming a realistic possibility. But then Woody fell to the bowling of David Payne – my England under-19s team mate – bringing Hamza Riazuddin to the middle.

At that stage we still needed 100 runs to win. Hamza and I put on 56 in 15 overs, leaving us needing 44 runs from the final six overs of the match. We'd need to go into one-day mode if we were going to win, and had I been a bit more confident with the bat, maybe I'd have just gone for it. But I was also conscious we did not want to lose this game, and that getting a draw would be like us winning it, having been 72-6 earlier in the day. So a draw looked like the most likely outcome, while my own personal milestone, that maiden first-class hundred, was just 13 runs away.

But then Gloucestershire seamer Will Gidman came on to have a bowl, bowled a straight one, and exposed that propensity I had for falling to straight deliveries, with the ball going right through me, and crashing into the stumps. Disaster. I was gutted as I felt I was nailed on for a hundred, and ultimately fell tantalisingly short. I'd done so much work on that flaw over the winter, so to fall in that way was really disappointing. Worse still, we ended up losing the game by 33 runs. We'd done so well to get back into it, only to give it away at the last moment.

ESPNCricinfo writer Ivo Tennant summed up my feelings perfectly when he wrote in his match report on that day, "Nothing seemed more certain than that Bates, in need of runs to ensure his club does not make any further misguided attempts to sign a more experienced replacement on the basis that he might bat better, would reach the first century of his career."

Ivo had obviously heard the Foster rumours the season before…

The changing room was despondent, and I was obviously gutted to miss out on a hundred and to have almost, but not quite, saved the game for us. Had we done so, it would have been a major boost for me personally, as I think it would have been a massive statement to my coaches and the other players that I could weigh in with runs at crucial times. But I was just batting for myself in that innings, riding the wave, not really considering the context of the game. I should have been more resilient, more aware of the game situation. But that was me as a cricketer – perhaps just a bit too indulged in my own game.

Dan Housego, playing for Gloucestershire in that game, and someone I grew to know quite well later in my coaching career, told me recently that he and his team mates had been really impressed with my keeping and batting ability in that game. "Who the hell is this?" is what he said the Gloucestershire players were saying after that match. So clearly I was making a mark, even though at the time I was still feeling quite insecure about my batting.

A few weeks later, in mid-May, we set off for a tough away fixture against Yorkshire at Headingley. We batted first up in Leeds and, as seemed to be the way that year, our top order again struggled with the new ball, and we were 83-4 before we knew it. Simon Katich played an absolute blinder in that first innings, showing all the class that'd made him a star of one of the best Australian Test teams in history. It was a joy to watch him building his innings, how he paced his knock, the shots he played, and the patience he showed in getting there.

Pretty soon I had an even closer view. James Vince and Sean Ervine both came and went, before I got my chance to share the middle with the Aussie legend with the score at 207-5.

Batting with Katich in that innings was a great experience. He had a real method for building a partnership. We were counting the runs off in tens, which really worked for us on that occasion. On the field Katich was really intense – he didn't say a great deal, he'd just literally say, "Right, three more runs until 20", "… 'til 30", "…'til 40", and so on. He was a man of few words, and those words were very focused. Some people I batted with like to have quite light-hearted conversations between overs to relieve the pressure, but with him it was very intense.

We reached close on day one still together, Kat on a mammoth 180 not out, while I was just 12 short of my maiden first-class hundred. When I came off that night, and got into the changing room, I remember feeling that Chalks and the coaches were pretty impressed with my knock. They were almost pleasantly surprised at how well I'd batted and what I'd achieved, both from a personal perspective but also in the context of the game, as by close we were in a strong position of 352-5.

At that stage I felt like my batting was flying. My innings against Gloucestershire was still fresh in the memory, and this was another big knock that, hopefully, I could convert into a hundred in the morning. It was only the beginning, but it felt like I was starting to fulfil that keeper-batter role for the team that everyone – the coaches, the captain, my teammates – wanted me to do.

Overnight was horrible, the tension unbearable. All I wanted to do was chalk off those final 12 runs, knowing there would be a hundred next to my name in the record books, no matter what happened in the future. When we came back to Headingley the following morning, I was obviously nervous. But I also felt so good about my batting, to the point where I was sure I'd get the runs needed for my hundred. And I was right! The runs came relatively easily, and I reached my maiden first-class century with ease.

It was an absolutely amazing feeling. The relief, all that work I'd put in the winter before, it all just melted away as I lifted my bat up and pointed it towards my coaches and team mates in the dressing room. I embraced Kat in the middle, and he said to me "Enjoy it, youngster", in his warm Aussie accent. I did listen to him, but I don't think I really took it in. Like so many other occasions in the past, I just took it in my stride rather than thinking about the magnitude of it all. Plus, I'd scored most of my runs the day before, I was only 12 not out on the day – so I didn't feel like I'd scored a hundred, in some respects.

But I had. I'd scored a first-class hundred at Headingley, in bowler-friendly conditions against a very decent Yorkshire attack. I was out soon after, and I was really cross with myself because I was run out and I felt like I'd just lost my concentration a little bit. Looking back, I probably should have taken a little time to get over the emotional high of reaching three figures, and then looked to go again, but it wasn't to be. Then again I couldn't grumble: 103 and 87 in the first few games of the season – I would have taken that at the start of the year.

Incidentally, a young Yorkshire batsman by the name of Joe Root was on the home side that match. And when I spoke to him in 2017, we reminisced about that game five years earlier. What he said was quite nice to hear. Especially coming, as it did, from England's Test captain:

> Having seen you play the way you did at Headingley, it's quite frustrating to not see you playing first-class cricket now. I'd love to have seen you be a bit more maverick even. Like you associate someone like Chris Read being; pulling balls off a length, slicing it over point, you don't know what length to bowl to him. Billings reverse-sweeping and you're thinking "What are you doing?" But actually, before you know it, he's on 20 or 30, the rate's gone up and bowlers are spewing, and the whole tempo of the game has changed.
>
> Being such a good keeper almost worked against you. Instead of comparing your batting to other players' batting, they were comparing it to your keeping, saying "His keeping's up here, but his batting's down here". But was it as bad?

When the England Test captain is saying that to you, you can't help look back and think, "Shit, he's right. Maybe my batting wasn't that bad after all!"

Not long after that ton at Yorkshire I scored 41 against Glamorgan at the Ageas Bowl. The ball was doing a fair bit in that game and the pitch was green, even greener than it had been for the Gloucestershire game. As I said, we were producing some seriously green wickets there that season, but the one for Glamorgan was particularly lush. We all knew that batting would be tough, so I was pretty happy with 41. I can remember feeling good out there, and I was annoyed with myself to give away such a good start. I was batting with Sean Ervine and I felt like we got the team rolling in that match, after another shaky start at the top of the order.

Keeping was very difficult in that game – unsurprising considering the state of the wicket. I was again throwing myself around, particularly when David Balcombe was bowling. He was bowling round the wicket to Glamorgan's left-handers, angling in for LBW. He was steaming in with good pace, but plenty of deliveries, obviously, were going down the leg side. "I felt sorry for him," Balcs told Tom, remembering that game.

> He was so busy, but his keeping was immaculate. In my opinion he was instrumental to our success at that time. He stood up to everyone. No disrespect to Wheats [wicketkeeper Adam Wheater,

who would join Hampshire the following season] but he just didn't have those skillsets. Batesy would stand up to Woody and Dimi [Mascarenhas] in the one-dayers, as well as the spinners, and it just put so much pressure onto the batsmen.

All things considered, I was delighted with how I'd started the season. My batting, supposedly my Achilles heel, was looking good and becoming pretty instinctive, while my keeping was solid. I would end up taking 57 catches in first-class cricket that season, the most for a keeper in either division.

But my batting was the area of my game I was most proud of at that stage. Knowing how hard I'd worked on it in pre-season, and the previous couple of winters too, it was really satisfying to see it clicking. Even in the busy schedule of the county season I was still hitting plenty of balls in practice and working as hard as I could to keep improving. I was desperate to keep working and cement my place in the first team for years to come.

As a team we had the perfect balance of youth and experience. Me and the lads from the academy had obviously played with each other for quite a while. We were a close-knit group and we all felt we were well set for the future – not just for that season but for the years ahead.

At that stage in my career, one of my main aspirations was to represent my country and play for England, I knew there was a long way to go to get to that stage, but I loved the idea of playing for the senior England side one day, and I felt it was an achievable goal. I'd played throughout the England age groups, so why not?

In fact, at the start of that season, when I was gloving it well and batting nicely, our head coach Giles White gave me a list of England Lions fixtures. He was careful not to get my hopes up too much, he just said "Have a look through these just in case something comes up". Simon Guy, the ECB wicketkeeping coach at the time, had been to watch a couple of our games early on that season. I think he was at the Yorkshire game. I don't think he saw me bat, but he saw me in the field. He also came to a home game too. It was all promising, but I knew I had to keep it going and keep working hard if England progression was going to happen, this was only the start.

Not long after that, a young Aussie by the name of Glenn Maxwell ("Maxi") came into the group.

When he arrived, we all thought, "Who's this asshole?" He was forever name-dropping these global stars that he knew and said he'd played with. He'd come over for the summer initially to play club cricket for a local side called South Wilts. He then came to train with us and was just teeing off in the nets from ball one. He hadn't even sized any of the bowlers up yet, and he was just smashing them to all parts from the get-go.

Again it was Tony Middleton who had heard about Maxi playing for South Wilts, and wanted to get him along to a session with us. Eventually Tony got his wish. Maxi signed and in his first game in the 2nds, he got a hundred off hardly any balls. Soon he was in our first team, and not long after that he was knocking on the door of the Australia ODI side, who were touring England later that summer. It was an incredible story.

Once I got to know him, I've got to say Maxi was a top lad. He was brash and confident, maybe with a touch of arrogance, but he was a solid bloke; funny, determined, a real team player, and became a hugely popular member of the squad.

* * *

As the season progressed, my batting fell away massively. From June onwards, I had a run of low scores and just lost all the momentum I'd built the previous winter and into the first half of the season.

I was gutted and was really anxious about it. How could I have started the season so well, and then just fallen off a cliff so soon after? Looking back now, I just feel like I didn't have enough of a method with the bat, one that I'd mastered over a period of years in 2nd XI games as well as in the nets, or in training academies overseas.

When things had been going well earlier in the season, I'd been fine. But when the going got tough, my technique struggled to hold up. I lost my discipline, the methods I'd worked on to stop me getting bowled all the time. They just weren't embedded in my game, so I started straying away from them when I was out in the middle.

Plus, the pressure of needing to score runs for the first team on a regular basis was massive. Our tendency to lose wickets up top was one that continued throughout the season, so I was constantly going into bat with us five or six down for not very many, meaning there was pressure on me to deliver some runs. So rather than batting with the freedom I'd felt earlier in the season, I was instead going in feeling tense, knowing I needed to score. The more pressure I put myself under, the more introspection I was doing, and the worse my game was getting as a result.

I've thought about this a lot since. That period, mid-season in 2012, was a massive point in my career. Had I been able to keep my batting at the level I'd reached early on in that season, I may well be writing this book as a current county cricketer – an international cricketer perhaps – who knows? As it was, I just couldn't get out of that rut, I kept making mistakes, and getting out cheaply.

At that point, I didn't have a lot of support around me. My coaches, Chalks and Tony, I just didn't feel like I could go to them and say, "Guys, I really need some help with my batting – I'm really struggling." I was 21 years old in my first full season in the team, and I needed someone to almost spot that I was struggling, and come and talk to me about it.

I should've felt comfortable talking to Chalks or Tony about it. But instead I was worried that they would immediately think I wasn't good enough, and reopen those discussions they'd had the previous year, about bringing a more experienced keeper to the club. I was determined not to let that happen, so instead I probably acted as though I was fine, that I was working through my issues and it'd all be OK the next time I batted.

At the end of the day, they were my coaches. They were the ones picking the team. I didn't want them thinking I couldn't cope, couldn't get through this difficult patch. Talking to Nic Pothas for this book, he's suggested that he should've been asked to stay at the club, and basically mentored me that season, helping me in the difficult moments – which would inevitably come – giving me the mental and physical tools to cope with the ups and downs of playing professional cricket. That would have been massive, and exactly what I needed. But instead, I was all on my own.

But the games kept coming, and instead of taking time out to get my batting back on track, I was still in the firing line, losing more confidence each time I went in to bat. Fans were talking about my batting woes, journalists were writing about it, I was getting a reputation for being a weak touch with the bat. It was horrible. "But I scored a hundred at Headingley", I kept thinking to myself. But sport is fickle; that'd been forgotten by most.

* * *

By June, the games were coming thick and fast. The one-day competitions – the Clydesdale Bank 40-over competition (CB40) and the Friends Life T20 (FLT20) – were in full flow, and we were expected to do well in both. I knew I needed to be on top of my game from a keeping perspective. And I also knew that, if required, I'd have to deliver with the bat, too.

The shorter format is probably the one I thrived in most; it's the format I felt I was best at, and the one I felt I could impact the most from a keeping perspective. As a team, we found a way of grinding out victories that season. When we were bowling, our general game plan, particularly in T20 cricket, was to take pace off the ball and suffocate opposing teams' run rates. How I performed as a keeper to the likes of Daws, Woody, Briggsy and Dimi was a massive part of that. But the great thing about our side that year, was that everyone recognised the importance of their contribution to the team, and everyone was good at delivering, on a consistent basis. Dimi and I discussed that 2012 team:

> You hear people saying "You've got to know your role." It's said a lot, but I'm not sure if it's really understood by some players. I didn't have to tell Ervine or McKenzie who was going in to bat next. They just looked at the situation, talked to each other, and then they'd go "Dim, Slug's going in", or "Macca's going in".
>
> I'd be like, "Yep, do it". It didn't have to come from the coach or me; they knew. "This is the situation, I'm going in". So that was pretty special. I've never played in a team before that's done that. Normally it's the captain, or from on high; it's never the players having a chat. And everyone was happy with that. Everyone knew their role. It wasn't time for McKenzie to go in, or it definitely was time for McKenzie to go in. And that was pretty special for us.

We got through our group pretty comfortably in the T20 competition, winning five and losing two. You'd take that at the beginning of the competition, but we definitely hadn't hit our best form yet, that was for sure. Our quarter-final draw was a pretty tough one – away to Nottinghamshire at Trent Bridge – where we'd have South African legend Neil McKenzie to thank for seeing us home in a tight game.

Macca had this uncanny knack of getting important runs when we needed them, and in a team containing so many inexperienced players, his ability to keep cool and deliver was absolutely vital. But watching him was never easy. There were times when he was just blocking balls, not scoring quickly enough and letting us drift behind the run rate. In the dugout we'd all be fretting, "He's really struggling here...". But time and time again he'd play a release shot that would get us back up to the run rate, and we'd be away again. It was like he was just immune to the pressure and he had this self-assurance that he could always claw us back into a game. Brilliant.

Going into the final over at Trent Bridge we needed 12 runs to win. Dimi was on strike, and managed to run a bye second ball. Then it was the Macca show. Needing 11 off the final four balls, he hit 4, 4, 2, 4 to see us into the final. Although we had the explosiveness of Carberry and Vincey up top, it was Macca's experience that day that saw us home. His 79 was essential to us winning the match, and took us to another Finals Day.

On 26 August 2012, we headed to the SWALEC stadium in Cardiff – as it was known then – for the Friends Life T20 Finals Day. It was late August – the business end of the season – and I was buzzing. I wouldn't say my batting form had improved massively by that stage, but my keeping was really strong and I was happy with my overall contribution to the team. Now we were fighting for two trophies – the FLT20, and we were also going well in our CB40 group – so there was no time to be wallowing in a sea of self-doubt.

I always enjoyed playing at the SWALEC – there was always such a great atmosphere there. It's a small ground with spectators close to the pitch, and there was always good banter going on from the stands, which was nice to tune into from time to time during the day. One of my favourite memories from that day was everyone in the stand opposite our changing room singing "Sweet Caroline" at the top of their voices. There was a great atmosphere in the place.

We played in the second semi-final that day, against our old adversaries Somerset. They had a good side, but we tended to do quite well against them most of the time. Going into that one we fancied our chances, and went into the match full of confidence as a result.

We bowled first and managed to restrict them to 125, which was a really good effort from our bowlers. And when we batted there were no mistakes, Carbs, Ervine and Kat all chipped in with 30-odds, and we saw them off with an over to spare. Ideal – expending as little energy and adrenaline on a day in which you need to play two high-pressure matches was the perfect scenario.

That set up a final against Yorkshire, a side I'd enjoyed success against earlier in the season, albeit in the longer format. This time we batted first, and once again our senior boys came to the fore. Jimmy, Slug and Kat all weighed in with decent scores, as did Vincey, getting us up to a competitive total of 150-6. As I said earlier, if you're getting 150–160 on the board batting first, particularly in a final, that's always going to heap some pressure onto the opposition. It's not a huge score, but it's competitive. But by the same token, with that score, the game was always going to be tight.

We were happy with our batting performance as we sat in our dressing room at the halfway stage of the match. Outside "Sweet Caroline" was still echoing around the compact SWALEC stadium. Night was falling and we knew it would be difficult for Yorkshire to bat in the failing light, with dew settling on the grass. But we also knew we'd have to bowl and field well if we were going to win the trophy.

And we got off to the perfect start. Dimi picked up a couple of key wickets early on, despite not being 100% fit. There were question marks over his fitness before that game, but he was never going to sit this one out. I took a pretty sharp catch to remove Bairstow, Briggsy finding his outside edge in the ninth over, and Yorkshire were 49-4 at the halfway stage in their innings. We were bang in the game.

Then, in the 11th over, there was a huge moment. Macca's fellow South African native and Yorkshire batsman, David Miller, clipped a Dawson delivery off his pads to Macca at mid-wicket. Macca took a low catch off the turf that we were convinced had carried. Macca was convinced too, but Miller wasn't so sure. He asked Macca if it had carried, and Macca said he was pretty sure it had. The umpires weren't sure either, so they referred it to the third umpire to review on the TV screens.

The tension around the ground was unbearable. If you've ever been to Finals Day, you'll know that the crowds are generally pretty rowdy all day, especially by the time the final comes around, as the vast majority will have been drinking all day. But the SWALEC crowd knew that this was a huge moment, and a tension-filled hush descended across the ground. The competition logo spun on the big screen while the third umpire reviewed the footage. We were huddled together, the temperature a lot lower now as it was pitch black. It was late August, and not a particularly warm night.

Finally the verdict came back from the third umpire – Miller was not out. It was a massive decision in their favour. Miller was Yorkshire's overseas player and a huge international star with the bat. At that stage Miller had just seven. The next over he hit Slug for four sixes – it was game on again.

From that moment onwards, it was nip and tuck all the way through. Miller showed his class with the bat, putting our bowlers well and truly to the sword. Slug came back on to bowl the 18th over, and went for 15 more, giving Yorkshire a glimmer. They needed 21 off two overs – very gettable, particularly with Miller still at the crease.

My old academy buddy Danny Briggs came on to bowl the penultimate over. Briggsy was another young lad, bowling at a crucial moment in a massive match. But it didn't faze him. It just goes to show, us academy kids weren't just making up the numbers, we were making match-winning contributions. And Briggsy did a brilliant job, conceding just seven from that over, meaning Yorkshire needed 14 off the final over to win.

That put huge pressure back on Yorkshire, for whom it was now shit or bust. Woody, another academy graduate, came on to bowl the final over. Woody just revelled in these sorts of situations – like a kid jumping into a massive ball pit. He just loved it. And he was such an intelligent cricketer too; he had this knack of raising his game and delivering when it mattered most. And it mattered most now. Instead of getting all worried about getting it wrong, Woody just puffed out his chest like a silverback, and cranked his performance up a level or two.

Dimi, our captain, and Woody set our field. I was keeping up to the stumps, as I had been pretty much all innings. Yorkshire needed 14 runs, we just needed to keep it tight. Woody did better than that. First ball, to England international Tim Bresnan – OUT. Bresnan attempted a slog and skied it to point. But Miller had managed to get on strike! Not ideal. Next ball, Woody bowled it full and they took one run. Miller was off strike again – that was as good as a wicket. We conceded just two singles off the next two deliveries, meaning Yorkshire needed 11 off the final two balls. Mathematically it was still doable, but we were massive favourites now.

I can remember crouching down in preparation for Woody's penultimate delivery thinking, "We've done this!" Miller was off strike, so it was down to Richard Pyrah to try to get a six and keep his side in the match. Woody ran in and... OUT! He bowled a full delivery and Pyrah played on. We *had* done this! But Woody had one ball to go. He ran in again and – you guessed it... OUT! Azeem Rafiq, my old team mate in the England age groups, scooped it to midwicket, and we were the champions!

Woody, with balls of steel, ended up with three wickets from that final over, handing us a memorable, 10-run victory. Cue fireworks on the boundary, our fans chanting "Haaaaaamp-shiiiiire" in traditional style, and the lads on the pitch running around like nutters trying to get hold of each other and celebrate – we'd just won our second T20 title in three years. What a feeling!

We'd played well all day and we thoroughly deserved our victory. Both wins were convincing and pretty much everyone, to a man, had contributed in some way. And that was the beauty of that team; not only did everyone know their roles, everyone was capable of contributing in a big way to the success of the team. If Carberry or Vince didn't score runs up top, Jimmy, Maxi, Macca or Kat would score later on. If Woody or Dimi didn't strike early with the ball, Briggsy, Daws or Maxi would pull it back in the middle overs.

And in the middle of it all, well at one end of the wicket at least, was me keeping up to all the bowlers, putting pressure on the batters, catching every half-chance that came my way and cleaning up anything that went awry from the bowlers. It was a great team, and we all contributed massively to our collective success. Dimi said this to Tom, in 2017:

> At first it was tough to justify playing a keeper who didn't really bat in the T20 format. But as the season unfolded we were treated to some exceptional dismissals, both off the spin and pace bowlers. With the brand of cricket we played and the make-up of our team, Batesy was definitely an integral part of that, and his keeping played a significant part in us winning trophies.

Aussie batsman Simon Katich added:

> The role Michael played that season was significant. We had a number of spinners which Michael had to be up to the stumps for; it's such a crucial role because there are limited opportunities sometimes in T20 on flat wickets and every stumping, catch or run out a keeper gets can be vital to slowing down the batting team. His glovework was consistently very clean and created huge confidence for the bowlers, knowing they could adjust their line and length to different batsmen without fear of costing the team any extras in the process.

Dimi, once more, reflected:

> For our team, having Batesy up at the stumps worked. If he was going to bat, it was going to be at nine or ten anyway. It didn't matter. If your keeper isn't going to bat six or seven tops, you may as well pick the best keeper you've got. It's such a skill. Especially standing up to the stumps – stumpings, catches up to the stumps off fine edges, thicker edges, it's a joy to watch – it was brilliant.

After the initial celebrations on the pitch, we gathered on the stage to lift the trophy. Dimi got his hands on it, and hoisted it high into the dark Cardiff sky. Behind him we cracked open the champagne bottles and covered him in Moët. It was party time.

After we'd completed our media duties, had some photos with the trophy and done a lap of honour to thank all the fans for their support, we headed back to the dressing room. We drank and did fines with Neil McKenzie the ring leader as always. We sang our team song, then other songs, then had more drinks. Just what you'd expect from a group of young lads who'd just won a trophy.

We left the ground late, I couldn't tell you the exact time, but given the game finished about 10pm, it must have been in the early hours. We got a coach back to our hotel somewhere in Cardiff. Some beers had been provided for the bus ride, so we continued the festivities while in transit. Then when we got to the hotel we found out that Rod Bransgrove, Hampshire's Chairman, had hired out the bar for the night, so the partying went on deep into the early hours.

It was a great night, and we were all buzzing about what we'd achieved. Some of the older lads were telling us to treasure the moment, but I didn't pay too much attention to that. I was just riding the wave, completely. I thought this was the norm – two trophies in three years and I was only 21, I thought it would go on forever!

Looking back, I wish I had savoured that night a little bit more. Great sportspeople have this thirst for success. It's like an addiction to winning, one they need to satisfy every time they compete. I was definitely a lot more relaxed about what we'd achieved, and totally took it in my stride. Maybe that thirst for it would come with time? Either way, what I'd been part of with this Hampshire team up to that point was very special, and I was keen to build on that success in the years ahead.

It was a fantastic team win, and it was a privilege to be a part of it. But our season wasn't over yet. And the day after our win in Cardiff, we had to leave our hotel early in the morning to get back to Southampton, to fly onto Durham for our final CB40 group game! As you can imagine, we were not in a great place after the night before. But luckily, when we got to the Riverside Stadium in Durham, it was pouring with rain and the game was duly abandoned. We got a point for the abandonment, which was what we needed to qualify for the knockout stages.

A good job too, as I think a few of us would have been drunk in charge of a cricket bat if we'd have played that day!

Chapter 7
Lord's 2012

Saturday 15 September 2012 is a day I'll never forget. A lot of people remember me best for "that moment at Lord's". But before we even get on to Lord's, I need to first tell you about the not-so-straightforward task of beating Sussex in the semi-final at Hove. Just a week after Finals Day, on Saturday 1 September, we had another huge game ahead of us. Sussex won the toss and decided to bat first, which as we'd shown already that season, was absolutely fine with us. Bowling at teams and suffocating their run rate was what we did best, and we had the batters who could then go in and chase down any total for us.

We restricted Sussex to 219-8, and that was in spite of a brilliant Luke Wright century. I'd taken a nice catch to remove my Sussex wicketkeeping counterpart, Ben Brown, which was a nice touch. Going into our innings, we were extremely confident of getting the job done, and reaching our second final of the season.

Vincey and Carbs, our trusty – and explosive – opening pair, set us on our way with a century stand. Then Jimmy and Kat saw us home with slick 40s, as you'd expect from those two wily old campaigners, to complete a thoroughly professional victory. To get to Lord's with such an accomplished display was extremely pleasing. We were heading to the Home of Cricket in a really rich vein of form, consistently winning key games in convincing fashion. That becomes a habit, and it was a habit we were determined to continue all the way to NW8.

And with one trophy already won, we were determined to add another one to the trophy cabinet back at the Ageas Bowl. But we weren't the only in-form team heading to Lord's, as Warwickshire had just won the County Championship. So both teams were flying and I guess it was no surprise that the final was a bit of a belter.

That was the first time I'd ever been to Lord's, as a player or a spectator, and the moment we arrived on match day was incredible. As a cricket fan, never mind a player, you know Lord's is the ultimate. So to be there for a match, to be playing on that fabled turf, in front of that gorgeous old pavilion, was a huge honour. A real pinch-yourself moment. Am I really here? Yes Michael, you are.

We headed to our changing room in the main pavilion, which is like a grand mansion with a huge stairway in the entrance, and corridors going off it in every direction. It was like a maze, and getting from the changing room to the pitch would be a challenge in itself! The changing rooms are plush, as you'd expect, with each player's bench kitted out with a green leather seat. Sitting there, I couldn't help thinking about all the legends of the game who would have been in that exact room as me, preparing for a game just like this. Alec Stewart, Bruce French, Alan Knott, Jack Russell, some of the greatest wicketkeepers my country had ever produced – my heroes. They would have been right where I was at that very moment. Surreal. Spine-tingling.

Then we went out onto the pitch for a look around. Out there, even with the stands laying empty, you could almost feel the atmosphere, that electric buzz that would soon emanate from the stands as the fans started pouring in. The place has an aura that you can't even see, feel or hear, but it's there. I remember noticing the slope running across the ground. Everyone talks about it on TV, but to actually see it with my own eyes was something else. Looking at it against the advertising boards running across the pavilion stand, I couldn't believe how much it drops away. But I must admit, at the wicket, it didn't really impact my game at all.

After our warm-up, we walked up the stairs through the members area, and back to the changing room through the famous Long Room. That was such an honour. The high ceilings, the light, airy space with windows covering the pitch-side wall, and paintings and pictures of legends of the game adorning the rest. It's like a museum displaying the history of our great game. It gives me goose bumps just thinking about it.

So many top, top players have played at Lord's over the years. And here I was, a young lad from Yateley, here to play in a cup final for my county. Not on some tour of the ground, or on a corporate event. But to play this great game that I'd loved since I was seven years old. Amazing.

Time and time again I've gone over the final in my mind. Guys like Jimmy Adams, our skipper, have literally dined out on stories from that day ever since, giving countless after-dinner speeches on the subject. What was he thinking in that last over? Did he think Hampshire would win? Did he tell me to stand up to the stumps? I don't blame him. It was an incredible game and for it to go down to the last ball after 80 overs was incredible.

As you will have gathered from the earlier chapters of this book – and if you watched me play during my career – in white-ball cricket I kept up to the stumps, pretty much to any bowler. In our 40-over side that year we had two spinners in Danny Briggs and Liam Dawson, while our seamers, Dimi Mascarenhas and Chris Wood in particular, tended to take pace off the ball. So me keeping up to them was therefore an option, and became a big weapon for that team. I was always in the game up there; I loved it, and I was good at it.

If you're keeping up, you can apply that extra bit of pressure. If you're good, it'll stop them playing their natural game. They're unlikely to skip down the wicket. They're in two minds whether to really commit to their shots. It's one way a keeper can massively influence a game, and for me that's the great benefit of having a specialist keeper over a keeper-batter, as we've discussed earlier.

So I kept up to most of the bowlers, but Kabir Ali was a slightly different story. Kabby wasn't as quick as he had been earlier in his career, but he still bowled mid-80s mph. It was lively, but I felt I could do it.

As the start of the game approached, my nerves were definitely jangling. Just like at the T20 Finals Day a couple of weeks earlier, the TV cameras were there, and the press box was heaving. The stands were full, with each set of fans hoping, expecting, their team to win. Before the game started, I located my family in the crowd, they were sat in the Edrich Stand to the right of the Media Centre as I looked out from the pitch. They gave me a wave and shouted "good luck!". I was buzzing and couldn't wait to get started.

In the warm-up I tried to be busy. I got some catches in, and just tried to familiarise myself with the two ends. As a group we were all calm, confident we could get the job done. In sport, you can only worry about what you can control, and we knew that our game was right on the money at that point in the season; the T20 win, not to mention the semi-final against Sussex, gave us that confidence. Sure, Warwickshire were a good side too, but if we performed well, we knew we could win the game.

Warwickshire won the toss and put us in to bat. Perhaps they'd seen us chasing down Sussex's total two weeks earlier, and thought that the best way to beat us was to get us to set the target. I quite liked that approach, because from our perspective it seemed like they were more worried about us, rather than trying to play to their own strengths.

We batted OK. There were moments when I thought we were going to put the game out of reach, when Jimmy was going nicely with Neil

McKenzie, and then again at the end when Sean Ervine and Simon Katich put on 69 together. Jimmy top scored with 66 – a man-of-the-match knock as it would turn out – and we finished our 40 overs 244-5, and those five wickets lost would prove to be really important later on. It was a half-decent total, but it was obvious it was going to be close.

I wasn't needed to bat, which given my troubles with my batting in the latter stages of that season, was a blessing. Sat on that cramped Lord's balcony, I was dreading having to go in, but our top order did really well and set a competitive total, and kept our tail away from the wicket.

Our bowling response started with Daws and Kabby. I felt good. Focused. But in Kabby's first over I completely misjudged one, which was a shock, for me and probably the rest of the team.

I was stood back, the wicket was a bit greasy and one of Kabby's first deliveries just skidded off the surface. The ball flew down the leg side, catching me completely off guard, and I ended up dropping it. Normally I'd take those all day long, but that's what nerves can do to you. It was a massive shock to the system, like when your sister hits you on the head with a cricket bat. I was normally so reliable behind the stumps, and that was a totally unforced error.

That mistake woke me up, made me realise I wasn't quite on it before then, and after that I was up and running. Maybe if that mistake hadn't happened, I mightn't have been as sharp when we got to the business end of the innings, which obviously I needed to be. So in a way perhaps it was a blessing in disguise.

As our innings earlier had done, the Warwickshire response ebbed and flowed. They started well with a half-century opening stand, then we edged back with a couple of wickets. Then another partnership between Ian Bell and Tim Ambrose got going. It was like that all day. They had a strong batting line-up, we'd get one wicket, but quickly another partnership seemed to take root.

In the 27th over the Bell/Ambrose partnership was finally thwarted. And it would be that man Chris Wood again, who'd do the damage, as Jimmy Adams explained to Tom.

> Chris Wood ran in from the boundary and said, "I *have* to bowl this over". Kat had just bowled, and Bell had hit him for a six. Kat bowling was a bit of a punt because Slug wasn't feeling very well, so we had to get a couple of extra overs in from someone else. But Woody ran in from the boundary and said, "I *need* to bowl this

over, I'll get you a wicket". And when someone runs in and says that to you, you're like – "Alright then".

Batesy came up to the stumps, they were both very comfortable with that. That was the beauty of those guys. They'd done that for years. We knew Batesy was going to do the same job up there – he wasn't going to miss one – and with all the added benefits of standing up. And sure as eggs are eggs Ambrose nicks one, Batesy takes the catch, we get a wicket, and the game changes again.

The next big moment was in the 39th over, with Woody bowling his final over of the game, Warwickshire needed 20 off the last two overs of the match. Woody bowled four really good balls to Chris Woakes and Ian Blackwell, conceding just five off them. I remember thinking, "If we can get away with conceding a couple of singles off the final two balls, they're going to need 12 or so to win, and this game could be ours." Then Woakes hit two boundaries off the final two balls, and the equation changed again. Suddenly we're thinking, "Shit". We were just playing it out almost, hoping for a miracle. They've still got wickets in hand, they've still got Blackwell, Woakes and Carter, all of whom can bat.

They needed seven off the final over to win, so they were favourites. I thought to myself that if we could just break that partnership of Woakes and Blackwell, we might just have a sniff. But Warwickshire were going to have to throw it away for us to win.

"I remember fiddling with the field a bit," Jimmy said. "Just because we had time, and I wanted to get everything right. Batesy coming up to the stumps to Kabby was something. He'd done it before, but they needed seven, so it became a no-brainer."

"I was up in the changing rooms watching it all unfold, because I was injured," Dimi added. "I couldn't sit, I was just pacing around the rooms watching each ball from a different position. It looked like we'd won it, then lost it, then won it again. I honestly had no idea which way it was going. Batesy came up to the stumps to Kabir Ali, who bowled at a good clip. 'Why is Batesy standing up? He should be back, shouldn't he?' All these thoughts were going around my head."

Final over. They needed seven runs, we needed dots and wickets.

Blackwell and Woakes exchanged singles, so they needed five off four. Then we got Blackwell out, having a bit of a hack at a straight one which he missed, leaving them requiring five off three.

In came Neil Carter, in the last game of his illustrious career at Warwickshire. I guess it was written for him to hit the winning runs and walk off into the sunset with the trophy under his arm. Well, not if we had anything to do with it. First ball he tried a lap-sweep which hit him on the pads. We all went up. Obviously we were desperate for the wicket, but it looked plumb from where I was – and I was very close.

No wicket, but crucially no run. Five from two. Next ball Carter hits a four, levelling the scores. 244 apiece. And that's when the wickets lost came into it; we'd only lost five to their seven, so if the scores remained all square, we'd win.

Last ball. The crowd's hushed. All our players were looking on, in a trance, wondering if the ball was going to go to them. If it did, they'd know they'd have to throw it in to me – or the bowler's end – really well, to ensure Warwickshire didn't complete the run and win the game. Talk about pressure.

Katich recalled:

> I was at backward point. I knew Kabir would be bowling another reverse-swinging yorker from around the wicket, so there was every chance it was coming my way low and hard from a slash, if Carter put bat to ball. I remember thinking, I can't get too deep as they would be running and I didn't want them to get the single, but I was also worried about getting too close and the ball racing past me for a four!

"I was at short extra cover," Dawson said. "I was put there for the run out, to run to the bowler's end if they were going to go for it, if the ball was going to be chucked."

We were all set. Jimmy had made his final field adjustments, Kabby was at the top of his run. I was squatting a yard behind the stumps, focusing 100% on the ball. Not over-thinking, trying not to predetermine where the ball was going to go. My brain was pretty lucid at that stage, although the yorker was the obvious delivery, it was just whether Kabby would execute it correctly.

Kabby set off on his run-up, going around the wicket, looking to spear one into Carter's pads. In the ball came. It was a full toss. All Carter needed to do was get bat on ball, and he could set off for a run – a run which would surely win the cup for Warwickshire.

But he missed it...

And, crucially, I didn't...

"There was that pause when it hit your gloves," Woody remembered. "I was looking for where the ball had gone and then I realised – Batesy's got it!"

"You made an unbelievable take," Dimi added. "Probably the best take you could think of, given the situation."

"When you caught it," Daws said. "I remember shouting 'Take the stump, take the stump!' But you'd already taken it."

"What amazed me about what you did that day was not that you caught it," Jimmy added. "Because we'd have been surprised if you'd missed it, or hadn't caught it cleanly. It was that you stumped him, and then pulled the stumps out as well, and that's unbelievable composure. Everyone else was running around going mad, and you still had the composure. And I can remember getting a bit twitchy, because before you did that, I was running to the stumps at the other end, because if Carter was in and you whipped the bails off, they could still run, and Warwickshire would win. So I was all over the oche. But they didn't run, then Carter walked off, incredible."

It all happened so quickly. Standing up meant Kabby could only really bowl in one place. As a batsman, Carter was probably thinking "Right, this is coming in the blockhole. All I have to do is get bat on ball and run, and we should win."

But he missed. And quick as a flash, I'd caught it. Realistically there was not a lot of adjustment to make from Kabby nailing the yorker, to him slightly over-pitching it, which is what it did. I think it hit my gloves on the full, so there wasn't a lot of adjustment required. If he was to have sprayed it down the leg side, I would have needed to make a huge adjustment, and I would have either been quick enough and skilful enough to do it, or not.

Instead it stuck cleanly in the middle of my mitts. Instantaneously I'd dislodged the bails, and it was game over. Well, not quite. Carter was still in his crease, so not out. Yet. The batsman then realised he had to attempt the run, or Warwickshire would lose anyway. At which point I ripped the stumps out of the ground, to effect the run out. They think it's all over? It was now, and we'd won the double!

"Proper skill, to be able to take the full toss in those circumstances," Dimi said. "There's not many players in the world that would have felt comfortable taking that. Foster, Dhoni. Those are the two I'd put up there, but not too many others."

Incredible. It all just happened. I was on autopilot, jolted into action following that blunder at the start of the innings. By the end of that game, I was completely in the zone. Time stopped. The noises from the stands silenced in my brain. I was still. Calm. In a state of nothingness. Then, I see the ball, move my hands, move my head, move my knees, all in tandem. Catch the ball. Remove the bails. Remove the stumps.

Then my senses all came flooding back. I heard the cheers and roars ringing out around the ground. My team mates were running about all over the pitch, grabbing hold of each other and hugging. It was utter carnage!

For it to have ended up in our favour like that was awesome. Those moments, when you're properly in the zone, there isn't really any conscious thought. Maybe after, on reflection, you might pick up on a few things that you were subconsciously thinking, but when you're in the zone you just do what you've always done.

Once we'd calmed down a bit, we started walking around the pitch, and waving at the fans. They were all still there – the stands were full. I was desperate to see Mum and Dad. Finally I saw them. They were beaming. They'd supported me all my life; all the lifts, all the emotional support, keeping me focused when I wanted to give up, pushing me harder, making me stick at it. Seeing them in the stands, looking so happy, so proud, was one of the best moments of the day for me. Someone took a photo of me with my parents which ended up in our local newspaper. It was such a proud moment for the whole family.

As was becoming a customary, well-trodden process for us now, we then went through our media obligations, before collecting the trophy and our medals. My first full season in the side, and two winners' medals to my name – it was insane.

After all the pomp and ceremony had died down, we headed back to the changing room for drinks and fines. The night of the T20 Finals Day victory was a heavy old session, but this was more contemplative. Winning at Lord's – that's pretty much the pinnacle in cricket. Aside from playing for your country, playing and winning a trophy at Lord's was as good as it gets. We soaked up the moment with a few drinks, but this was about reflecting on a job well done this season – a double-winning season, one we wouldn't forget in a hurry.

* * *

As the dust settled after that Lord's victory, it suddenly came into focus that the season was over. All in all, it had been an excellent first full season for me in the first team. I'd come in and kept really well, and while there was clearly still room for improvement with the bat, there was also enough promise – certainly with my form in the early part of the season – to suggest my batting could develop and be good enough for first-class cricket.

But analysing my season's performance would have to wait for a bit. First, we had some celebrating to do.

First we had the PCA (Professional Cricketers' Association) do in October, straight after the end of the season. That was the first time I'd been to that event where I felt everyone knew who I was. Chris Read, James Foster, they all came up to me and complimented me on my performances that season, particularly that final-ball moment at Lord's. It was the first time I really felt like I belonged, like I had arrived at that level.

Later that month, we headed to Johannesburg for the Champions League, our reward for winning the T20 final that season. It was a massive tournament, with teams from around the world qualifying having won, or come second, in competitions in their respective countries. The great and the good from world cricket were in attendance; Brendan McCullum, Sachin Tendulkar, Shane Watson, Jacques Kallis – they were all there.

All the teams were staying in a stunning, all-inclusive hotel, and because it was quite a dangerous area we had to stay in the hotel all the time. To be honest I was a bit overwhelmed by the whole experience, and probably didn't make the most of the situation. People like me, Daws and Woody – absolute minnows, rubbing shoulders with those guys. I don't know whether the occasion just massively overawed us, because based on our form that summer, we should have done much better in the tournament. As it was we underperformed, and didn't even make it through the qualifying round.

Out there the wickets were hard and fast. Dimi was getting nothing, and neither were Briggsy or Daws – nothing. In England, Dimi would typically bowl his four overs through at the start, go for no runs and pick up a few wickets to set us on our way. In the whole time I played with him in England, I only ever saw Dimi get taken down once or twice. Out there, Dimi was going for loads of runs and picking up no wickets in every game. When your senior guy wasn't in the game, the rest of us were just out. It was game over.

It was gutting as we had been in such good form just a couple of months earlier. Also the format of the competition that year didn't help us. In 2010 we couldn't go and in 2011 we messed up Finals Day. In both those years, we'd have gone straight into the competition proper had we gone out there. In 2012, we had to qualify first, and we screwed up. Somerset went in 2011 and didn't have to qualify, and they ended up going quite far in the competition. They earned loads of money for the club and made a success of it.

We messed it up, but you win some, and you lose some. It was a learning experience, though not a particularly enjoyable one.

That aside, 2012 was a great year – for us as a team and for me personally. In December, just before Christmas, we went to the BBC Sports Personality of the Year Awards ceremony, as a nominee for the Team of the Year award. How insane is that?

It's probably the best event I've ever been to, and probably ever will. It took place in a huge converted warehouse in London's Docklands. There were two big bars either side of this massive open-plan room, with loads of tables and chairs in between. But no one was sitting down – everyone was standing in between all the tables, and chatting in groups. There were no paparazzi, everyone was just there having a great time, partying hard and having a laugh.

It was 2012, the year of the London Olympics, so we were there with all the Olympic winners. I had my picture taken with Mo Farah; Bradley Wiggins and Jessica Ennis were there too! David Beckham was standing on the other side of the room, getting hounded by everyone. Every so often you'd see a really famous face; Gary Lineker was presenting. All the great and the good of UK sport, and some other famous faces were in attendance, too.

"I was honestly thinking, what the hell are we doing here?" Daws said, with a smile across his face. "What was the point of a county cricket team being there? What were we doing when there's Bradley Wiggins, Jessica Ennis, David Beckham all there?"

And then you had us, these tiny little fish in a massive pond. We just ended up chatting among ourselves. What are you going to do? "Ah, there's David Beckham over there – I'll just pop over and have a little chat!"

We felt like we were inferior, like we shouldn't be there because we saw these other guys as being properly famous, especially after the success of the London Olympics. We were nobodies compared to them.

But we'd won two domestic trophies that season; the equivalent of winning the FA Cup and the League Cup in the same football season, and you'd definitely expect to be picking up some awards if your team had won those two accolades.

Cricket often gets downplayed a bit, doesn't it? It's not always seen as the most popular sport, and certainly when you see the crowds at some County Championship games, it's easy to think that no one really cares about it. But cricket is still a fantastic sport with a really loyal and passionate fan base, so to be there that night, it was a massive compliment us, but also to our sport, and perhaps us being there just reminded us all just how much love there still is in this nation for county cricket.

One chap I would have loved to have seen there – I'm not sure if he was but I didn't see him – was tennis player Rafa Nadal. Out of all the sportsmen and women out there, he is probably the one I look up to the most. He's just such a fighter. He's fit as anything, fiery, hits the ball really hard, and has clearly worked his absolute nuts off his whole life to get to where he is now. He wasn't the most gifted; he was no Federer, for example, for whom tennis is almost too easy. So Rafa had to properly fight and graft, and I love that. Maybe there's a bit of me that associates with that – I had the ability with the gloves, but I certainly had to fight with my batting.

It was a great night, and a fantastic way to end what had been a superb year. The work I'd put in pre-season, travelling down under, going to the Caribbean and then the season itself. The trophies we had won, it had been amazing, almost dreamlike.

A dream from which I was about to be rudely awakened…

Chapter 8
Wheater

In and amongst all the partying and awards ceremonies in the autumn of 2012, I managed to squeeze in my end-of-season performance review meeting, with Jimmy, Tony and Chalks. Once again I headed to Rod's office, upstairs in the Atrium at the Ageas Bowl. I was reasonably confident going into the meeting. I'd had a good season with the gloves, and there were real signs of progress with the bat, although admittedly it had tailed off a bit in the second half of the season.

I arrived at Rod's office and there in front of me sat Chalks, Tony and Jimmy. Tony led the meeting, saying he was really happy with my keeping, and that he was pleased I'd gained some plaudits for my contribution at Lord's. He reiterated that I had a huge part to play in our one-day success, and that up to the point at Lord's, I perhaps hadn't earned the acclaim I deserved.

It was certainly him doing most of the talking, with Chalks chipping in from time to time. And to be honest, the whole time I was at Hampshire was like that. He definitely put the most into me, in a coaching sense. Tony had brought me up, through the whole academy programme, and despite certain issues in our relationship, in terms of the lack of support I felt he showed me at times, one thing I could never deny was that he was always on my side. He wanted me to do well, and I always appreciated that.

My batting, and my tendency for getting bowled, was also mentioned. They raised it as an issue and threw a few stats at me, and said it was something we were going to have to focus on over the winter. Chalks and Tony were good at raising these issues, but weren't so forthcoming when it came to actual solutions. So, there was no training programme suggested, no special drills or approaches that I could work on to help me address those batting frailties. It was like that the whole time I was at Hampshire. And it was quite frustrating, because I knew I needed to work on my batting, no question, but it was like they were out of ideas on what they could do to help me.

They also mentioned, in general terms at least, the lack of runs scored by our lower-order batsmen, and how that was something they were looking to address for the next season. My view was, and still is, that run scoring is the responsibility of the whole batting unit, in red-ball cricket especially. If the whole team isn't scoring enough runs on a consistent basis, I'm not sure how you can blame only the keeper and bowlers. Fair enough if this was a criticism for the whole batting unit, but this wasn't. By singling out the lower order, it was almost as though the top- and middle-order batters were absolved of any blame, which looking at the batting averages for that season, wasn't right. We'd all struggled.

I mean, we had a formidable-looking batting line-up, but we were always susceptible to batting collapses in Championship games. If you look at the club today, that's still very much the case. Personally, I think it's because the club puts such a huge emphasis on their one-day teams. It's ingrained in the players from a young age, hence why perhaps the likes of Daws, Vince and co. have struggled in England's Test team. Although that's a debate for another book.

Yet despite disagreeing with the coaches on this one, me being me, I just accepted the criticism. I nodded and agreed and the conversation moved on. The meeting ended soon after.

With those end-of-season reviews, there was no follow-up process as such. I know some people in the corporate world who tell me they have end-of-year reviews which are fully documented, with both the manager and the individual making comments on their performance, before both signing the document. They then agree on an overall rating for the year, with follow-up actions agreed if needed, and objectives set for the following year.

In cricket, certainly during my time, there was nothing that formal in place. Obviously both parties knew about the review, and I'm sure from the club's perspective it was probably logged somewhere that a meeting had taken place and I'd attended. But there was no report, no written instructions on what to work on over the winter, no hard evidence as such to back-up the coaches' points, positive or otherwise. No written objectives, no targets as such. So it was a pretty half-baked process, if I'm being honest.

Memory is fickle at the best of times, but I know I came out of that meeting with an impending sense that the future wasn't looking quite as positive as I thought it was when I'd gone in. This was disappointing because 2012 had been such a great season for us all, and for me personally. I'd gone into that meeting thinking I was developing along the right lines, with work still to do, of course, but heading in the right direction. Now I was fearing for my very future at the club.

And that was far from ideal, not least because I was also in the middle of contract negotiations. Originally Hampshire wanted to give me a one-year contract extension. I argued back saying I wanted more security. Looking back, they were obviously thinking of another wicketkeeping option already, and didn't want to commit to me.

In the end I secured a two-year deal, but during the negotiations I had a strange encounter which, if true, was going to affect my entire future at Hampshire. What happened was bizarre, totally confusing and, to be honest, I'm still not quite sure how it came to pass, or who was behind it.

This is dead set – I swear to God, even though it reads like a plot-line in a whodunnit, this is the stone-dead truth...

I received an anonymous letter through the post at my parents' house in Yateley. It asked if I was aware that Hampshire had approached Adam Wheater about playing for Hampshire next season as their wicketkeeper?

It freaked me out. I didn't know who it was from – to this day, I still don't. Lots of people I've talked to about it have given their view on who was behind it. Some suggest it was a stalker, some think maybe a fanatical follower. Some think perhaps it was someone at the club who wanted to give me a heads up of something happening that was real, and had the potential to really impact – potentially derail – my career.

For what it's worth, I think it was someone looking out for me, as opposed to someone being malicious. A fan of mine, perhaps. Maybe it was Ivo Tennant, the ESPN reporter, because he was always writing nice things about me. I jest, of course, but my hunch is that it was a friend looking out for me, rather than a foe trying to hurt me.

I was totally bamboozled by this letter. Obviously at that stage, I had no idea whether it was actually true or not, and it wasn't the sort of thing you really wanted to take in to the coaches and ask them about. I tried not to give it too much thought, it was so out of the blue that it had to be rubbish, didn't it? Although with that and my lukewarm end-of-season review meeting, I was starting to feel a little insecure about my future.

Despite all that, I signed my contract and sent it back to Hampshire in the post. When Chalks received it, he summoned me to a meeting. What's going on here, I wondered.

So off I went, along to this meeting – in Rod's office, as always – completely in the dark about what Chalks wanted to talk about. I'd signed the contract, we were all good in that respect. We'd discussed my performance from the previous season, and by that stage we now had a bit of an idea of what my winter was going to look like. Tony had put some training plans in place which, we hoped, would address my issues against the straight ball.

Chalks kicked off the meeting, saying he was pleased that I'd signed the contract. His voice was stern and his face looked troubled, and I knew something else was coming.

"However," Chalks continued, "within the envelope you sent back, there was also this letter…"

"What letter," I asked. "What are you on about?"

I looked at Chalks, genuinely bewildered at what was happening. He looked serious. Solemn. The room was silent for only a second or two, but it felt like a day had passed. I stared into his eyes, desperately searching for clues. I was freaking out, what could I have done to have annoyed him so much? What the hell was going on?

Then Chalks revealed the letter – the anonymous, Wheater letter that I'd received at home. He started describing what it said, but by then, I knew. I knew he had the anonymous letter, I knew what it said, I knew it all.

Oh my God. How the hell had that got in to the envelope? To this day, I still have no idea how – it certainly wasn't a cry for help from me. The only thing I can think of, is perhaps my Mum, Dad or my sister put the letter in a pile with my other paperwork on the kitchen table, including my contract, not knowing what it was, but knowing it was mine and to do with cricket.

Even if that were true, I'm sure I would have checked what I was sending back to Hampshire before I sealed the envelope. I mean, everyone checks what they've put in an envelope before they seal it up, don't they? I was devastated. Distraught. It was so embarrassing, I just wanted the ground to swallow me whole.

Slowly, the embarrassment lifted a little, and my mind switched to the massive elephant now in the room; were Hampshire actually going to bring Wheater in to replace me? I wanted Chalks to say, "Of course we're not getting a new keeper – you're our number one. You've had a good first season in the team, there's some work to do, but we'll get there."

Those words of reassurance never came. Instead, before I knew it, my worst fears were realised. Yes, Hampshire had indeed approached Wheater, and yes he wanted to come. There were a few contractual issues on both sides to work through, but the deal was going to happen.

I was numb. Even though I'd achieved so much that season, it seemed like my club had given up on me. I'd just turned 22 – I was still learning. I felt there was still so much to come from me. My keeping had obviously earned plaudits already, I'd got praise from fans and the media alike for that final-ball moment at Lord's, and my fellow wicketkeepers at the PCA dinner had been quick to praise my work, too. I felt really valued by my team mates, particularly the bowlers, who were always saying how good my keeping was, and how it really benefited the team, particularly in one-day cricket.

OK, my batting still had a way to go, but it was getting there. It was a work in progress, but it was good enough – I'd shown that at the start of that season. Plus I'd been at the club all my life. Was this really the end of the line, already? After just one season in the first team? All that investment from the club, I'd been in the academy setup since the start, were they really going to throw that all away? I'd been in the England age groups all the way through too, did that count for nothing?

All those thoughts were hurtling through my jumbled mind, as I sat across the desk from Chalks. He told me I still had a future at the club, particularly in white-ball cricket, but the writing was on the wall. You don't invest in a new player – who would be commanding a much bigger salary than I'd just agreed in my new contact by the way – without thinking that he was going to be the first-choice keeper.

I came away from that meeting not knowing how to feel. I think I just kind of hoped that it wasn't going to happen. Maybe Wheater's contract issues wouldn't be resolved and he'd end up staying at Essex. I buried it, didn't want to address it and I just tried to carry on as normal.

And that was really me all over during my time at Hampshire. I glossed over issues and acted as if they weren't happening, or didn't matter. Whereas internally, I was gutted. Chalks had said I was still in their plans, and while I looked at that with a degree of scepticism, I wanted to believe it so much that I ended up telling myself it was true. I bottled up these issues, I was never very good at opening up, to my folks, my sister or my girlfriend at the time. I stored it all up, hoping upon hope that it'd be OK in the long run, even though I knew there was a good chance it wouldn't be.

Daws has said to me since how I always seemed so positive around the club. Inwardly I was really insecure, but I never showed that. I needed support, yet it was never forthcoming. Instead I just tried to sweep it under the carpet and pretend it wasn't happening.

The idea of rotating Wheater and I was one first suggested by Jimmy, Chalks and Tony, in conversations immediately after it emerged that Wheats was joining. That instead of being the second-choice keeper, I'd actually be used for specific games, as Jimmy explained to Tom:

> We had hopes of being able to marry the two, but that was wishful thinking in hindsight. We went through a stage of talking about rotation, but it's easy to talk about that in pre-season. Then you realise that you're not dealing with objects, you're dealing with people. When they're in form they want to play, when they're tired they often won't say because they're worried about losing their spot. All the insecurities which come with being a sportsman come out.

I wanted to buy into what I was being told by the skipper and the coaches. And on the face of it, I probably came across as though I'd accepted it. But again, deep down, I just didn't see it happening. How could we both play together in the same team in the long term?

That's where sport is so fickle. One day you're on top of the world, the next you're down in the gutter. And that was the thing that hurt the most. We'd had an amazing season in 2012, and I felt that my talent behind the stumps had more than played its part in our success. Sure, Lord's was the stand-out moment, but me keeping up to the medium-pacers and spinners in general was an integral part of our white-ball success.

I came across a *Sunday Times* interview with Jose Mourinho recently, which struck a chord with me about my plight at Hampshire at that time. In the article, Mourinho talked about how he prioritised winning the Europa League and the League Cup over finishing fourth in the Premier League when he first joined Manchester United in 2016. Mourinho wanted to develop a culture of winning within the club. The players, the staff, everyone at the club would be used to that success, and strive for it even more.

It resonated with me because we'd been so successful in that 2012 season, and part of that was our strategy in white-ball cricket, to strangle the life out of batting teams. I was pivotal to that, yet here I was being phased out. It struck me that, while Hampshire were looking for more lower-order runs in first-class cricket, they perhaps hadn't considered the impact me being out of the side would have on our white-ball team, which in turn would impact our success at the club. If it ain't broke, don't fix it. As it was, Hampshire would have to wait until 2018 before they'd win another one-day competition. Make of that what you will.

Jose Mourinho's take is quite relevant to that idea, so here's what he said:

> The first step [was] to try to bring the football team in the right direction. Of course in the first season I was trying to improve [this], but I also felt the club need to feed — at least emotionally — the fans, the self-esteem of the players, the motivation of the people. And you can't do that without some success. That's why I fought hard for trophies. And that's why I prefer a Europa League victory than a third or fourth spot in the championship. Because the best way to accelerate the process is to do the process winning. Because winning gets you smiles, you get better atmosphere, you create better empathy with the people, you can demand more from the people, you can persuade the people to give more.

Our team had won two out of the three trophies available to us that season, and success breeds success. Maybe if Mourinho had been our gaffer, I'd have been kept on at Hampshire. My keeping was central to our team philosophy in white-ball cricket. I just couldn't believe my batting, at 22, had essentially been discarded.

Obviously I wasn't happy with the club's decision to sign Wheats. It was nothing personal but I felt I'd done enough, in what was – let's not forget – my first full season behind the stumps. Shouldn't my performances have earned me another year at least?

It was no use. Wheater signed for Hampshire on 1 March 2013, less than six months after we'd completed that amazing double at Lord's. It was a controversial move, in more ways than one. Essex coach Paul Grayson was clearly unhappy, saying "Hampshire have given him [Wheater] assurances that he will be first choice [keeper]," which was obviously not great to hear from my perspective.

Chalks denied the claims, but in his press release said, "Adam will add competition with the gloves and comes with an impressive first-class batting average," so it was clear that run-scoring in red-ball cricket was the primary consideration behind the move.

Media reports at the time claimed Wheater had bought himself out of the remaining year of his contract at Chelmsford, and he'd left because he was the third-choice keeper there, behind James Foster –

yes, the same guy Hampshire had considered signing the season before – and Ben Foakes.

His arrival was causing controversy at our end too. Fans couldn't believe it, and I saw plenty of angry messages on social media aimed at the club for bringing Wheater in. And my team mates were shocked, as Dimi Mascarenhas explained.

> I thought it was a crazy decision to bring in a new keeper for the next year, given that they had just sacked our best wicketkeeper-batsman in all my time at Hampshire [Nic Pothas]. Also the fact that you'd shown good signs of improvement with the bat and surely deserved an opportunity to carry on and see what you could do in the coming season. You went behind the stumps and we won two trophies – there really was no need to change anything. Unfortunately for you, they brought in Wheater. And I think I said at the time that I thought it was the wrong thing to do from Hampshire's point of view. They should have given you another season. It probably didn't work for either of you, to be honest.

There was also plenty of media reaction to the move, with *ESPNCricinfo* reporter, George Dobell, writing: "Bates may consider himself unfortunate. While the 22-year-old is a batsman of modest ability – first-class average of 19.66 – he is an exceptional wicketkeeper. He played a pivotal part in Hampshire's CB40 success last season, taking the final ball stood up to the stumps against the pace of Kabir Ali."

So I had massive support, which was great and I really did appreciate it. At the same time however, the powers that be at Hampshire had made their decision; they'd forked out a hefty wage for Wheats to come in, putting their reputations on the line in some respects. So I knew, deep down, that I'd struggle to get a look in the following season, even though Jimmy and Chalks were assuring me I'd play white-ball cricket at the least.

It was a horrible time. I was numb, bitter, frustrated. I was gutted, depressed, disillusioned. What the hell was I going to do now?

Regrettably I did the same thing I always did, and tried to pretend everything was OK. I almost didn't allow myself to have thoughts on it, I just tried not to think about it, or, if I did think about it, I would think about what Jimmy and Chalks had said, that I was still in their plans for white-ball cricket at least, and used that to boost myself up. "Well

Jimmy and Chalks have told me I'll be used in the white ball stuff, so it'll be fine," I used to tell people. "I've just got to keep working hard, and keep believing."

Deep down I knew it wasn't as easy as that. Hampshire had invested in Wheater – it was a big deal to sign him. So he was obviously going to be their main man, otherwise what would've been the point in signing him? Chalks and the guys behind his arrival needed to prove the move was a successful one. In a weird way, even though I'd been at the club since I was a kid, they had more loyalty to Wheats now because they needed their signing to be a success, for their own reputations.

Although I've got to say, I always got the impression Tony wasn't particularly in favour of the move. I don't know that for a fact, but just the way he was towards me at the time, and since. When you think about it, Tony had worked with me from a young age, all the way through the academy setup. I'm sure his preference would always be to promote from the academy, because he had that emotional attachment to us, and he believed in our ability. Even if that was his view, it wasn't one that was shared by the others.

When Wheater actually came into the group, meeting him was obviously quite an uncomfortable, unpleasant experience. Again, it's important to note this is not a personal vendetta against the guy. This is elite sport and this is what happens. However, as the one whose position was most under threat by his arrival, I was always going to be the one most impacted. For batters and bowlers, you have more than one position in the team to fight for. When you're a specialist keeper, like me, there's only one spot you can occupy in a team.

Wheats was quite a canny operator. Everything he did and said seemed quite tactical, quite calculated. I can't help but think that he tried hard to get me on side right from the word go. He played a very good game. I don't think he ever had any animosity towards me as such, but I can't help but feel like the way he was towards me was fairly superficial. To be fair, that's probably to be expected. He would have known it was my position he was coming in to take, so getting me on side would obviously make his integration into the group a damn sight easier. He wouldn't have known the group dynamics within the changing room, but it doesn't take Einstein to realise that we'd have been a close-knit team. We'd won two trophies the year before, and a lot of us had come through the academy together. Therefore coming in and ruffling feathers would have been a stupid move.

I've sat down with Chalks and Tony in recent times and asked them if they thought they gave me enough support, both before the news that Wheater was signing, and after he'd signed. They said it was a tricky one as they never knew if I needed support or not, because I didn't show it. I didn't go to them, they didn't come to me, so it was kind of a stand off.

It's so difficult, looking back, to know if I could have handled it any differently. I could've kicked up a right stink about it, but that just wasn't my style. Chalks and Tony said they didn't think I needed support because I didn't ask for it, but did I really need to ask? I never felt like I was really struggling the season before – my keeping was good all year and my batting showed enough potential. Sure I'd had a bad run in the middle of the campaign, but everyone goes through lean spells. And by the way I wasn't the only one who'd struggled with the bat that year – especially in red-ball cricket where we'd stayed in Division Two – quite a disappointment given the quality of our squad.

Clearly there was a pattern. I didn't speak to the coaches. I didn't speak to my family, or my girlfriend. I was a lone wolf, I suffered in silence. Well, did I suffer? I think what I actually did was just reassure myself that everything was going to be OK. I was a bit delusional perhaps. Or maybe just too damn trusting, taking the coaches' assurance that'd I'd still play in white-ball cricket way too literally, when common sense suggested that was unlikely. Wheater was a big-money signing – he wouldn't want to be benched so that I could play the white-ball stuff.

It was all just really disappointing. I was gutted with the situation I was facing going into the 2013 season, and to be honest, I felt let down by the way the club had handled it.

Chapter 9
Dealing with batting failure

Most of us know how it feels when someone new joins the team you are working in, who is in direct competition to you, and the job you are doing.

It's hard. As humans, we're in a tricky position where you have to be civil, welcoming, while at the same time maintaining a distance, appreciating that the individual is, essentially, a predator to your position.

Dealing with the arrival of Adam Wheater at Hampshire made me face up to my insecurities and weaknesses in the game, most notably my batting. Over the years I'd always been aware that my batting was slightly behind where it should be, but by the same token I always felt I could get it to the level required, given time.

However, time was something I no longer had. With Wheater arriving, I knew my career at the Ageas Bowl was now under threat, and holding my place in the team was not something I alone could effect by playing well. I'd now need to rely on Wheater being injured, or playing poorly, as well as myself playing well in the seconds.

It was a hammer blow. My batting had long been a weakness for me, of course. But it was something I felt was progressing. Now this new signing put more pressure on me to deliver with the bat, rather than allowing me to build on what I'd achieved in the first half of the 2012 season. Dealing with that blow was tough. Acknowledging that this was all down to my batting failures, was uncomfortable. Upsetting.

At that stage, I no longer enjoyed batting. I liked it as a kid, but the older I got, and then playing in the first team, it became harder and harder. It was more about enduring it, trying to make the best of the talent I had. Trying not to fail, rather than really doing a job for the team. That's not a great starting point mentally; set a team up not to lose and invariably, they'll lose. I was setting up not to fail with the bat, and invariably, I was failing more than I was succeeding. Batting was always thus. Every cricketer would say their batting failed more often than it succeeded. But for me, the failures seemed to far outweigh the successes.

It's back to my point in the introduction, of cricket being a series of individual battles within a team sport. Batting, perhaps, the most exposing discipline of all. You could bat for 100 balls, play well, keep your wicket intact, score some runs. Then one lapse in concentration, one unlucky bounce off the wicket, one inside edge onto your stumps, one good ball, and you're gone. Out. You reached 41, but you didn't convert it to 50. Your career stats won't capture a 41 – it'll capture a 50, but not a 41. Little things like that. Little details. 87 against Gloucestershire. Yes, but instead of two hundreds against my name in my career stats, there's only one. In many respects batting, and cricket more generally, is one of the most exposing games in pro sport. Certainly in team sport.

And I knew that, if I failed with the bat, everyone else would be thinking that I'd failed. Again. And in a county cricket season, you just don't really have the time to work on the reasons you're failing, because the games come thick and fast. You don't want to start deconstructing your batting technique in the middle of the season, with your next game never more than a couple of days away. You wouldn't drive your car out of the garage with the bonnet still up and tools hanging out of the engine, would you?

Plus we're in the unique situation with cricket, of having to jump between three different formats, almost on a weekly basis. One week you're playing red-ball cricket, and your batting is all about occupying the crease; bat long, don't give your wicket away. The next you're playing a 50-over game; you have to up your scoring rate, bat sensibly but more aggressively. Then the week after the T20s come around, and you have to up it another gear.

You work hard practising for each format, but the reality is you may have only a couple of training sessions between matches. Sometimes only one. Sometimes none. Sometimes you finish an evening T20 match, and by the time you get home afterwards, it's midnight, or 1am. Then the next day you have practice for a one-day cup game the day after. It's relentless.

You also have to consider travel time. Sometimes we were heading up to Durham, Manchester or Leeds for a game – that all takes time out of your training schedule. To factor in work on your technique on top of all that is pretty much impossible. So instead, you almost have to learn out in the middle, in the matches themselves. And that's obviously very difficult.

Plus, if you start your cricket career with poor form with the bat, your batting average will start low and very quickly it's making for painful reading, even though in your own mind, you're only just starting out.

In my case, I had my wicketkeeping. And yes, people may think "Well, he might take a stumping, or a catch that wins the game," but people won't actually see that reflected in your stats. "He might average 20 with the bat, but he's taken four one-handed catches, or he's taken three stumpings out of the rough that's completely changed the game." That goes back to not being able to accurately quantify the contribution made by a wicketkeeper in a game of cricket.

Personally I think I was pigeonholed quite early on as being a keeper who wasn't as strong with the bat, and I was forever trying to drag that back. Fans, the media, everyone would say "He's a good keeper, but he can't bat."

Once people start hearing that, it's such a difficult thing to shift. I would have to go above and beyond what was required of me with the bat just to change people's perceptions. Even if I changed people's minds temporarily with a couple of decent performances, a couple of failures would soon take them back to their original opinion. I felt that from my coaches as well. I always felt like they were judging me, and I always felt like they agreed with general consensus; that my batting just wasn't good enough.

Ironically, people used to say to me, "You worked so hard on your keeping, why didn't you work harder on your batting?" But I did work hard on it. I just don't think I addressed the key issues, most of which were mental. And I don't think I'd had enough time to nail down my own method for batting. I came into the first team at 19, at a time when others, like Billings, were at uni honing their batting. Or Buttler, who was at Somerset, playing as a batter behind Kieswetter. I was first-choice keeper at Hants, I had to be focused on my keeping every single game. I had to focus on my keeping. I didn't have the mental capacity, or the time, to really nail down my batting.

One technical flaw in my batting was pushing too hard at the ball, and too far out in front of my pad, leaving too big a gap between bat and pad. So if the ball nibbled off the wicket a little bit, I was a goner. Even now, playing club cricket, if I get a straight one I can just feel myself pushing my bat out too far in front of me, to the point where I feel this sensation in my body because I know I shouldn't be doing it. But somehow my reflex reaction is to lurch forward towards the ball, leaving a gap which the ball would find its way through, and onto the stumps.

I needed to remove that neurological link of my brain telling my arms to push the bat forwards whenever a straight ball was bowled. It was more of a psychological issue, and a change of mindset was required. But all I did at Hampshire was continually hit balls, in the hope that I'd just get over it eventually, through practice.

Another issue was that I never used a trigger. My front leg did move as the bowler came in, and it was sometimes in the air when the bowler actually released the ball. Ideally, you want to be dead still when the bowler releases, but I was usually on the move. I was moving my front leg down the wicket probably 80% of the time, which is huge. Alastair Cook does that a lot, too, and there's been a lot of coverage on that when he's not playing well.

If you're already moving when the ball is bowled, then you can't react again to the delivery. Either you should trigger before the ball is bowled, or stay dead still. Either way, you want that movement after the ball is bowled so you can react to the length and line of the ball coming down towards you. It's all about that base position, going back to my wicketkeeping masterclass chapter. Ironically my base behind the wicket was really good, really solid. But my batting base was anything but.

When I play club cricket for Wokingham now, I do trigger. It's something I wanted to try out and it works for me. I reckon I'm more still at the point of delivery now, because that trigger movement sets me up to be static at the point the bowler releases. That's where, as a coach myself now, I look back at my time at Hampshire and question why that wasn't picked up, because all the signs were there.

If I was thrown into a first-class game now, I think I would be much better prepared to deal with the mental side of batting. I think physically, it would take a bit of time adjusting to the speed of the game again – the bowlers in county cricket are that bit quicker, or spin the ball that bit more than they do in club cricket. But mentally I would be a lot better equipped now. Part of that, of course, is because I'm older. When you're young and cricket feels like the be-all and end-all of life, that threat of failure is huge and something you don't even want to consider. As a youngster you don't even want to think about a life outside of, or after, cricket. If you do, perhaps, you have more perspective on life, and as a result, put less pressure on yourself when you're playing.

In reality, not many young players actually do that, and that's in any sport. How can you? From a young age, all you've thought about is being a professional sportsperson. So when you actually start getting games in the first team, you're going to obsess about being the best you can be. It's only natural. But the best players, they have that experience, even at a young age, to take that pressure away from themselves. To bat in the moment.

Remember what I was saying earlier, about bottling up that innocence of youth, of batting without fear? That's what you want to achieve, and the best players, from a young age, they do that. They thrive in those high-pressure situations. In my mind as I write this, I'm picturing Joe Root, who, from an England perspective, is perhaps the best example in recent times of a player coming into the England team and completely thriving in that environment. Sam Curran is another. Not many can do it like them, but if you can, you're on to an absolute winner.

Dimi Mascarenhas told Tom:

> It's belief in yourself, and belief in what you can do. It was evident that Batesy was brilliant behind the stumps, and he owned it when he was there. But it was a different story when he had a bat in his hand. It wasn't a lack of talent, because he showed it. Maybe not as consistently as he would have liked, but he could score runs with the bat.
>
> In first-class cricket, he didn't look the most comfortable out there. But he could get the job done, if he'd just relaxed, played and not worried. I think he just looked like he was worried all the time.

On a personal level I felt like I was always trying to improve with the bat. I put a lot of effort into it, but in hindsight, I'm not sure that effort was directed the right way. I often found myself tweaking my technique, putting loads of energy into a lot of different things as opposed to working with what I had and trying to build a method for scoring runs with my technique.

Did the coaches do enough to work on my flaws? No, I don't think they did. I kind of wish they'd said to me, "These are your flaws, this is what we're going to do to work on them. I'm going to spend two months with you on your batting, and we're going to nail it." When Tom spoke to him for this book, Jimmy recalled a time when he and the coaches discussed what to do with my batting.

> There was a period where Batesy's batting was earmarked. "Let's work with him through the winter on his batting," because we

felt, Tony felt, that we could get it up to a level. We saw glimpses of what he could do. That hundred against Yorkshire, for example. And then possibly a feeling that it stalled a bit. But looking back now, I mean geez, we've all had dodgy half seasons, you know? Maybe that was Batesy's. I think cricket was starting a phase where it got a bit more brutal and ruthless with its selection and squad sizes. When I started, people were given a bit more time, I think now guys are ready so much earlier that a blip isn't given the same patience as it was.

I just remember nothing really changing from a training perspective, even when my batting form dipped. I was receiving throw-downs in the nets and getting told, "Yup you're looking good, you're looking good." But all I'd received is what I'd do in a game, mixed-length balls coming down for an hour, rather than spend that time trying to address a specific issue, or mental coaching, sports psychology, to address the weakness I had in my mind, my decision-making.

One county player we spoke to told us of a conversation he'd had with his batting coach. He said he was told that his batting coach had noticed a weakness in his technique having watched him over the course of the previous three (yes, three) seasons. "You've known that for three years, why have you never told me?", the player told us. "And rather than say 'let's go to the nets and work on it', it was like 'here's a hundred balls, hit them how you see them.'"

It doesn't take a coaching course to realise there's something wrong there. If there's a flaw in a player's game, something that's consistently causing him problems in matches, surely it's the coaches responsibility, and in the club's interests, to help him address that specific issue.

I wish I'd have taken more ownership of my game, and been more proactive in going to the coaches and saying to them, "This is what I want to work on. This is what I need to work on." But I believed what Chalks and Tony were working with me on was the right thing. Even if at times I thought we should be focusing on other things, I trusted my coaches because they'd looked after me my whole career, and so surely they'd be doing the best for me now?

And it wasn't that they didn't want to help. But obviously they saw the option of bringing in an alternative wicketkeeper as an easier, more beneficial option for the team in the long run, than helping me to develop my batting. I spent a lot of time on my batting but, by and large, it was time wasted. I was almost not working on anything. It didn't really go anywhere. Which is really frustrating and it didn't get me to where I needed to get to with my batting.

At that age you need guidance. Actually I think you need guidance the whole time. People talk about ownership, about players needing to take ownership of their own development. And of course that's true. But I also think you need that support from your coaches all the way through your career.

I can remember reading an article by Adam Gilchrist in which he said how you don't want to show your vulnerabilities to your coaches. He was saying how he was in a dark place with his batting form, but the last thing he wanted to do was tell his coaches about it. I totally got that. I didn't want to show the coaches I was vulnerable, for fear it might be held against me. I'd be dropped, discarded, rather than developed. In the end I was dropped having not divulged anything to my coaches anyway, so perhaps I was doomed either way. Jimmy Adams told Tom:

> I wonder whether perhaps Batesy worked so hard on his batting, that he got into that horrible thing where he was almost trying too hard. Batesy was an incredibly hard worker, he was always a guy who you wanted to do well. You wanted him to play. You knew that there was no stone left unturned.
>
> I wonder if perhaps he just spent too long worrying about his batting, almost to the detriment of his keeping. But then again he was the victim of his own success. You see some of the ridiculous stuff he did [behind the stumps], and it becomes the norm, and the reality is that it can't be that level all the time.
>
> The difference between a younger player and the more experienced player is the bits that don't go to plan, and raising the bottom of that level up. So when there is a rough trot, they find a way to get out of it quicker. You turn up in the morning and you think "I don't feel good today", yet you still find a way of doing it.
>
> When Batesy was in form he could do what he wanted, and fill that batting role at seven. If not higher at times. And you knew he was a strong boy, you knew he was able to do it at the end in one-day cricket. But it was making that a bit more consistent, as Batesy himself has said. And that's the trick. Maybe that comes from having a little more time to work on the skills without it being in the spotlight, and sometimes being exposed, because it's a very cruel world in cricket.

County cricket isn't as bad as Test cricket, but we had it with Vincey and England, where he was out playing the same shot twice, then suddenly they're picking him apart. He gets out again like that, and you're thinking, is it because he's now thinking "Do I, don't I?" And it's a similar thing. I imagine with Batesy, he knows. None of us want to miss balls, but you don't score a hundred at Headingley, against a good attack, without being able to bat.

A lot of it is emotional and mental, because you can have an indifferent technique, like Chris Rogers perhaps, or Simon Katich. I mean they're far better players than I'll ever be, but you wouldn't model your technique on them if you were doing your level four coaching badge. But [their success] is purely because they've got an exceptional mental game. Sure, there are always technical elements that can be tweaked, but at some point you've got to leave that behind, and just say "I've got to go out there and play with what I've got."

But the thick and fast nature of county cricket, and in 2012 Batesy playing every game, that does make life tough. There's nowhere to hide. You can't get away if you're going through a rough trot – and you will, whether you like it or not. You're going to have a period where you get a couple of good balls, you make a mistake. And there's no coincidence, when you see players coming back from little injury breaks, they come back and they have success. Being mentally fresh makes such a difference. But you don't get that in the county cricket season. County cricket almost becomes a war of mental toughness. Of course skill level is important – the more skilled you are, the more you may be able to ride a bit on that. But even the most skilled players get to that point in the season.

I think Batesy had a very good mental game. But when you're asking a 21/22-year-old to do that, that's really tough. It's no coincidence that players tend to improve with age, certainly they become more consistent through their late 20s, early 30s.

Looking back, it was only Neil McKenzie who I really talked to about my batting. I chatted to him a lot when he was at the club, but I don't think I really got what I needed. That wasn't his fault, and it wasn't through a lack of trying, but I just felt I hadn't really worked it out, in the nets, or in my mind.

When I was batting well in 2012 it was a bit of a surprise to me, to be honest. And I couldn't really articulate why I was playing so well. So when it did go wrong later that season, neither could I articulate what it was I needed to do to get back to my decent form. I didn't have a process to fall back on. I didn't have coaches saying, "You've stopped doing this", or "You've started doing that".

Also, I got into a vicious circle of negative thinking in the second half of that season. I was never dropped, basically because there was no one else who could come in. I knew I wasn't playing well with the bat, and I knew that, on my batting form alone, I should probably be dropped because I wasn't delivering. But I kept playing, I kept getting picked, and I knew that was because there was no one else and that compounded my negative mindset even more.

Unbeknown to me, it must have been around this time in the middle of that 2012 season that Hampshire first came across Wheater. Jimmy Adams told Tom the story of how they discovered the man who would become my successor at Hampshire in a game against his Essex side.

> Essex needed three or four to win and he holed out to long on, but Wheats had taken them to the verge of winning a game they should never had won. And that made us think, "Woah". At that time we knew he was a keeper, but we hadn't looked overly hard at his batting. Batesy had been going through a bit of a rough trot with the bat, and I know from my own experience of, if I'm batting poorly, then my slip fielding is usually less resilient. And maybe Batesy's keeping hadn't been at that level we'd maybe been used to.
>
> Then a few weeks later we were on the balcony at Bristol and I was speaking to Dimmer [Dimi Mascarenhas] and we'd had another top-order collapse, or maybe we'd had a start but the middle order hadn't really performed. And we were saying, "we want to play in Division One, what do we do?" It was something we mulled over a lot and Batesy's batting used to come up. We weren't able to give him a buffer really, he was batting at seven sometimes, maybe eight with no one below.
>
> I said, "Dim, where do we go with this?" And he felt strongly that we needed another all-rounder, shall we say. And all-rounders are hard to come by. We couldn't find a bowling all-rounder, and we felt that the all-rounder we could find was along the lines of a Wheater.

And so my future was being sealed, and I didn't even know it. On the field, my issues with the bat definitely affected my keeping. I'd have games where I'd say I kept pretty well, but there were games where it was all over the place, especially in the four-day games. In the one-day games I was still keeping pretty well.

The feeling of getting out for nothing, over and over again is so, so draining. When I look back now and people ask do you miss playing, I think back to those feelings and think, it was so tough mentally. Do I really miss that? I was massively up and down. The start of the 2012 season I hit the ground running, I was batting brilliantly, and then soon after I hit rock bottom. I was so wrapped up in my own world, stressing so much about my own game, that I didn't give much thought to what was coming up ahead from the team's perspective. We had some massive games on the horizon, and half the time I wasn't even thinking about them, or it would only be the day before when I started really considering them.

The worse things got, the bigger the bubble around me grew, and the more oblivious I was to everything and everyone else around me. The season is so hectic you don't have time to think about anything. You're jumping from one game to the next, and as soon as you lose a bit of control, it snowballs.

I'd gone from being understudy, playing plenty of cricket, to being the main man within a six-month period. It was bound to catch up with me. I was, after all, still just 21. That's where, had Nic Pothas been retained as my mentor, it could have worked quite nicely, because he could have supported me, both physically – giving me a breather from the first team when I needed it – and also mentally, teaching me how to cope with the demands of being the first-choice keeper and my first full season of county cricket.

What made it all the more frustrating, when Tom spoke to Nic, he told us he had the whole 2012 season planned out for me, had he been asked to stay:

> I would have seen my role at the time to mentor Batesy, to help him transition into the modern-day wicketkeeper... Because he certainly didn't need any help keeping. Where I could have helped, it would have been, right let's put a plan together. How does he manage his energy? He's kept wicket for 120 overs, OK he batted a little lower down so he would have had time to rest, but how does he rest in the changing room? – and I mean mentally, not physically. Have some time away so that when he batted, he's

got that energy. How does he manage his lifestyle?, how does he manage his training? You know wicketkeepers, we come into the ground first and leave last. It's not like a bowler who comes in and some days he bowls, some days he doesn't. For us it's a really hard workload.

Let's put a career plan together as such, rather than, you just go and hit a ball and catch a ball. That's not the way it works. Unless you've actually been there and done that, as a keeper on the county circuit, it's very hard for people to understand that it's not just about batting and keeping. It's about managing yourself, and your game, and knowing how to go about something when you're out of nick.

Batesy was never a primary batter, but he was put into a situation where he was just expected to score runs straight away. That was never gonna happen, with all due respect. There could've been a really good technique, but it was about how he went about using that technique and training in different ways in order to make him an effective batter, rather than a good-looking batter.

How do you manage a whole season? How do you put a batting average together? And that's where I helped Ben Brown at Sussex. What Ben Brown is doing now is very different to what he used to be doing. By out-batting the bowlers, he's improving his average by being not out at the end of an innings. Being not out, some people see that as selfish. People used to say to me "You get a lot of not outs." That's what I trained to do in the nets. I don't know any batter in the nets who trains to get out. Our role down the bottom is to play with the tail, which I know I was very successful at.

One thing Tom asked was whether Nic could have stayed on at Hampshire in a coaching capacity, to help me transition into the first team. Hampshire never asked him to do that – how did he feel about that?

I was upset. When you move a youngster up into the first team, he's got to have some sort of mentor, someone that he can go back to that's going to help him out. The technical stuff wouldn't have been an issue, as Batesy had Bobby Parks [Hampshire's wicketkeeping coach] there. It was how are you going to get your keeper, how are you going to get Michael Bates, to score runs?

> It was never provided as an option [from the club]. Even if it came down to a cut in salary, that was not an issue, because I would have 100% understood. I was transitioning out of my career, I'm playing a lot more second team cricket. There was going to be a transition so we could have just opened up a new conversation about what would that pay structure look like, but my primary role would have been to make sure Hampshire cricket had the best keeper in the country playing and scoring some runs. Instead the poor bugger's out of a job. And that just isn't right.

So Skeg also felt that him being my mentor for that 2012 season would have been a good option, both for him and me. Yet the club never spoke to him about it. In fact, having spoken to Jimmy about this since, I don't think they ever considered it as an option. "Actually, I hadn't thought about that," Jimmy revealed. "Both from a skill level, and a mental freshness level. Sometimes you forget that when they're young, bright eyed and bushy tailed, you [think they] can do everything. But you still find that come September, it's not that you're excited for it but you're quite looking forward to a break from it. But that could well have been an option, goddamnit!"

It's a shame all round. I would have benefited hugely from Skeg's experience. It would have helped Nic himself transition out of his playing career and been a first step on the rung of what is turning out to be a very successful coaching career for him (he's already coached Sri Lanka and the West Indies, so he must be doing something right). While for the club, there would have been continuity in the position, an experienced pair of hands they could call on if and when my form did dip, while also giving me the best chance possible to make a success of the position I was being put into.

What else would Nic have worked on with me from a batting perspective?

> Batting is a tough gig, you get one chance. If you were a young bowler, you would have had a far more extended run, because you may bowl 120 balls in a day. As a keeper, you did a very good job, but when you go out to bat you get one chance. And where you batted down the order, you probably faced that new ball quite a lot, and that makes it tough as well.
>
> Part of it is mental. Every time a straight ball comes down, in your body there's a tension and an anxiety so you're not going to

execute on that. So we've got to give you tools, and that's mental and physical tools to sort it out.

It was a view shared by Simon Katich, the great Aussie batsman and one of my team mates in that 2012 season. He told Tom:

> Nic was a fine player and competitor. Having had a number of chats with him over the years, we both felt he should have been allowed to play another year or two longer, to be around to mentor Michael and give him that little bit more time to develop in the shorter formats, while Nic played four-day cricket. I think that extra time would have allowed Michael's batting to develop at the lower level so that he wasn't judged as harshly as he was when he got his chance. As a result, I think things could have been so different than the way they panned out for him. It really disappoints me to see what happened to him at Hampshire.

Now, when I'm batting, I definitely try to be more relaxed. I listened to the great Kumar Sangakkara on TV not so long ago. He was talking about a conversation he'd had with Jason Roy in the summer of 2017. He said that from day to day, how you feel and how you move is going to be completely different. How ever you feel when everything clicks, chances are the next time you bat you'll feel completely different. So rather than getting frustrated that you can't replicate the form you had when you batted well, you have to somehow find a way to play the way you did when you felt good about it, even when you don't feel so good.

I completely got that, and I would totally have to develop that side of my mentality if I was going to have any chance of reclaiming the gloves from Adam Wheater in the 2013 season.

Chapter 10
Fighting for my career

Having received the Wheater bombshell from Chalks and co., I set about preparing for the 2013 season as best I could. I decided to stay in England for the winter. I didn't really fancy going down under again, plus I wanted to work on my batting with Tony, as we'd done some really good work together in the first half of the previous winter. We did more of the video analysis we'd done before, and worked on my backlift, aiming to get it higher before impact with the ball. It was nice being at home for the winter for a change, although the Wheater rumours were constantly doing the rounds at the Ageas Bowl, and in the local media, which was doing my head in. Obviously I knew the club were after him, but hearing everyone talking about it constantly, and reading more about it in the local paper, was really annoying.

In the end I had to wait pretty much the whole of pre-season before it was finally announced. Then, all of a sudden, there it was. On 1 March 2013 the club confirmed that they'd signed Adam Wheater from Essex. I knew it was coming, but still it was a massive blow. In my own, introverted way, I always hoped the deal would fall through; the contractual issues wouldn't be resolved, or perhaps Hampshire would have a change of heart. No such luck.

The timing of Wheater's arrival was such that I didn't actually meet him until we went on our traditional pre-season trip to Barbados, just days after he'd signed with the club. Meeting up at the airport was extremely awkward; we were civil and said hello to each other, but I didn't really engage in much conversation.

In fact, we didn't really have anything to do with each other on that trip. He didn't make an attempt to introduce himself. Obviously I knew who he was, but I certainly wasn't going to go out of my way to interact with him. We kept ourselves to ourselves. And when we got to Barbados we certainly didn't socialise, and we trained separately.

In fact the whole trip to Barbados was a nightmare for me that year. I was in such a low place, both in terms of Wheater's arrival, and also some girlfriend issues going on at the time. We were going through a rough patch when I'd left for the Caribbean, so I was generally pretty miserable. In addition, I wasn't doing all that well with the bat, despite all the work I'd done with Tony that winter. Whenever something would go wrong with my batting, I'd fly off the handle and get really stressed.

To his credit, Chalks did come and talk to me while we were out there. He wanted to check that everything was OK. He asked was it because Wheater was there? I mean, obviously that was a factor, but I was just generally pretty pissed. As usual I was introverted. I didn't give a lot away, and basically played the conversation away with a bit of a forward defensive. At least this time, I didn't get bowled...

Dale Benkenstein (Benks), our new first-team coach, had a chat with me too. Benks actually intimated that, had he been at the club the year before, Wheater possibly wouldn't have been brought in. "I've got to play with the cards I've been dealt," was the gist of what he said to me. I got the impression Benks was a little bit puzzled by the decision that had been taken to sign Wheats, and he wasn't alone in that view in the dressing room. In there were my mates, but a lot of them – especially the bowlers – were grateful for the work I'd been doing behind the stumps, and weren't overly happy about Wheater's arrival.

Hampshire bowler Chris Wood told Tom:

> Batesy was huge for my career. Other keepers wouldn't be able to keep up to my pace. I'd be half the bowler I am without having had him up to me. I knew that, if I did bowl one down the leg side, it's just going to be one rather than five. That's massive. If you have someone standing up behind the stumps that's not great, you're thinking "Shit, shit, shit". It effects a bowler's confidence massively.

Liam Dawson added:

> You knew that if you did get something wrong, he'd save you as a bowler. That gives you confidence. You know if you put it down the leg side, or you chuck it wide, you'd back him to tidy that up. And that's one of the best things you can have as a bowler. You have more room for error. If the batter runs down and you lose track of the ball a bit, you'd still back Batesy to stump him. As a bowler at the top of your mark – and as a team – we knew that.

Sadly for me it wasn't Daws or Woody picking the team. And when we returned from Barbados to the cold, damp, early spring days back home, I knew I was in for a long, hard season fighting to get back into the first team.

* * *

As expected, I started the season off in the twos. It was so demoralising dropping down to that level, especially after what I'd achieved the season before, but obviously I had no choice. All I could do was play well, and try to put pressure back onto Wheater, and give the coaches a decision to make.

Thankfully I started the season really well. I scored a lot of runs, averaging over 50 in the four-day format. Wheater on the other hand wasn't really performing in the first team, so I felt my chance may come sooner than expected.

But sadly it never materialised, no matter how well I did. I played the odd first-team game in place of Wheater when he was injured, but on the whole my performances in the twos seemed to be going unnoticed. It felt like the coaches were being quite stubborn in changing things. They obviously wanted their big signing to work out, and I totally got that. I didn't like the decision to bring Wheater in, who would in my position?, but I did understand that, after he joined, the coaches would want – and need – to give him every opportunity to succeed. By the same token, they'd told me they wanted me to compete for the gloves. So if I was performing and he wasn't, surely something would have to change? It was a really difficult situation for all of us in the end. I wasn't close to Wheater, but it can't have been easy for him, constantly being reminded of how good I was by fans, local media, pretty much everyone apart from the coaches picking our team. It can't have been easy for Jimmy either, captaining us both, knowing we both wanted to be playing every week. In fact Tom spoke to Jimmy about the situation as it unfolded that season:

> It was pretty clear there was going to be a battle on for the spot. It was very clear that Batesy was the better keeper. It was reasonably clear that Wheats was the better batter. And the frustrating thing was it was clear that with one player – Batesy – day in day out, you knew where they were at. Whereas Wheater, he was a bit more of a maverick. On his day he was unbelievable, but on the other days you weren't sure whether he was there. We went with the maverick in the hope that we could get a more consistent maverick, and we did actually at times – but saying "at times" probably says it all.

> Dale especially got frustrated with the keeping side [of Wheater]. Perhaps we'd been spoiled by having Batesy. He was an "Energizer Bunny", he'd tidy up everything that needed to be, he was great for the fielding unit.

There was a lot of negative noise around Wheater; the fans weren't happy and he wasn't performing, whereas I was scoring runs in the seconds. When I was playing, I was producing, and I felt that my form warranted a place in the first team.

Despite my own turmoil at the club that season, the rest of the lads were playing some good cricket in the white-ball competitions in particular, and we managed to progress to another T20 Finals Day. That one, held at Edgbaston, didn't quite go to plan – pretty much from the get-go.

We were playing in the second semi-final, so unlike the previous year when we'd stayed in Cardiff the night before, we decided to drive up on the morning of Finals Day itself. That morning, we packed our bags in the changing room at the Ageas Bowl, and wheeled them out to the coach. We chucked our bags into the hold, and then got on board ready for the off.

When we got to Edgbaston we all went to retrieve our bags. Everyone got theirs out, and soon the hatch was empty. Yet there was still one very sheepish-looking Michael Carberry standing, staring at the empty hatch with a bemused look on his face. Turned out Carbs' bag was still in Southampton. I think he'd thought that someone else was going to put his bag on the coach for him. But no one did. In the end, Terry, our kit man, had to pick Carbs' kit up from the Ageas Bowl, and drive it all the way to Edgbaston himself to drop it off.

When Terry got to Birmingham, Carbs realised he'd collected the wrong kit bag! So Carbs ended up having to borrow some kit, which, as you can imagine, he was none-too-impressed about. That's the thing about elite sport. For all the intensity, pressure and hard work, there are moments of complete farce – like any job – which make you laugh out loud and just totally lighten the mood.

Going to Finals Day was a weird experience for me that year. I knew I wasn't going to be playing, so I was a lot more relaxed, soaking up the atmosphere of the event, as opposed to mentally preparing for the game. While the guys were warming up for the semi-final, I came across Alec Stewart, who was there with his Surrey team, our opponents in that match.

I got chatting to Alec and he was kind enough to offer some words of encouragement, telling me to hang in there, and to keep going. It was fairly evident from the chat that he knew my game, was aware of my situation and, I felt, rated what I could bring to a team. I felt pretty boosted from our chat. He was my childhood hero, and it's always good to hear nice words of encouragement, especially given the season I'd had.

I ended up doing a bit of warm-up with Wheats before the game against Surrey. It was good to be involved, but it was almost from the other side of the fence, as a coach rather than a member of the playing staff. I wasn't going to be on the field helping the team. I was going to be cheering the lads on from the changing room.

It was a pretty average day for me, and so it turned out for the guys playing too. We scored 142-9 from our 20 overs, which always felt a bit under par. Then Surrey went out and reached that total pretty comfortably. Glenn Maxwell, our team mate the year before, scored 26 from 21 balls for Surrey and helped his new side to an easy win.

Wheats managed just two with the bat that day, which hardly backed up the coaches' decision to go for the keeper-batter instead of a specialist keeper like me, in the biggest game of our season. Batting aside, I knew I would've put more pressure onto their batters from behind the stumps, as I'd done the year before.

Was that the reason we lost that semi-final? Impossible to tell, due to the lack of data on wicketkeepers we've touched on earlier. But I felt I would've definitely added something to that game, no question. But as was becoming increasingly clear to me, that wasn't a view shared by my coaches.

* * *

My form on the pitch wasn't helped by events off it that season. Around that time, I finished with my girlfriend.

It was such a difficult time for me. I'd been with her for a few years, and it had developed into a serious relationship. I'm not sure if the situation at Hampshire put a strain on us, or me, or whether the relationship just ran its course. Either way it ended, and it was really hard to deal with. Especially while, at the same time, trying to stay focused on the cricket.

I mean, I knew this was such a huge moment for me in my career, and I had to be completely on it, to make sure I was delivering as best I could. But this was the first time something outside of the game had really distracted me like this, and it was definitely hard to stay focused.

Players are going to have relationships, that's obvious. And for the main part, they're encouraged in pro sport. England and Liverpool footballer Adam Lallana is a big cricket fan, and he used to come down to watch Hampshire a lot when he played for Southampton. He's a similar age to me, and he'd often tell me about how the football clubs he'd been at – including Southampton – had always encouraged the young players to settle down as early as possible. The idea being that if things are settled at home, you could concentrate more on the pitch.

I'm not sure if a more settled home life away from the cricket would have really helped me at that point. Obviously having a support network is incredibly important to people in pro sport, and in my case I'd lost that somewhat with the breakdown of my relationship. But I still had my parents, my sister and my wider family. And in any case, I wasn't one to really take my stresses from work home anyway. Maybe I should have, and I think me letting out more during that period would definitely have helped me. But I didn't do that, so from that point of view, our relationship ending didn't change things.

Perhaps surprisingly, given everything that was going on, I'd continued to bat well for the twos all through the season. I hit 180 or so against Northants on the Nursery Ground at the Ageas Bowl, and 140 against Surrey at Wimbledon. Maybe that prompted the coaches into a change of heart, I don't know. But eventually I did get a bit of a run in the first team, with the coaches deciding to play both Wheater and myself. I was given the gloves, obviously, which must have gone down like a lead balloon with Wheats, while Wheats himself played a specialist batsman.

In reality, the season was over for us. Finals Day had been and gone, and all we had left was a handful of Championship games at the back end of the season, with promotion already out of the equation. So I was probably picked as a way of keeping me happy, while having both of us in the team meant we could have a bit of a playoff against each other, in the final few games of the season.

Even though Wheater was playing, in my mind I was trying not to turn it into a straight shoot-out between us. It was pretty obvious what the hierarchy was doing, but I tried not to succumb to the pressure. The more pressure I put on myself, the worse I played, so I tried to put the duel – if you want to call it that – to one side.

And in one of those end-of-season games, against Northants, it worked a treat. I scored 71 while Wheater, who batted before me, was out for 19. I was batting with our skipper Jimmy Adams, who was on his way to a big double-hundred. I batted nicely, passed Wheater's score and was going along well. Jimmy was telling me to keep focused, and go onto three figures. "Don't throw it away," he was saying. I felt pretty relaxed throughout really, and it was great having Jimmy's support up the other end. It must have been tough for him that season too, having to manage both Wheats and I. But here he was cheering me on, hoping I'd do well. He was such a legend, was Jimmy.

Sadly I did throw that one away in the end. It was a poor bit of cricket all-round; Azharullah bowled a slower ball that got stuck in the wicket, and I came down the pitch and just lobbed it up to cover. It was disappointing not to capitalise with a big score, especially after Wheater had failed.

Neil McKenzie was playing in that game, and after I batted he told me he felt I'd improved a lot since he'd last seen me bat the year before, which was nice to hear. I also remember him telling me about batting against spin, saying to bat on off stump, and to go towards the ball. It was great having Macca there, backing me and believing in me, and giving me advice on how to improve.

A week later I scored 41 at Worcestershire. Again Wheater had failed, but equally I couldn't quite convert it into a big score. I think, in hindsight, I should have been more ruthless to convert both those scores. But back then, I was just relieved to get to 40, 50 or 60 in the first team, rather than pushing myself on to reach three figures and really boost my batting average.

Coaches tell you about getting a start, and in both those games I'd done that. But I needed that ruthless streak to get myself to three figures. It's about being able to pace the innings, to be resilient at the crease and to not be content with a start.

It'd been nice to play a few games, but before I knew it, the season was over. I'd done OK at the back end of the campaign, but it was pretty clear I wasn't going to get as many opportunities as I was hoping for in the following season.

That 2013 season was an act of defiance. I wanted to show the coaches what I could still do, and take the fight to Wheater. I was determined to stay positive, to try not to sulk or moan about the decision. I wanted to work hard and show everyone that I was good enough for the first team. I'm still not sure whether that was the right approach to take or not. Maybe if I'd have kicked off at the decision more, I might have alerted the coaches quicker to my frustration, and maybe that would have put more pressure on them to play me more. Who knows? When Tom spoke to Daws for this book, he had an interesting take on that particular personality trait of mine.

Batesy was always positive. He probably was down inside at times, because everyone does naturally do that and people show it in different ways. But Batesy would never take his batting into his keeping. If he didn't bat well, he wouldn't take that into his keeping. If I'm batting shit I'll bowl shit. But Batesy wasn't like that, and that's a great trait to have.

Or is it? Because maybe by being like that, the coaches think there's nothing wrong and so didn't say anything. Maybe he should've been more miserable like me!

* * *

Looking ahead to 2014, I knew it was going to be a huge season for me personally. Not only was it the second year with Wheater around, it was also the second – and final – year of my contract. The contract I'd agreed with the club at the end of 2012. Wow, how times had changed, and in such a short space of time. I knew I needed to impress if my stay at the Ageas Bowl was going to be extended.

For pre-season, Hampshire were encouraging me to go back to Perth, this time to work with a batting coach named Noddy Holder – no, not the Slade singer. A few of the Hampshire boys like Michael Carberry and Jimmy Adams had worked with him in the past. They'd got on well with him and their batting had developed, so it was a good option for me. To be honest it was nice to get away from Southampton.

I headed to Perth just after Christmas, and spent all of January and February 2014 out there. I got on really well with Noddy; we worked on lots of aspects of my batting. And by the end of the trip my batting was getting back to the level it had been at before the 2012 season, when I was absolutely smoking it.

Noddy was a big fan of a high backlift, as he felt that would help you generate more power into your shot. If you look at Carbs' or Jimmy's technique, they both play with a high backlift still now. Jonny Bairstow is another, although I'm not sure if Jonny ever worked with Noddy specifically. We did a lot of bowling machine work, Noddy getting me to hold the bat almost like a baseball bat, to try to generate more power through my shots.

Noddy and I spent a lot of time with each other that winter, and we became really close. I told him about the Wheater situation back home, and he was great at offering me some advice. He was really complimentary about my ability, and was also good at motivating me. He'd talk about when I got back to Hampshire, I'd really need to nail it, and take the fight to Wheater from the off. We'd talk a lot about having a positive mentality when I went back, about believing that I could achieve it.

It was good advice, but I felt I'd done that the season before, and that hadn't exactly won the coaches' hearts and minds over. It was tough. I'd been trying to stay positive for the last 12 months and, to be honest, by then I was starting to get fed up with it all.

I didn't really feel like Chalks had done much to help me address my batting issues himself at Hampshire, and had instead given up on me a bit. Sending me to Perth felt like a bit of a cop-out to me. I wanted to stay at Hampshire that winter to work through the issues with my batting, with the coaches who knew my game best. Noddy had a great reputation, but he wasn't necessarily renowned for fixing issues like the ones I had.

I tried consoling myself with the fact that at least the club were still investing in my development, by sending me out to Perth. But at the same time it felt like I was being palmed off a bit. Ushered out of the way, almost. I was trying to tell myself that going to Perth was the right thing to do. But I made a lot of decisions around that time that, when I look back now, I feel like I took just because I thought that was the right thing to do, rather than because I actually wanted to do them. Perth was one of those. So while I enjoyed the experience, deep down I had some cynicism towards the trip.

Perhaps staying at Hampshire would have been worse though, as it would have meant having to spend more time with Wheater, and that would have just wound me up further. So there was no real best-case scenario for pre-season that year, and I think working with Noddy was, on balance, the best of a bad bunch of options.

When I went back to Hampshire at the start of March 2014, I felt like my batting had improved. I was hitting the ball harder and scoring a bit quicker, but my weakness to the straight ball and my propensity for getting bowled was still very much within my game. I still felt like I didn't really have a go-to method that I could rely on when batting, so all those doubts were nagging at me when I was batting, right from the start of the season when I wanted to feel at my best.

And that really showed as the season unfolded. I felt OK, like I wanted to turn over a new leaf, but it was a bit of a false dawn. I stumbled and struggled my way through games, particularly with the bat. There were times when I played well and scored some runs, but I was really inconsistent. It frustrated me, never mind anyone else.

One day I'd be on fire. Like when we played Surrey in a seconds match at Guildford. I scored probably the best 40 of my life that day. I was absolutely smoking it, and there were some glimpses of what I always knew I could do. Craig White, the twos coach, was really impressed, as was Alec Stewart, who was there watching some of the Surrey lads. Alec came over to me for a chat during that game, and had a similar message for me as the one he'd had at Finals Day the year before; to keep going and stay positive.

Whether word of that knock got back to the first-team coaches, Chalks and Benks, I don't know. But soon after that there was a spell when I was playing alongside Wheater – me with the gloves and Wheats as a specialist batsman.

We played at home to Worcestershire in May 2014, when the weather was generally dull and chilly throughout the four days. I did really well, taking four catches on a day when the ball was nipping about a fair bit. *ESPNCricinfo* reporter Alex Winter wrote a nice piece on me, entitled "Bates gives keeping masterclass", saying, "He reminded Hampshire that they possess a very special talent who is surely too valuable not to be selected on a regular basis."

Reading articles like that was nice, of course it was. But without wishing to sound big-headed, I was hearing that a lot. I knew I had the backing of a fair percentage of the fanbase, a lot of the squad and plenty of the media. But ultimately I knew why I was out of the team; my batting wasn't rated by my coaches. And coming in and out of the team definitely dented my confidence with the bat. It was hard, impossible even, to leave those worries, those doubts, at the boundary rope and go out and bat with a clear head. I'd get starts, but I wouldn't capitalise.

It was nice to be given the game time, but I wasn't sure how long it would last. Ultimately, Wheater and I were both wicketkeepers, and while I may have been perceived as a stronger keeper, ultimately Chalks and Benks had a decision to make – pick their man, and stick with it.

As the season progressed, I was acutely aware that my contract was running down, and there had been no conversations with Chalks about a new one being offered. In that scenario, where you're in the last year of your contract and an extension has yet to be offered, you begin this appraisal process. It's a player's right, in that situation, to have an open dialogue with the head coach of director of cricket, in order to get a better understanding in terms of the club's position on the player's future. Each player has three appraisal meetings throughout that final season, which in my case would be with Giles White – Chalks.

I had my first meeting in mid-season, around the time I was getting game time. It was a pretty cordial conversation. Chalks said I'd be given opportunities and it would be up to me to impress in those matches. Clearly that's why I was being played alongside Wheater around that time.

It wasn't a massively inspiring meeting, but it set out the process, that there would be two further meetings later on in the season, and my future would become clearer as those meetings came along. I felt I was getting a pretty clear picture already, to be honest.

My second meeting was scheduled for August. Along I went to Rod's office, the same place I'd had all of my end-of-year reviews in the past. The place where I'd been told I was being given my first ever pro contract years earlier. The place where I was told I was getting that contract extension in 2012. This, though, was a very different meeting. One I never thought I'd be having. Not yet anyway.

Walking into that meeting, I knew what was coming. In my heart of hearts, I just knew. I opened the door, and Chalks stood to greet me. We sat down. He looked nervous. I knew what was coming, and pretty quickly, there it was. Hampshire had a new direction they wished to take in the wicketkeeping department going forwards, and I wasn't going to be a part of that journey.

The meeting itself was very brief, and very brutal. I had been released, and there was nothing I could do about it.

I could tell it wasn't what Chalks wanted to tell me. Ultimately he was the main man, and it was his job to make those calls. He'd obviously been part of the Wheater signing, and while perhaps ours hadn't been the closest of relationships over the years, there was a mutual respect between us and I knew, deep down, that this would have been a tough message for him to deliver.

But that didn't stop me feeling utterly hideous as a result of what he said. I was livid, gutted, upset, furious, broken. I didn't really say anything back, just grimaced, shook my head, bowed it slightly, and closed my eyes for a second.

"I'm sorry, but we're not in a position to extend your contract," is what Chalks said, I think. But it was a blur by then. As soon as I heard about the change in direction, I'd hung a left out of that conversation. I was gone.

Of that decision to release me, Jimmy told Tom:

> In terms of his career path, we felt he needed to play. He's that kind of guy, and given hindsight where he's at, I don't see Batesy

as one to look too far in the past and dwell on it. If we'd have had the luxury to do it, you'd almost keep him as part of a 24-man squad and have him when you need him. But that would almost be doing a disservice to the keeping side of his ability.

There was a sense of inevitability with the decision Hampshire took, particularly when you look at the way the previous two seasons had unfolded. But that didn't make that moment any easier to deal with. Neither did I feel it was the right decision, a view shared by my predecessor at Hampshire, Nic Pothas:

> I think you've always got a responsibility to your local talent which is, in my opinion, local talent should get a longer gig. I know people want results, and I totally understand that. You've got to have a variety of characters sitting around the table, people that have the ability to think outside of the box and challenge conventional thinking. Saying "we don't have runs with this bloke, we better go and sign someone else" is just too easy. That should be a plan C.
>
> It is unfortunate, but it's also life – it's professional sport, and it's pretty tough. You learn lessons, and even as an outsider I learned a lesson. I would have done it differently, of course I would have. But when I look at that situation I think, "What would I have done differently?", and if something similar happens in my career, hopefully I can handle it differently.
>
> The other thing that has to go on record is that I wasn't in that room. I can quite easily talk from the outside and say I would have done it this way, but I wasn't privy to every bit of detail in the club, the finances at the time, the ethos at the time, the culture at the time. There are so many things that go into making a decision, but one thing I am 100% certain of, and I would have thought the club would admit, was that they didn't handle it in the best possible way they could have.

After that hammer-blow, I finished the season off in the seconds. Chalks allowed me to start contacting other counties, to try to line something up for the following season, so I immediately got to work with that. I spoke to lots of counties, and a lot of the coaches I spoke to wanted to help me, saying they'd love to be able to give me an opportunity, but there was nothing they could do at the time.

The end of the season – my final season, with the club I'd represented since I was a boy – was fast approaching. In Hampshire's last Championship game of the season, they secured promotion to Division One with a tense final day victory at Glamorgan. I was invited up to Cardiff to celebrate, along with David Balcombe, who was also leaving the club – although in Balcs' case his story was happier in that he was signing for Surrey.

We were expecting a Hampshire victory on that final day, but as we travelled up to South Wales, we saw on social media that the win was a bit more imminent than expected. James Tomlinson had ripped through Glamorgan on that final day, taking 6-48.

By the time we got to the ground it was all over – Hampshire had won and were promoted. It was a weird feeling. Obviously we were both leaving, but we'd been with the guys all summer, and in my case especially, for years before. Knowing how we'd struggled in red-ball cricket over the years, I was delighted for my mates at the club to have finally secured promotion. But also knowing that I wasn't going to be a part of that journey the next season was really disappointing.

Balcs and I got off the train in Cardiff and got a cab to the SWALEC – the scene of that great T20 Finals Day victory two years earlier. As we approached the away dressing room, Balcs and I chatted and joked, excitedly predicting the mother of all parties going off behind the door we were about to open. But instead when we walked in, we were greeted by a scene of silence. Blokes slumped over chairs, heads in hands, or leant back on the wall of their changing areas: they were all absolutely knackered.

Eventually the party got going. Balcs and I joined in, got a couple of beers down us and caught up on the game. After a while, Balcs and I were each presented with a commemorative frame with a few pictures of us playing, which the boys had all signed. There were some really nice messages written, and I won't lie, I broke down. In fact, I was absolutely bawling my eyes out.

Sitting in the changing room with the lads that night, it felt quite poignant. We'd been here two years earlier winning the T20 trophy, that golden year for us, and probably still to this day one of the most successful seasons in the club's history. I couldn't believe what had happened to my career since then. Couldn't believe it.

After beers at the ground we went out into Cardiff. It was a proper night out, I can tell you. We all went out in our whites, so I had to do a John Terry and put my whites on for the celebration. I went into town with a sleeveless jumper and whites – I must have looked ridiculous.

A night out is a night out; they're great while they last, but eventually the laughter stops, the music ends, and it's time to go home. And then, just like that, my Hampshire career was over.

Dimi recalled, with the benefit of wistful hindsight:

> You never know what could've happened if you'd played for the next two years that we signed Wheater. You could have found your way with the bat, rather than just trying to get forward and defend. You could still be playing now. You were phenomenal behind the stumps.
>
> Hampshire's style in one-dayers now it doesn't look far off what it was back then, so you could still be an integral part of that team. It was a shame to lose you behind the stumps. You're right up there with Foster, and there's not many who get close to you. You just hadn't worked out a fall-back option with the bat. I didn't work that out for years – it takes time. I was lucky that my bowling kept me going, because I had my best season with the bat the first year I ever played, then I didn't get that many runs ever again. It's hard work, it takes time to find stuff out about yourself.

I certainly found out a lot about myself in those two years, while trying to save my career at Hampshire. Leaving was the most painful thing I'd ever been through at the time, and while I had spoken to other counties, I had nothing lined up for the 2015 season.

I was facing a winter of uncertainty. For the first time since I was 14, I was no longer a Hampshire player, and therefore no longer had an end-of-season review. No longer had pre-season regime to undertake. No longer had hopes and dreams for the following season.

Instead I had a winter of isolation, loneliness and misery to look forward to. What on earth would I do next? How would I get my career back on track?

Chapter 11
Finding another county

As my hangover faded post-Cardiff, thoughts moved onto my next task – moving out of my flat in Southampton. That was such a low point. I'd bought that flat with my win bonuses from our CB40 and FLT20 successes in 2012. Given that I was now unemployed, however, I took the really difficult decision to rent it out to make some money, rather than having to sell it altogether. So off I went back to Mum and Dad's in Yateley, with my tail – and my bat – between my legs.

What a fall from grace this was. I'd been a pro cricketer at Hampshire. I thought I'd made it. A couple of years earlier I'd been playing cup finals at Lord's, winning trophies, attending the BBC Sports Personality of the Year ceremony alongside David Beckham and Mo Farah.

Now I'd left the club I'd represented since the age of 14. The dream was over. The bubble burst. It was shattering – easily the hardest, most upsetting thing that's ever happened to me in my career. And the worst bit was, I still couldn't believe it. I still didn't feel like I'd been given a fair crack of the whip. One season in the first team, that's all I'd been given. Then discarded like a used tissue – it just seemed so harsh.

My parents were amazing back then. They were more than happy to have me living with them in Yateley, while providing much-needed shoulders to cry on, whenever I felt the need to open up. Which, now I was out of the cricket bubble, was happening more and more.

When I saw people I hadn't seen for a while, they'd ask, "How's the cricket?" I'd then have to explain to them that the dream job I'd had, the one I'd been working towards since I was a kid, was now over. Meanwhile when I saw my uncle, he'd keep saying, "How can someone as good as you be out of the game?" To this day it still annoys him that I'm not still playing. I loved the sentiment, but conversations like that only made it harder for me to move on.

Of course you expect your family to support you, to back you up when you're at your lowest. When we started interviewing people for this book, what really struck me was how so many of my ex-colleagues, team mates and peers were totally with me on this one too:

"Why not keep both of them?" Liam Dawson asked Tom, at a round-the-table-chat which included Woody and myself, in the Ageas Bowl Atrium in 2017. "Especially as Wheats was scoring so many runs. He could easily have played as a batter. Financially you should be able to keep two wicketkeepers on your books."

"I was really disappointed with how they dealt with Batesy's batting," David Balcombe told Tom. Balcs continued:

> I have no doubt he should still be playing now. His keeping was the best out there, and his batting was improving. How was he going to improve if he wasn't given the chance to bat – particularly in the one-day stuff? Skeg had done wonderful things but they [Hampshire] obviously wanted to change direction. They could have transitioned Skeg into a player coach, which when you look at where his career has gone since, is what he wanted to do anyway.
>
> Batesy has lost a part of his career which he'll never get back. He never got to make that decision to transition out of the game – it was something he was forced to do.

Some were angry with the club itself. Dimi Mascarenhas, our T20 skipper during my time at the club, was pretty miffed at my departure, but also at the way Hampshire as a club had treated all three keepers at that time – Pothas, Wheater and myself. "They hurt a lot of people," Dimi said. "All three keepers; Skeg, Bates and Wheater, they fucked them all up, which was the disappointing thing for me."

Speaking of Skeg, he wasn't impressed either. "Batesy was a phenomenal wicketkeeper," Nic said. "And that's where the sadness of the situation comes from, because for a guy of his skill and ability not to be playing professional cricket now is a very, very sad situation."

Dimi and Skeg weren't the only ones to question Hampshire's actions around that time. Simon Katich told Tom:

> I was disappointed to see what happened to Michael after the 2012 season. Although given something similar happened to me, it didn't come as a surprise. The reason I say that is because I don't think the judgements that were being made on players after what was a very successful season [in 2012], were correct. As a result I ended up at Lancashire the next season so that I could play all three formats, even though I loved playing at Hampshire in what was a fantastic 2012 season, winning two trophies.

> To have seen so much junior Hampshire talent end up elsewhere now after that season is a reflection on the direction of the club and what it stands for. Winning teams need to be developed rather than bought, and that is what it has looked like from afar. The camaraderie between the playing group in 2012 was as good as I've experienced in my professional career and as a result it was a true team that played for each other and enjoyed each other's success.

I agreed with what Kat said to a point. But as one of those lads to come through Hampshire's academy at that time, I will always be loyal to the club and grateful for the chances they gave me, despite what happened. But that was the view of someone within my changing room, so it's only fair to reference it.

My issue was that I was still so young for the club to make a decision on whether my batting would ever be good enough for county cricket. I was only 24 when I was released, 22 when I was replaced by Wheater. I was still nowhere near my peak, something Dawson was quick to highlight when we chatted.

> When do you know your game? You don't know your game until you're, like, 28. That's when you start potentially dominating, and you can do that for like six years. There's only a select few that can do it from a young age. You think Joe Root, but he's a freak. He's dominated from the age of 22. There's not many people who can do that. The normal people, in any sport, you don't know your game until mid-20s at least, maybe even 30. And that's the tough thing in Batesy's case. Frustrating even. But you also have to have a bit of luck. You need a lot of luck, you need to be stuck with [by your coaches] even when you're not doing very well, and sadly that's part of it.

But perhaps the biggest surprise of all those conversations came when Tom spoke to Jimmy Adams, Hampshire's club captain at the time I was released. Not because I didn't expect him to be gutted for me – not that I was looking for sympathy in any case. What struck me was the effusive nature of what Jimmy said, the sincerity with which he spoke. That's what really got me.

> His skill was exceptional, but the person was exceptional too. There are people that glue a changing room together, and he was

one of them. And that was one of the hardest parts there, because we lost a strong bit of glue when he left. You talk about the keeping and the batting, but you realised pretty quickly when he wasn't there that there was a bit of a hole. And that's one of the bits I'd like to change, if I could.

It was a horrible decision to make [letting Bates go]. Not that I was making decisions directly on Batesy's career, but I'm well aware that the decision I was involved in, to bring in Wheats, indirectly – but as close to directly as indirectly can be – had quite a clear correlation to where Batesy ended up. And that will always be a bit of a sticking point for me.

Maybe that marvellous crop of players that came through together were victims of their own success. They'd come in and been so brilliant that people's expectations of them grew. And to maintain that, that's really hard to do.

The shame of it wasn't that Batesy's batting was poor; he had a first-class hundred and he'd scored runs at crucial times – you knew he was going to fight for you. But maybe the make-up of the team, maybe if we'd had a genuine all-rounder, things would've been fine. In the team we've got now, perhaps you could have him in there batting nicely at eight, and everything would be fine.

Once we signed Wheater, it got to the situation where it wasn't fair for Batesy. We felt he should be playing, and it was a luxury to have both. Sitting here now you think, "Wow, maybe that's one we got wrong?", but you can't change it, unfortunately.

I've been asked at after-dinner speeches, what was the hardest decision I was involved with at Hampshire. There were two; one was Tommo [James Tomlinson] not playing at Lord's, and the other was Batesy, and how that panned out. Because you wanted him to play. But then you wanted to find a balance in the team that you felt could perform, and that involved having a keeper that batted six or seven. To speak about it is brutal, but that's sport. Never have any of us wanted someone to come back and haunt us [more than Batesy], but it just hasn't quite happened. I thought something would be there for him, but it just hasn't quite worked out. It's a very strange one. If someone had asked me, "Who was the best keeper you played with?" I'd say Michael Bates. But he's not playing anymore, and that's a very strange thing.

Even though I was gutted by what had happened, I was convinced I was going to get another county. I was desperate to. Cricket had been my whole life for as long as I could remember, and I hadn't finished with it yet. I had so much more to give. If I didn't get a county straight away, I was prepared to play for a minor county instead, and play club cricket at the weekend while I carried on looking. I was willing to do whatever it took to prolong my professional career.

In the weeks and months after I left Hampshire I was calling around the counties myself, speaking to as many directors of cricket as I could. I spoke to Dougie Brown at Warwickshire quite a lot, and a few others, and the gist of what I was being told was that people would like to help, but they didn't really know what was happening with budgets for the following year. Or "So-and-so is still our number one choice, but once he retires – or if he leaves – then you never know...".

It was frustrating, but understandable. Counties were being loyal to their keepers, and I didn't blame them for that. From my perspective however, I needed to look out for myself. So I decided to get in touch with an agent who was recommended to me by Dale Benkenstein, Hampshire's first team coach.

Phil Weston worked for a worldwide sports agency called Elite Sports Properties (ESP). It would be down to Phil to take those conversations I'd started with counties forward, hopefully on to the next stage. He was very experienced in what he did, and would be able to have more targeted conversations with counties than I ever could. Like in football, the way a cricket agent gets paid, is if the cricketer he represents gets paid. That's to say, if he managed to get me a contract with a county, Phil would then take a cut of my monthly wage for his efforts. If there were sponsorship deals, the same would apply.

After a couple of months of having conversations with various clubs, Phil called me at the start of 2015 to say he'd managed to sort something out at Essex for me. I guess you could call it an informal trial, whereby I'd train with Essex over the winter months, on an ad hoc basis. There were no guarantees, but obviously if Essex coach Paul Grayson saw something in me he liked, he could make it a more formal arrangement.

It felt like a foot in the door, but to be completely honest I just never really felt right at Essex. I flitted in and out of their off-season programme; I'd be asked along one week, then not the next. When I was involved I'd have to kip on a mate's sofa, who lived near the ground in Chelmsford – hardly an environment conducive to me playing my best cricket.

The group was constantly chopping and changing. Players were abroad at different training camps, or away with their national teams on tour – the usual stuff I'd encountered at Hampshire. Only I didn't have a pre-season programme or agenda now, I was unattached, unfamiliar, unknown, all the while trying desperately to fit in.

And that was difficult. When I was at Hampshire, I was a well-known member of the squad. I don't mean I was famous, but I'd walk around the ground and everyone would know me, and I'd know everyone. I'd have chats with people, the receptionists in the atrium, the guys in the ticket office, the stewards: "How's it going?", they'd ask. "How's the family?" I was part of the furniture there, and had been since I was a kid. This was a totally new environment, and it was hard to fit in, no question.

Also within the changing room, I felt a bit like I was on the outside looking in. The Essex boys were all top lads, and I knew a few of them from playing on the circuit in previous years, as well as going on training camps abroad together, as in the case of Jamie Porter. But still, I was an outsider, trying to work my way into an established group. A lot of the chat went over my head, I didn't know the gags, wasn't part of the banter. I guess it's like that going to any new club, but as a trialist, not knowing whether I was staying for the season or not, it was definitely harder.

In March, as always, the group started coming back together. The likes of Alastair Cook were coming back from international duty with England. The weather was improving, so we could start doing some work outside at last.

One day, the bowlers were having a bowl in the nets outside. It was one of those early spring mornings when the sky was blue, the sun was shining, but it was bitterly cold and there were plenty of layers being put on by us all. Despite the cold I was really looking forward to getting outside and having a bat. As we walked out, Paul told me and a couple of the other trialists to "just chip in where you can". What that meant, I don't really know. But what happened was, we weren't really involved in anything.

Then a bit later, seeing we weren't really doing much, Paul came back over and told us to head to the indoor centre and use the bowling machine. I felt like I was a spare part. Paul didn't know what to do with me, and I wasn't getting anything out of the experience.

"Fuck this", I thought. No disrespect to Paul, but "this", whatever it was, just wasn't working out, for either party. Clearly Paul didn't see me as a feasible option for his squad, otherwise he'd have asked me to have a bat to the bowlers outside. I was fed up and pissed off. So I headed to my car, put my stuff in the boot and without fanfare, I drove out of the ground.

I literally left, without even telling Paul I was going.

Almost immediately I felt terrible about my behaviour. I hadn't even told Paul I was leaving. So later that day I called him up and said sorry for walking out. He was really understanding. I think he realised where I was coming from and empathised with my situation. It wasn't easy, having to try to earn the right to be signed by another county, having been at another one for so long. And to his great credit, Paul gave me a second chance, asking me back to play some games for the twos. Maybe my theory about kicking off at the coaches was one I should persevere with after all ... or maybe not.

Sadly it was a false dawn. My performances in the twos weren't really up to the standard Paul was looking for, and he advised me a permanent deal wasn't going to happen. I didn't blame him. I knew I hadn't quite been at the races, and, by then, I was just happy he'd given me a go.

My winter preparations had been lousy. In previous years I'd been away to Australia for two months or more, worked incessantly on my batting, played domestic cricket out there, and got myself razor sharp for the upcoming season.

In 2015 I was kipping on a mate's sofa like a dosser, going in for training with a bunch of lads I barely knew, as a trialist – it was just awful. Nothing against the Essex lads, who were a great bunch, but I was just nowhere near good enough, mentally or physically, and it felt like the Essex experiment was always doomed to fail. It just came too soon after Hampshire. Getting released was still so fresh, so raw, I just wasn't ready for it. But I needed to sharpen up, because with just a few weeks to go until the 2015 season, I had no county sorted, and time was quickly running out.

And while I was still confident – well, hopeful – that another county would come calling, I was also aware that I needed to start making ends meet. I'd been living off the rent from my flat in Southampton, while also dipping into my savings, and that couldn't go on for much longer.

So instead of heading to Barbados on a pre-season jolly, I was lugging bricks around my uncle's building site for a few extra quid. Next I tried my hand to a bit of marketing, working for my mate's firm. And finally I followed in my Mum's footsteps, pulling pints in a pub in Yateley.

Working behind the bar wasn't great. Nothing against the guys I was working with, who were predominantly students just looking to earn a bit of extra cash to support their studies. I'd spent years training those hands for professional sport, now they were pulling pints and picking up glasses in a local boozer. What a waste.

It was a tedious job. I'd stare at the clock on the wall, counting down the minutes until my shift was over. I'd chat to my colleagues, as you do on those slow midweek afternoons when there's three men and a dog in the pub, sipping their pints of Best like they've got to make them last 'til closing time.

"What's your story then, Michael?", my new colleagues would ask me. This wasn't the banter of the dressing room I'd been used to for years, but it would have to do. I'd begin by explaining that I used to play professional cricket for Hampshire and England under-19s, and their jaws would practically hit the beer pumps. Their faces would be a picture, a combination of shock and bewilderment. "Well what are you doing here then?", they'd ask. It was a good and fair question.

They were good people. And when I told them about what'd happened, they were all genuinely sympathetic. They'd say how sorry they were to hear it, and how they hoped it would work out ok for me. "I'm sure it will", they'd say, in that blindly optimistic way in which people offer reassurances, even when they haven't got the foggiest idea what you're talking about!

I know people have much worse things to worry about in life than whether their career as a professional sportsperson is going to continue, or not. I heard plenty of stories working in that pub that really put things into perspective. But by the same token, cricket was all I'd ever known. It was me, and without it, I wasn't me.

Every time I started to talk about cricket, about my story, my failure, it took a little bit more of me away. The pain, the disappointment, the embarrassment. And what do you say back to someone who says, "I'm really sorry to hear that?"

"Err, thanks?!"

My social awkwardness aside, I was at least earning some money now. And as the cricket season started, more good news was to arrive as I was named as one of the pros at minor county Wiltshire County Cricket Club. Wiltshire CCC manager Neil Shardlow told the *Daily Echo* at the time.

> We've signed Michael for the season. But he still wants to play cricket at first-class level and we'll obviously support him in that

should the opportunity arise, which I'm sure it will. It's a shame no first-class county has taken him on so far, but it's worked out well for us, we're thrilled to have him. He's a brilliant keeper.

Having played at the highest level all my career, it was really hard to adjust to life at Wiltshire. It was minor counties cricket, so a decent standard still, but it wasn't up there with county cricket. I was playing for Wiltshire Sundays to Tuesdays, while also playing for club side Oxford on a Saturday. So I was playing plenty of cricket, but definitely not at the standard I wanted to be.

I was still in a bad place mentally following my departure from Hampshire, and my winter preparation had been awful, so I just wasn't feeling my cricket at all at that stage. And as a result, I pretty much hated both experiences. Both changing rooms were full of good lads, but as had been the case at Essex, I just wasn't in the right frame of mind to play my best cricket.

Things were looking bleak. Essex had been a nightmare, and now this. It was going from bad to worse. I'd prepared terribly for the season, and as I wasn't getting any county cricket in, my performance levels were dropping off by the week. So if I did get a chance to play first-class cricket, I'd be further and further away from where I needed to be, the longer the season went on. There was no phone call from Phil to say, "Batesy I've got the perfect thing for you." No opportunity to just walk into a county and start playing pro cricket again. And it seemed like there never would be.

Then, in early April, out of nowhere, Phil did get in touch to say he'd managed to get me a trial with Somerset. What a relief. It was a six-week deal to play in their seconds to see what I could do and then, well, who knows.

This was the opportunity I'd been waiting for. A chance to get some decent game time in, and really try to impress the coaches at a county. Suddenly, and finally, my mood was on the up. For the first time since Hampshire, I was happy again.

My first day at Somerset was great. Being in and around a group of lads again was brilliant. They were a great bunch, and really made me feel welcome. And that buzz, that energy from the group, the banter in the dressing room, training together in the gym, working on our cricket all the time – it was like oxygen to me. I could breathe again.

OK, so I was on trial again like I had been at Essex, but this time felt different. I had a six-week contract, and that gave me a little bit more security than I'd had at Chelmsford. All the people working at the

County Ground were lovely too. The office workers, the media people, the ground staff, they were all great. And everyone outside the club just loved their cricket, so it was a really positive environment in which to play.

The County Ground at Taunton is a beautiful old ground dating back to the 1880s, with a lovely pavilion at one end, overlooked by the Church of St James to the side. It's picture perfect; a great deal smaller than the Ageas Bowl, which was a big, modern, purpose-built international cricket ground. Instead, the County Ground was small, pretty and quaint. Instantly I felt at home. I was training hard, playing matches for the twos, and I just felt like I was back where I belonged.

But then in late May, as quickly as it had started, it was all over again.

I don't know what happened, but it all went very wrong, very quickly. All of a sudden I was told they didn't want me anymore, no more games for the seconds, no contract extension, nothing. I was out. No reason, just "We don't need you anymore".

It was brutal. A third knock-back in less than a year, and in some respects this one hurt the most. I was an emotional wreck, utterly fed up with it all. So I gave Matt Maynard, Somerset's head coach, a call to find out what was going on. I had nothing to lose, so I just went for it and told him how I felt. I said I was pretty disappointed not to be given more of an opportunity, but if he changed his mind I'd be very happy to come back and give it another go.

Incredibly, not long after that call, in early June, Matt did give me a call back. Their keeper, Alex Barrow, was having an absolute stinker in the first team, while their backup keeper James Regan had broken a knuckle. So they needed someone to come in and play against Nottinghamshire in the County Championship on 14 June. Matt wanted me to come in for a month or so, play every game while Regan was injured, and see how things went from there.

So there I was, going from the pits of despair, wondering if I'd ever play first-class cricket again, to playing a Championship game against Nottinghamshire, within a matter of days. That's the life you lead as a sportsperson, when you're out of contract and therefore available on the loan market, I guess.

The game against Notts went well, and we won by two wickets. We were chasing down a massive 401 to win in our second innings, and it came down to the ninth wicket pairing of me and Abdur Rehman to get us over the line. I scored an undefeated 14, not a huge number of runs, but it did get us over the line to secure us a massive win.

The week after, we were off to the Ageas Bowl, to play my old teammates at Hampshire.

It's funny how things happen in sport. Who'd have thought I'd be back playing cricket at the club I'd been released from less than a year earlier? It was great to go back. I was made to feel really welcome by everyone at the club, my old team mates, the coaches and all the fans. Knowing that I had been given a chance to restart my career elsewhere, I think everyone at Hampshire were probably happy and relieved with how things had turned out.

The game itself ended in a pretty comfortable win for Somerset; we'd enforced the follow-on and needed just 64 runs in the second innings to secure the victory. I scored 14 in the first innings, before being bowled by a straight one from Jackson Bird – which was typical me. With the gloves I took five catches in the match and generally kept pretty tidily, so it was a regulation Bates performance, to be honest.

Generally things were going really well. My batting wasn't on fire, but then I wasn't actually getting much action with the bat. Especially in one-day cricket where I was often unused and down the order at number 11. But Somerset were happy enough to extend my contract, asking me to stay until the end of the season.

As part of my contract, Somerset asked me if I wanted to move into a flat at the ground, which was where they put all the new players if they need somewhere to stay. So I was able to move out of Mum and Dad's for the first time in about nine months, which was a great feeling in itself. A few of the players were living in those flats; Jack Leach was in the flat above me, so we hung out quite a lot between training and games. It was so good to have a bit of independence back, and for the club to give me a flat, really made me feel like they were in this for the long haul. As, of course, was I.

In total I played six County Championship games for Somerset that season, three Royal London Cup games and two T20 Blast matches, and generally felt my performances had been pretty good. But similar to the situation at Hampshire, it was fairly obvious that my glovework had outshone my batting.

Soon after our last game, as usual, I went to my end-of-season review meeting, this time with Matt Maynard. I was quietly optimistic that he'd take a chance on me, and sign me up for the following season. I certainly hoped so, anyway.

Sadly Matt had other ideas, and our chat ended up with a very similar outcome to the one I'd had with Giles White 12 months earlier. Matt was a little bit more forthcoming with praise for the good things

I'd done with the gloves, but the outcome was essentially the same. Thanks, but no thanks for next season. This was the end of the road for my Somerset journey.

It was another shattering blow for my career. How many blows can one man take? I was like a boxer, with punches raining down on top of me as I lay, vulnerable, across the floor. How many more times could I climb up off the canvas?

Looking back I do feel like my reputation with the bat preceded me a little bit, certainly in Matt's eyes. I would have needed to have done exceptionally well to convince him that I was worth persevering with in a batting sense. Ultimately I didn't do enough to change his mind, and that was the most disappointing thing.

I'd come in on a three-month contract, halfway through the season and thrust straight into first-team matches. Obviously I was thankful of the opportunity, but equally it was a huge ask for someone who'd been out the game at that level for nine months, to come straight into the team and be ready to perform.

That's what elite sport demands though. That's professional cricket. I knew it wasn't going to be handed to me on a plate. Matt needed a keeper to come in and hit the ground running, and I hadn't been able to do that. There were reasons for that, but ultimately they were just excuses. I simply hadn't done enough.

Having said that, I'm not sure Matt was ever 100% sold on me. Even when Phil, my agent, had his initial chat with Somerset, his feeling was that Maynard was quite reluctant to take me on, even though it was pretty clear they needed wicketkeeping options.

The other coaches at Somerset were great and I felt they supported me, perhaps more than Matt did. The likes of Steven Snell, who was on the coaching staff at Taunton, really liked me and was really trying to push my case forward. I'd known Steve from the Skillsets days with the England age groups, so he knew all about me as a player. Jason Kerr was another great coach at Taunton. Had it been up to Jason I think he would have taken me on, too.

Matt on the other hand seemed to have that perception of me as a player, and I clearly didn't do enough to change his mind.

Not long after I was released, Somerset signed a young keeper called Ryan Davies from Kent. I was surprised, because Ryan was a very similar keeper to me in many respects. He was strong with the gloves, but inexperienced with the bat. He was more of a specialist keeper in my mould than a multi-dimensional like, say, Phil Mustard, who was also being linked with a move to Somerset at the time.

I would've understood a move for Mustard. He had all that experience and was an established batsman, proven at that level. Instead they went with Ryan, someone with similar skills to me but with even less experience. I couldn't understand the thinking behind both my departure or Ryan's arrival, and I was pretty despondent with Matt's decisions as a result, to say the least.

A couple of years on, Ryan has been replaced by Steven Davies behind the stumps at Taunton, which backs up my view that perhaps he wasn't the right choice. Whatever I thought was irrelevant, however. The decision had been made and once again: I was moving on. I packed up my stuff and moved out of my flat at Taunton and took the long, lonely drive back to Yateley, and to Mum and Dad's house. Again. What the hell was I going to do now?

Chapter 12
Life after cricket

The days after that meeting with Matt were some of the lowest of my life. Obviously I'd been released from Hampshire the year before, and that had been unbelievably painful. But there was a sense of injustice with Hants; I felt they'd made the wrong call on me. This time it felt different. In essence Matt's was the same message that Chalks had delivered to me 12 months earlier. My batting wasn't good enough. And no matter how good I was with the gloves, it was my batting which had cost me.

The Somerset rejection felt worse because, well, it was another county giving up on me. Another coach thinking I wasn't good enough. This was the third county to release me, or not re-sign me. I was running out of chances, and I knew it.

I was in a horrible place mentally. I felt like I'd lost my identity. All my life I'd been a cricketer, right from when I was seven years old playing for Yateley Cricket Club's under-9s. All through my life, my friends and family had known me as a cricketer. When my parents went out for dinner, their friends would ask them, "How's Michael getting on, is he still enjoying his cricket?" What were they going to say to their friends now?

I'd had some great moments in my career. And winning those trophies, particularly the one at Lord's, were moments my parents could retell a million times to the people they knew. But this latest low point, of me being released – again – it was a horrible moment for all my family to see me go through. Of course, they didn't care about the trophies – they just wanted me to be happy. But seeing me at my lowest, bereft of all confidence, with no direction or purpose in life, it can't have been easy for them to have seen me like that.

I didn't know who to turn to.

My mates still playing cricket? They were still in that bubble. They didn't understand what it was like to be in my shoes, because they were all still there. At the cricket club every day, training, playing, basically just existing in that all-consuming cricket bubble.

The people I knew outside of cricket – my family and friends away from the game? They didn't know what it was like to play professional sport. To train for a living, to work constantly at your game addressing tiny imperfections in your technique. The media scrutiny, fans talking about you as you walk around the cricket ground – some praising you, some slagging you off. You don't get that sort of attention in many other lines of work. Maybe if you're Theresa May, or Piers Morgan… OK, that's a little bit above where I was as a cricketer, but you get the point.

Of course it's to do with that fame thing or being in the public eye; people thinking they know you and thinking they have the right to analyse and criticise you. And in some ways they do, because they're paying their hard-earned money to come and watch us play. So they are perfectly entitled to their opinions. But that doesn't make it any easier to deal with. And it doesn't mean that, when all that stops as it had done for me, it doesn't leave a gap.

If you ask any ex-sportsperson if they miss it, I guarantee the vast majority will say they do. They may not miss the pressure, the scrutiny or the endless hours of training. But they will miss the buzz of the changing rooms, of being with their team mates all the time, of travelling, touring and playing everywhere. They'll miss winning. They'll miss celebrating. They'll miss laughing. Crying. Cheering. Cursing. They'll miss loving every minute of it, because when all's said and done, it's an absolute privilege to play professional sport. To get paid for doing what you love, that's the absolute dream.

That psychological battle, of leaving professional sport behind, was a massive one for me to overcome. I'd only experienced professional cricket for a few years, and maybe that made it even harder for me to leave because I knew I should still be playing. I wasn't injured. I wasn't too old. Just supposedly not good enough. The thought of not playing again was horrendous, but something I knew, realistically, I'd have to start thinking about.

I spent a lot of time in the autumn of 2015 wallowing around at Mum and Dad's house, wondering what I was going to do next. I read Andrew Flintoff's book, in which he talked about his struggles with leaving the game behind. He talked about how he will always be a cricketer, no matter what he's doing now, and how the void of never playing again will never be filled. I totally got that.

I met a guy around that time called Jon Pitts, a neuropsychologist specialising in elite sport. Jon actually worked at Somerset before I was playing there, and he now works with the Red Bull F1 racing team, among other elite sporting outfits including the Western Storm women's T20 team. So his credibility in sports psychology is beyond reproach.

As a bloke, Jon's a ball of energy. He's like a big kid at times, very excitable. He's lean, quite tall with short, smart, dark brown hair. He was forever drinking Diet Coke, something I regularly took the mickey out of him for. He's a good guy, someone I've got to know really well as we now work together for the Western Storm, which I'll come onto later.

Jon and I have spoken at length about my playing career and how it all unravelled, first at Hampshire and then at Somerset. Jon didn't think I was given the right level of support, both mentally and psychologically, when things had been tough for me. I suppose it goes back to what Nic Pothas had said about my time at Hampshire – that I would have benefitted from having an experienced keeper mentoring me through that formative 2012 season in the first team, teaching me how to recover from a day in the field, how to switch mindsets between keeping and batting effectively. Most of all, how to find a way of mentally coping with the rigours of professional cricket, finding ways to perform well with the bat, even when things weren't going so well.

Jon linked my situation back to his time at Somerset when he worked with batsman Nick Compton, who was dropped from the England squad in 2013 in pretty brutal circumstances. Jon felt the way Nick was cast aside by England was harsh, and tough for the player to get over. Nick wasn't given any feedback from the ECB on what he should work on to get his place back, they just dumped him. Obviously I knew what I should be working on – my batting. But perhaps, when I was at Hampshire, we were looking too much at the physical traits of my batting and my tendency to get out to the straight ball, rather than considering the mental aspects, which were perhaps more of a contributing factor in my case.

Jon also talked about Craig Kieswetter, who was vying for the gloves with Jos Buttler at Taunton during Jon's tenure. Craig used to get frustrated when he wasn't scoring runs, and that frustration would make him overbalance and he would become more susceptible to getting out LBW as a result. John gave Craig some methods to deal with that frustration to stop him overbalancing, which helped Kieswetter massively.

His work with Craig in particular illustrated the benefit of having someone helping a player with the mental rigours of professional sport. Sure, I'd had interventions from batting coaches throughout my time at Hampshire. But I don't think it was ever a physical problem I was facing. It was more in my head. I saw a straight ball and immediately tensed up, pushed too far forward at it, leaving a gap in my defence and getting bowled. Jon's convinced that if he'd worked with me at the time, I'd be still playing. In fact, in the summer of 2017 when we first worked together at Western Storm, Jon wanted to work with me on my batting with a view to me getting back into the game.

Jon's area of expertise, clearly, was on the mental side of the game. A county season is long, and dealing with those endless hours on the field, when you have to be the heartbeat of the side and keep everyone going for whole days at a time, can be tough.

As Nic Pothas said, wicketkeepers arrive at the ground first and leave last. When the team is fielding, you're in the game every delivery. You need to focus on every ball, because any time the batter misses, you need to be there to catch the ball. You need to run through overs, ensure that the over rate is maintained, ensure the fielders are switched on, gee up the bowler, keep the batter on his toes. The role is never-ending. And then, when it's your team's turn to bat, if there's a top-order collapse, which was quite commonplace in that 2012 season at Hampshire, you then need to quickly switch on mentally, so that you're prepared for when you need to bat.

That's a lot to cope with, especially for a 21-year-old. And perhaps because I did leave so much out on the field mentally when I was keeping, there wasn't enough left in the tank when I went out to bat. If I'd had someone alongside me like Nic, or Jon, someone I could talk to about those challenges, someone to put an arm around me when I needed it, who could give me some strategies for dealing with the mental fatigue that you don't even realise you're battling, I honestly think my career could've turned out differently.

I talked to Jon again more recently, and when we got to the end of the chat-cum-interview, he asked me why I wasn't playing any more. Batting issues aside, he can't believe I'm in the situation I'm now in. As he said, at one stage I was close to the England setup!

The coaches at Hampshire had clearly identified a talent in me – I was involved from the academy from the outset and went all the way though to make my first team debut at 19, so I was clearly rated. But having started well with the bat at the start of that breakthrough season in 2012, I didn't have anyone to turn to for advice when my form with the bat dropped off, in the second half of that season. And that's my biggest disappointment.

Sure, I had Chalks, Yorkie Chalky, Tony, the wicketkeeping coach Bobby Parks and senior players like Jimmy Adams to talk to. But none of those, as Nic said, had kept wicket in first-class cricket. Well, not in the last 20 years, in the case of Bob.

***

One other aspect that may have influenced my career being cut short, which we haven't really explored thus far, is the question of finances in county cricket.

You don't need to be a fully fledged cricket badger to realise that the game at domestic level isn't exactly awash with money. So far in my story, I've talked about my career in terms of my playing ability, and my mental fragility. But finances must also have played a part.

I enjoyed some incredibly privileged moments in my career, not just on the field but off it too. Some of the hotels we stayed in were magnificent, in the Caribbean, South Africa, Bangladesh and New Zealand. These were luxurious 5-star hotels, places normally reserved for the rich and famous. We'd walk into these stunningly grand buildings to be greeted like royalty, with the hotel staff lined up in the foyer, welcoming us in with drinks and snacks. The food was delicious, often made with fresh produce from the local area. The rooms were stunning, like our hotel in Barbados where the patio doors opened out onto the gorgeous, sandy Bridgetown beach.

As players, we were treated really well, and that's just at domestic and junior England level; imagine what it's like for guys in the senior England squad.

Yet you only have to look at the empty stands at a County Championship match to realise that the county game is struggling with its finances. There's usually a smattering of members in for Championship games, while even the one-dayers struggle to sell out, at some grounds at least.

We spoke to numerous people and we kept hearing the same thing: "You can't have two keepers in your squad in county cricket. It's not like football where you might have three keepers. That's the nature of the game, it's not the way it should be, but that's the way it is."

A lot of what happened in my career was influenced, in part at least, by the financial constraints at both Hampshire and Somerset. Nowadays, sadly, clubs just don't have the money required to have a large squad. So instead they try to get as much out of each player as they can.

From a club's perspective, if they're paying a certain amount for a player, and then feeling like they're not getting the required level from their batting, it might be a case of examining whether the club getting enough out of the player for the money they are paying him. Under my second professional contract at Hampshire, I was earning about £30,000 a year, plus £75 per day for first-team appearances. I also got competition bonuses, particularly in that 2012 season when we won two trophies. The players received a percentage of the total sum earned by the club for winning both competitions, depending on how many games we'd each played in the competition.

Obviously I was still quite a junior player, even when that second contract was agreed, so other players would have been on a lot more than me, I'm sure. I'd be surprised if Wheater wasn't on a lot more than what I was on when he arrived from Essex. He may have had more performance-related bonuses written into his contract too, because mine was quite a basic contract.

When I first broke into the first team, our squad was a great deal bigger than squads tend to be now. Back then, and we're only talking 10 years ago or so, second teams would be full of contracted players – quite a few of them senior pros. Whereas nowadays it's completely different, with only a couple of pros in the seconds, while the rest are trialists or academy players. It's sad to see, but the financial constraints have made it that way.

T20 cricket is where the money's at, even in county cricket. Which is why you see so many counties blowing huge proportions of their annual budget on T20 superstars from around the world. Counties know that reaching Finals Day can be extremely lucrative for them, while if they're playing exciting cricket with international superstars in their side, they're more likely to sell out their grounds.

The knock-on effect of that, however, is that there's less budget for the pros already at the clubs; the guys that are there all year, every year, and who have the best interests of the club at heart. It's surprising therefore that there's not more cynicism within the counties, towards how the regular pros are paid in county cricket. Or maybe there is...

"There's a lot of people in county cricket who would just play one-day cricket, and not even bother playing four-day cricket," one current county cricketer told us. "The only reason some players play four-day cricket is the financial side of it. The way white-ball cricket is going now, that should have more of an impact on how much money you earn."

That same player told us that salaries at their county were weighted depending on their contributions in both formats; two-thirds for their red-ball contributions, and only one-third for their white-ball appearances. That seems bizarre when you consider how much more money appears to be in the one-day formats. It's no wonder more and more players are signing white-ball-only contracts nowadays.

Logic suggests that counties are going to pay the highest salaries to those players who can contribute the most in all formats. That limits the case for me, a specialist in only one discipline. Is a county really going to pay for a wicketkeeper they feel is only really contributing with the gloves, even if those contributions are of a really high standard? I'm reminded at this stage of Jon Hotten's point, about how big an impact a specialist keeper can have on a game of T20 cricket in particular. You could argue my contribution therefore was worth more in that format.

From a county's perspective, however, they could invest in a multi-dimensional keeper, put an academy keeper into the seconds, and save themselves a bit of money which they could redirect into the budget for the big overseas T20 players. It's cynical, but at the end of the day, it's business. The big names sell, they bring in the crowds and that's ultimately one of the challenges facing the counties.

The backup keeper probably isn't going to play in the first team anyway, as Adam Rouse found out when I was playing at Hampshire. If the first-choice keeper gets injured, a county could just get a keeper in on loan anyway, which was the reason I was brought in at Somerset after all.

As an example, Hampshire's first-choice keeper in 2017 was Lewis McManus. The 2nd XI keeper was Callum Dickinson, who did well in white-ball cricket – he looks a gun batsman – but he wasn't played in first-class cricket as the keeper, even when Lewis was out injured. Instead Hants opted to play Tom Alsop as a keeper, and left Dickinson in the twos.

That's not really ideal for anyone; it doesn't do Dickinson's confidence any good, he's the backup keeper but he doesn't get a game when the first-choice keeper is injured. And it also burdens Alsop, who's a decent batsman. And, when you look at it, is it ideal from a team's point of view?

I guess it's a way of streamlining a squad, equipping it with more multi-dimensional players who can do more than one job, if required. That's really hard for someone like me, an out-and-out specialist, to say. But that's the reality of the modern game, and probably goes part of the way to explaining why I'm not still playing today. I'm convinced I was good enough, but counties obviously didn't want to waste their money on a player who, as they perceived it, had too much development still to do with his batting. Especially when they could instead bring a more established, multi-dimensional option in.

I know it's different, but think about how many bowlers a county has in their squad. They have room for all those specialist batters and bowlers, eight bowlers maybe? Yet only one slot for a full-time wicketkeeper. And you're not talking £75k, or even £55k for a wicketkeeper. Most keepers would happily take £30–45k a year, depending on their experience, international aspirations and so on.

What Jos Buttler told us is relevant here, because his theory was that it wasn't enough to simply be a wicketkeeper, or for that matter, just a batter. You needed to be able to perform as many different disciplines as you can to a really high standard, so that you're contributing more to the team:

> You look around at the England team now, there's myself, Jonny [Bairstow] and Sam [Billings]. We could all play in the same team, and one guy would keep. It shows the level that the batsmanship is perceived to need to be at before a guy can play. You look around at a lot of the counties, a lot are playing with three guys who could potentially take the gloves. It's definitely changed from your Bruce Frenches who were real specialist wicketkeepers and never missed a chance, but weren't going to score as many runs.

Back in 2013, when Wheater was brought in at Hampshire, I was a young player who'd progressed through the academy. I wasn't on a huge wage, something Nic Pothas highlighted when we spoke to him. "It's not costing them [Hampshire] any money," Nic said. "Bates wouldn't have been on much cash and then you go away and spend a lot more money on Wheater. You're always going to pay at least 20% above market value to bring in someone from the outside."

**

Gradually as the autumn in 2015 turned into winter, I started emerging from my pit of despair. I'd done a lot of thinking, a lot of worrying, a lot of crying. As Christmas approached, I was starting to feel like it was finally time to move on with my life. Although in my heart I still saw myself as a cricketer, in my mind I was starting to wise up to the fact that my future might lay away from playing cricket.

I still loved the game, and coaching was the obvious option for me to refocus on. Ironically when I was at Hampshire our PCA representative, Nick Denning, was constantly telling all the players that coaching might be a viable post-playing career option. At the time I had absolutely no interest whatsoever. But things had changed. Massively. And now it was something I was seriously considering for the future.

But before I had complete closure on my playing career, and really started knuckling down with my coaching qualifications, I was privileged enough to have a chat with an absolute legend of the game...

We talked at length on all things wicketkeeping; he asked me about my career, and I asked him about his. We both concluded that we had an awful lot in common as keepers, and a love for our art was palpable. That, for one, gave me a huge sense of pride, that while my playing career perhaps hadn't ended the way I wanted it to, I could still be very proud of what I'd achieved, and how I'd gone about it. And while I had regrets in terms of the way it had all ended, there were none in the sense that I'd played the game in the way I wanted to, which was the only way I knew how.

I can't quite believe I'm writing this in my own book. But ladies and gentlemen, boys and girls, please allow me to introduce, Mr Adam Gilchrist...

Chapter 13
Adam Gilchrist

No modern wicketkeeping book can be written without referencing the profound impact that Adam Gilchrist has had on the role.

It's by no means an exaggeration to suggest that Gilly revolutionised wicketkeeping as we know it. Before making his debut in 1996, Australia had been used to a wicketkeeper in Ian Healy who was immaculate behind the stumps; if he scored runs – which he could do – it would usually be considered something of a bonus. Healy was the archetypal specialist keeper.

By the time Gilly retired from international cricket in 2008, every team in the world was scrambling around their domestic teams for a keeper just like him. Someone who was still phenomenal behind the stumps, but who could also bat like a top-order batsman.

The truth is, Gilly was something of a freak, and it's difficult to name one player who has replicated his complete brilliance – in all disciplines – since. Just look at his batting numbers; 5,570 runs in 96 Test matches including 17 hundreds and 26 half-centuries, at an average of 47.6. When you consider Gilly's skipper and one of the great batsmen of recent times, Ricky Ponting, averaged 51 over his Test career, you'll see how utterly incredible Gilly's numbers were.

But unlike some modern keeper-batters, Gilly's keeping was just as good. Gilchrist recorded 416 dismissals in his 96-Test career, compared to Healy's 395 from 119. And Healy was considered the specialist keeper...

As a wicketkeeper, I've always been fascinated by Gilchrist. How was he able to be so consistently strong with both his batting and his keeping? How did he allocate his training time to both disciplines? Did he see himself as a batter first and a keeper second, as Alec Stewart had done, or was he a gloveman first and foremost?

Moreover, is he aware of the seismic shift in expectation his career has had on wicketkeepers playing now? I mean, I can't imagine anyone thinks of themselves as being a catalyst for change in that sense, no matter what line of work they're in. But looking back now, how does he reflect on his wonderful career?

Through a couple of major coincidences, both Tom and I had mutual connections who knew Gilly. In my case Australian batsman George Bailey, who was playing at Hampshire in 2017, offered to get in touch with Adam on our behalf. In Tom's case, his friend Glenn Beavis manages Aussie F1 driver, Daniel Riccardo, both of whom are friends with Gilly. "I was only with him in Perth the other day for a catch-up," Glenn told Tom when the pair spoke – it really is who you know...

After months of messages, emails and attempts at speaking – only for work commitments to get in the way – we finally got on a Skype call with Gilly one Friday in September 2017. It was a warm, spring evening in Perth for Gilly, who was sat at his home supping a glass of red wine having put his kids to bed. While I was at home in north Hampshire, nursing a warm cup of tea as the British autumn made itself known.

What a treat it was that he agreed to speak to us – pure poetry for any wicketkeeper, or any fan of the art of wicketkeeping. We kicked off by discussing my career, and it was really nice – and pretty morale-boosting – to learn that Gilly was aware of me, and my career.

What follows is our conversation, pretty much word for word and in its entirety. Two wicketkeepers chatting about the beautiful game; it just so happens one is the greatest of all time.

* * *

Adam Gilchrist (AG): So has it been good fun going back through your career stuff?

Michael Bates (MB): It has. It's actually made me miss the game a little bit. I'm just getting started with some coaching and I'm loving it, but I'm sure there'll always be, as I'd imagine you'll agree, a part of me that misses playing. Just recalling it all has brought it all back, but it's been good.

AG: Whether it's more difficult for you or not, I don't know. You're still young, and you clearly had the skills to be at it for a lot longer, so it must be tough.

MB: You're right, and going through this process has kind of made me wonder whether I could give playing another go. I've tossed that idea around a little bit, but I think it's probably time to draw a line under it and just focus on the coaching 100%. I am young, which I think is a big benefit for my coaching. So, do you know how my career panned out?

AG: Yeah, I've got an idea. Before this contact, I was very aware of your name, and friends would mention you and reference this guy Bates, this fella who was clearly known for being one of the best glovemen in the UK. The discussion was always about the quality of the gloveman balanced up with the batting in the new era of the game. But I was aware of your name. So I looked into it a little bit more, and there's some amazing pieces written about you, like some of the stuff you've achieved in finals and that to me is where keepers can normally get a bit overlooked, so that's a hell of a compliment to you.

I reckon in the last 10–15 years, and since probably Stewie, Alec Stewart, two or three names have been thrown out there that, at the time, have come out of nowhere. You never saw them in an England shirt, and you hear people saying "He's clearly the best in county cricket, but he's not going to get there because he's not quite good enough with the bat." That's a real shame.

With your career finishing in first-class, I gather that's because you didn't get offered another contract, or was it that you said "I can't be doing with this anymore?"

MB: I would have carried on playing if the opportunities were there, definitely. Hampshire didn't extend my contract at the end of 2014, so that's when I finished there.

AG: Did you play anywhere else?

MB: Yeah, I played for Somerset for a little bit, in the second half of the 2015 season. But I never really found my feet there to be honest. The previous winter, having been released by Hampshire and not really being in a good place mentally, I didn't train and was probably a bit rusty and didn't quite find my form. Then I was told Somerset weren't going to extend my contract at the end of the 2015 season either. After that I was on the hunt for another opportunity but they just never really came about – no one seemed interested.

AG: Ah right.

MB: So that was that really. So in 2012 we won the T20 and the List A competition over here – the CB40 as it was then known. Then literally straight after, in the 2012/13 winter, Hampshire signed another keeper, Adam Wheater from Essex. Once he came on board it was always going to be difficult to get myself back in to the team.

AG: Where is he now, is he still there?

MB: No. He didn't really go that well at Hampshire either. He's now back at Essex, actually not playing regularly as James Foster is still there. So he's not a regular feature in that team at the moment. Hampshire basically decided to go in a completely different direction when replacing me; Wheater being very much a batter who's manufactured himself into a bit of a catcher and was obviously on the other end of the scale to me. That was the decision they made, it was always going to be difficult to drag that one back from my perspective and that's how it panned out.

AG: That's tough. How old are you now?

MB: 27.

AG: You're obviously more mature now, maybe you'd do better now if you were playing?

MB: Well this is the thing, since doing this book we've spoken to various people. We spoke to Joe Root and Sam Billings as those are guys I grew up playing with at England under-19 level and they kind of said similar, that they're disappointed I'm not still playing first-class cricket. They asked me why I'm not. I'm with you: in that 2012 season, my first year as the first-choice keeper at Hampshire and playing all formats, I learned a huge amount. Over the last few years I've grown up and matured and I do feel like, were I to have the same opportunity now, I would definitely perform differently. Better. But as you said, people mature at different stages don't they?

AG: Is it worth saying again to other counties, "I am available"? I stand to be corrected, but I can't believe that every county would be so well served by a quality keeper. Regardless of the batting aspect of it, and I'm sure it's not that much of a drop-off between what they can see is required as a batting component to what you're able to provide. Is every county fully stocked?

MB: How counties tend to operate now, is they have a first-choice keeper of a really decent standard and well established, then they kind of use the second team as a platform for the younger guys, not necessarily paying their second-team keeper a lot of money. Generally, when you look at the other counties, most have a fairly well-established first-team keeper. A lot of the counties saw me as better than a second-team keeper but felt they wouldn't be in a position to offer me what I deserved, if that makes sense.

That's how a lot of them saw it. Not being able to offer me first-team cricket, but seeing me as someone capable of more than just second-team cricket, so it was a difficult one. But I reckon all the counties were aware of my situation, I had an agent working for me and I trusted he did all he could. There were a few people interested along the way, but their interest just seemed to peter out unfortunately. So that's that.

AG: So this book may take you on a different tangent potentially?

MB: Absolutely. And I guess that leads us on to the obvious question, how do you reckon the keeper-batter role has changed over the last 10–20 years?

AG: I see the first catalyst to change was actually the birth of limited-overs cricket in general. The first touch point I can think of was in 1970/71, the first one-day international.[9] From there the ODIs started. And I think, for me, and no one would have been aware of it at the time, that was the point the wicketkeeping role significantly changed. Simply because of limited-overs cricket and what that came to stand for. There's a limited amount of deliveries that a batting team can score runs from, therefore all of a sudden, the whole XI become accountable to contribute some runs.

Then, in 1996, the next significant change was what the Sri Lankans and the New Zealanders brought to the World Cup in India that year. Lee Germon probably wasn't the best keeper in New Zealand at the time, but he got thrown in there to give it a whack with the bat, because that's what they wanted from their keeper. Then the Sri Lankans changed the landscape further by picking Romesh Kaluwitharana, slotting him up the top of the order, and he just teed off. He probably wasn't that fussed about the keeping side of his game, although he was still a very decent keeper. He had 100 international stumpings so he was no fool with the gloves. But it was a definite change in emphasis towards a batter who could keep, as opposed to an outstanding keeper per se.

So that was significant, and probably opened up my opportunity. Maybe I remember that as the landmark more than anyone else because I think that changed the dynamic and the thinking within

---

[9] The first ODI was played in Melbourne in January 1971 between Australia and England, after three days of the third Ashes Test between the two sides were lost to rain. The teams agreed to play a one-off, 40-over match for fans, so that they could see a contest between the two sides, which would go through to a conclusion. And thus, completely by accident, the advent of one-day cricket had occurred.

Australian cricket, which gave me my opportunity. After that World Cup, Australia decided to have a separate one-day and Test team, with Heals [Ian Healy] remaining the first-choice keeper in the Test team, and me promoted to the number-one position in one-day cricket. So that was obviously the landmark moment in our setup and for me personally.

Then the final phase of the evolution was the introduction of T20 cricket, with all of the focus on runs as opposed to necessarily high levels of keeping skills. This made teams look for a batter-keeper if you will, as opposed to a specialist keeper.

MB: So, when you broke into the Australian team, did you see yourself more as a batter who kept or a keeper who batted ... or both?

AG: That's a really good question. Through my whole career, my primary focus was to be the best wicketkeeper I could be. That's what I judged my game of cricket on. Scoring a hundred but dropping a catch or missing a stumping, I'd be pretty flat. But the other way around; miss out on the runs but keep perfectly and take any opportunity that came my way, or if there weren't any chances but feeling like I took everything clean and moved well, that was good enough for me.

My mindset was purely about keeping and I trained about 80% on my keeping and 20% on my batting. There's 11 batsmen in a team, everyone gets the chance to bat, and pretty much anyone could have a bowl. But I needed to be on point with the gloves. That was my mindset – that's what I loved most.

I was slotted in at number seven initially, for 10 games or so, so clearly my job in my mind was keeping; keeping to Warney, keeping to McGrath, keeping to those guys. I didn't stop and analyse it or over-scrutinise it too much. But Heals had done such an amazing job, so I just wanted to keep really well.

Then, for whatever reason, I was promoted to the top of the order and had an extra part of the job description so to speak, to score some runs with the bat. I think because of the way I'd been introduced into that team – Steve Waugh had given me a bit of a licence to go and play some shots with some freedom. But I still always thought, "Well, I'm the keeper". So I think he has to take some credit for introducing me into the team like that, telling me to play my natural game.

MB: So did you feel secure that the role was yours throughout your career? Or did you ever have any doubts towards your approach?

AG: I was aware of the debate all the way through it, about whether or not I was the best gloveman in Australia. Perhaps Darren Berry was the better keeper, so the purists thought, and again I'll fast forward to now, I think he's possibly one of the best three keepers I saw anywhere around the world. He was a pure gloveman. But fortunately for me, I was the one they picked.

There was always that discussion throughout my playing days. No matter how much I'd fight it, there was always this backdrop of whether I was being picked purely as a keeper, or whether my batting persuaded the selectors to put me in there.[10] In my mind, I tried to tell myself that I was being picked because I was right for the backdrop of that Australian team at the time. But looking back now, there's no doubt my batting helped get me into the limited-overs team first, above anyone else, because that was what they wanted. And I think it was more the foundation that I laid there, and the fact that I'd had others saying "Oh he must be good enough nowadays as a keeper" to warrant moving into the Test team.

I suppose the general theory might be, because of limited-overs cricket, that there is still a balance point between value of runs scored versus wicketkeeping opportunities missed. And I think any captain and selectors will always have that in mind.

MB: I find it fascinating that you perceived yourself more as a keeper who batted. It's interesting – and quite reassuring I guess. I always assumed you'd see yourself more as a batter. Did the fact you had such a big part to play with the bat ever effect your keeping?

AG: If my confidence was up in one, it was up in both. I remember Heals telling me that very rarely did he find that if he was keeping well, he was batting well. He found it very hard to keep both skills up, which I think tells a bit more about personalities than skills or capabilities. If things were going well for me then life was good. If I was scoring runs, it probably meant I was happy in myself, and I probably had a more relaxed approach to my keeping. And you're more likely to let your skills come through when you are relaxed and vice versa. If I was

---

[10] What I find interesting here is how Gilly himself admits to having doubts, or worries about his place in the team. We're talking about the best wicketkeeper in the last 50 years at least, and yet he wasn't always confident he'd even make the team sheet. Incredible.

struggling a bit, 2005 was the absolute epitome of that,[11] I'd be down with the bat and then my keeping went down. Everything just spiralled out of control, that's more mentally than skill.

MB: How did you get yourself back up then?

AG: I wound down over a beer! The 2005 Ashes series in England was probably the worst tour of my career personally. After that we had a summer at home against South Africa. I had doubts, felt like I hit rock bottom. I thought about giving up. I mentioned it all to the people who are important to me, and they convinced me that I shouldn't.

Then in 2006/7 we had the return Ashes series, when England came out here, and we ended up winning 5–0. At one point in the Second Test, I decided "I'm retiring." I was done.[12]

But then I got some runs in Perth – my home ground – and that was a huge relief. Probably that innings was more important to me than any other. It was just the fun of batting, the reason you play the game. That had become so clouded. That day at the WACA, it was like I remembered the reason why I started playing cricket in the first place. It allowed me to rediscover my love for the game. I then fortunately went on to play for another 18 months after that, which was good. So the way I got through that was simply reconnecting with why I got into the game in the first place.

MB: Which is easily lost, when you're under so much pressure.

AG: Big time. And I'm sure that happens in any profession. But I had to reconnect with it and fight my way through that.

MB: It's interesting isn't it? In my case, throughout all the one-day success we had whilst I was keeping at Hampshire, I rarely batted, particularly in the 20-over competition. Yet I was still able to influence the game with my gloves; I was up to the stumps a lot, bowlers were taking pace off the ball, I'd be putting batters under pressure all the time.

---

[11] 2005 was the year of England's famous Ashes win over Gilchrist's side. England won 2–1 at home, handing Michael Vaughan's side the urn for the first time in 18 years. England played well, but several senior Australian players were criticised, Gilchrist included, with accusations that they were past their best.

[12] Australia emphatically won the 2006/7 Ashes series 5–0, but Gilchrist's series was mixed. He scored 0, 64 and 0 before that match-winning hundred in the second innings at his home ground, the WACA in Perth.

So you could argue if you've got an exceptional keeper who's going to make such a difference with the gloves and you can afford to bat him lower down the order, he might not get a chance to contribute with the bat anyway.

AG: Absolutely. I totally agree with that. Although I just wonder whether it falls on deaf ears because the only guys that seem to bat later are bowlers. A spinner who creates a lot of chances, they rely on the keeper being high quality, in order to take catches up at the stumps. Other than that, most catches are taken in the outfield or on the fence anyway. You have to save your number 11 slot for your bowler, like a Muralitharan, who in T20 cricket will probably only get 10 hits across 300 games. So maybe there should still be room for a specialist keeper, but then it also comes down to the overall balance of your team.

MB: So that said then, do you think there'll ever be a time when it'll go full circle? T20 is very specialist now, with specialist coaches coming in. Do you think it will ever flip on its head, and we'll have specialist keepers favoured in the shortest form of the game again?

AG: I think that's started already. There's signs in all formats that there's a lot more focus on specific roles. T20 cricket, ideally you'll have a very good spinner in your team, if not a couple depending on what the conditions are.

Batters can play 360 [degrees] around the ground, so you need that variation. Yeah, I think that wheel is already in motion, there's no doubt about it. As to where it all settles, I mean T20 cricket is still in its infancy, in comparison with how long cricket's been around. The world of cricket is still figuring out where it fits in, how to go about it. But that specialist role has already began.

MB: So do you reckon it's more important to have a specialist keeper in the shorter format, or the longer format?

AG: Speaking as a keeper, I would say all formats. But it would be interesting to see what captains and coaches who aren't keepers say to that. But I really think that ideally, you'll have a keeper who is a specialist. Show me a part-time keeper who's any good. A manufactured keeper, he can go and practice keeping, but I wouldn't be chucking him gloves. Maybe in a one-off T20 international, but I wouldn't be throwing him into a T20 World Cup, where you know you're playing four or five games to try to win a cup.

I think there still needs to be a specialist wicketkeeper picked. And then, if you want to look at the batting component of it, I think that's the reality where times have changed. But it shouldn't be ruled out that maybe it's not the wicketkeeping position where you should be making sacrifices, maybe it's the bowlers. Even if your keeper bats at 11, if he's so good that he's not going to miss anything, or miss very little, then maybe look at your bowlers, and work out who's more important there. Is there another bowler who has a bit more all-round capability, and can they bat at six, eight, nine? Like I said earlier, balance of the team comes into it for sure.

MB: Did you ever have a preference, batting or keeping?

AG: I loved both equally. I thought of myself more for my keeping, but in terms of enjoying one or the other more, no. Scoring runs was awesome, but to me having a scrap behind the stumps, whether you're facing a spinner or whatever, there's no better place to be. It's just so much fun, and being the focal point of the fielding team, they were the best times on the field.

MB: Do you miss playing?

AG: No, I don't. I love the game still, I love watching it. I love being at live games, at any standard. I love doing the Big Bash commentary, I love going to a packed stadium. When I was playing I was usually nervous, so I love going there now without the nerves. I know I can stuff up calling the match, but that's neither here nor there.

I still have that passion for it, but I haven't really thought about or longed to be out on the field at all. Which is quite nice. It's comforting to know that I probably pulled out at the right time. I played the IPL for six seasons, which helped me wean myself off cricket if you like, so no I don't miss it too much.

MB: Do you think your career was helped by the fact that you were part of such a dominant Australian side?

AG: My natural response would be yes. It was an amazing group of guys to play with, in the same setup, at the same time, it was pretty incredible really. I've never been one to compare eras, so how I would've gone now or 10 years prior, I don't know.

I watch the current Aussie team and there's things I think "Shit, really? Are you sure about doing that?" And that's when I've got to step back and think, "Hang on a sec". I was pretty fortunate to play with a group that things went really well for, most of the time. It wasn't plain sailing, and of course we worked hard for our success. But ultimately, they're just different eras, and you can't help the fact that those incredible players were all available to Australia at the same time.[13]

I was very fortunate to be among that era. And being around those guys, yeah I'd have to say I benefited, because it drove me to go higher and higher.

MB: It's widely accepted that you single-handedly changed the way wicketkeeping is perceived. Looking back on your career now and recapping on everything we've discussed, do you agree with that statement?

AG: It's a pretty humbling thing that people say. I can understand why people may look at it that way. I think the easy statistic to look at in order to make that call is how many runs I scored, or what I averaged, how many hundreds I got. Which I get, that's what people will be drawn to, because that was a new benchmark that hadn't previously been in place for a wicketkeeper.

But for me, what I would hope legitimises that comment is that, by the time I'd finished playing, I held the world record for dismissals in Test cricket, and in one-day cricket, at the time.[14] I effected as many if not more dismissals off Shane Warne than my rival, Ian Healy. That's not saying I'm better than him, but I like to look at those sort of stats. It's the keeping component that legitimises that comment, not just the fact that I scored a lot of runs.

Without getting too self-indulgent and again going back to my original point, I always saw myself as a keeper. Ultimately for me the catalyst to change I truly believe was limited-overs cricket coming into the game. Whether it was me, or someone else, eventually it was going to change the paradigm a bit and that was always going to be through limited-overs cricket.

Then maybe people started to think, "OK, let's start tinkering with our Test line-up," and the only reason why I think people may have

---

[13] Far from criticising the current Australian team, Gilchrist is really just making the point that the great team he was part of was unique. It's so rare to have a setup – in any sport – where there's so much strength in depth, in every position. Australia were blessed with once-in-a-generation players throughout the team, all playing at the same time.

[14] Gilchrist held the record for the most Test and ODI dismissals for a wicketkeeper when he retired, but has since been overtaken by Mark Boucher and Kumar Sangakkara respectively.

changed their mindset there, is because of the effect limited-overs cricket had on scoring rates in Test cricket. That wasn't just our era as cricketers. Suddenly, scoring at 3, 3.5 an over in Test cricket was the norm. That was the effect of limited-overs cricket slowly filtering across into Test cricket. So you get people saying, "Well we need to score runs, we need to score quicker, to allow our bowlers enough time." That's just the way the game changed.

So yeah, of course it's humbling when people say that I changed the face of keeping, but I think really it was the introduction of the shorter format that was the true catalyst to change, not me. If it hadn't been me, it would have been someone else.

MB: But you're most proud of your keeping stats, is that what you're saying?

AG: Absolutely mate. Haha. Absolutely.

MB: That's good enough for me, I love that.

* * *

Talking to Gilly was an absolute pleasure. Anyone who's heard him on TV commentary will have seen what a nice guy he is, and from our Skype conversation, I can tell you he was every bit the legend you'd expect him to be. He's incredibly knowledgeable and having the opportunity to chat to him about all things keeping was a fantastic experience.

I was surprised, and pretty chuffed, at how much focus he put on his keeping. It was immensely reassuring, and we both sounded like a couple of wicketkeeping geeks at times as we indulged in discussing our glovework. When he talked about being really happy with his work behind the stumps even when he wasn't in the game, moving really well, taking the ball cleanly, I totally got that.

The key message I took from our chat was that even the man considered the best keeper of modern times sees the need for the wicketkeeping specialism to continue – even in today's game, so dominated as it is by the need for big runs. Obviously Gilly was having a conversation with me, a specialist keeper, so he was unlikely to completely dismiss the idea of specialist keepers still having a role in the game. But what I got from him was his passion for keeping, and I can't help but think that with more people like him, or I, coaching in the game, perhaps the art of specialist wicketkeeping will prevail after all.

Chapter 14
Coaching

Facing up to a career beyond the boundary rope was daunting. Playing cricket was all I'd ever known, and all I'd ever wanted to do. Through the winter of 2015/16 I had to face the fact that I wasn't going to be a professional cricketer any longer, no matter how much I wanted to be. And no matter how many times people told me I should keep going, I realised that it was time to move on.

It was October 2015, and I had just turned 25. I wanted to start living again, rather than waiting around for an opportunity that may never come. So I decided to reconsider Nick Denning's suggestion about giving coaching a try. When I was still playing, coaching had never appealed to me. At the time I was so obsessed with my own game that the thought of having to worry about someone else's freaked me out. This is a shame really, because if I knew then what I now know about coaching, I'm 100% certain that it would have helped me improve my own game as a player. Coaching makes you think more about how the game works – the wider context of a match rather than obsessing about your own specific role within it. In addition, it helps you see that sometimes, a player's issues are mental rather than physical. Both those lines of thinking would have helped me while playing, for sure.

I'd learned the hard way how important that relationship between player and coach is. There were aspects of the coaching I'd received throughout my playing career which hadn't really worked for me; the stand-offish nature of some of the coaches at Hampshire, the ability to highlight an issue, but then not provide a possible solution, was another. These were all factors I could certainly draw on when I became a coach.

I've learned so much about the mental side of the game since I finished playing. My approach to batting back then was to aim for perfection, to try to bat at the same level that I kept. That was impossible for me, and totally the wrong mental approach. Now I realise I should have been concerned with what I could give to the team; to be clever, to occupy the crease, to protect the tail, to boost my average and weigh in with key runs, however they came. Nic Pothas talked a lot about that, and he was spot on. No wonder he's gone on to enjoy a successful coaching career since he left Hampshire.

Those negatives would definitely allow me to empathise better with the batters, particularly when they were struggling with the mental side of their game. With wicketkeeper coaching it would be slightly different. Sure there are key technical aspects that are pretty fundamental to keeping wicket really well, like having a strong base, good alignment, whether you catch the ball under your nose or with your hands out in front for example, which I knew I'd be able to cover off pretty comfortably. But that mental aspect of learning to love the process of taking every ball really cleanly, is probably the hardest thing to teach a keeper. So that was definitely something that if I could nail that in my coaching, it would be a massive asset to me, as my old England keeping coach Bruce French told us in early 2017.

> If Batesy can think of a way to get that into players ... I've been battling with that for years. The technical side is there, staring you in the face. But what goes on in the mind ... most of wicketkeeping comes down to what you're thinking about each ball. Are you able to stay in that relaxed state? Are you able to just watch the ball? It sounds simple, and that's probably in all sports. The tension just kills you, because you can be in the moment one second, and then in the next, it can be different.

I certainly think the experiences I gained throughout my playing career – good and bad – have enhanced me as a coach. My old skipper at Hampshire, Jimmy Adams, certainly felt I had something to offer. He told Tom:

> I've watched a bit of Batesy coach, and the impression I get is it's not a broken-down, "get the camera out, let's analyse and work it out" approach. It's very Indian. The way the Indians talk about batting is as if it's an art. And I sense there's an element of that with Batesy's coaching method. It's finding a way of getting it done, and getting it done well. It's fluid. I always felt with Batesy, that keeping was his way of expressing himself. It was a case of "I want the ball. Whether I'm fielding a throw, this is all part of my remit."
>
> And everything about Batesy is positive. Yeah, he made mistakes, but that's part and parcel. It's wonderful to hear that he's talking to players about that ability to clear your mind before

each delivery, because that's the stuff that's so hard to do. The stuff you don't see. Batesy could well be a Bruce French-type coach, and I hope that is the case.

* * *

I took my level two coaching badge in those painful autumn months in 2015, immediately after I was released by Somerset. It was a no-brainer really as it was a pretty basic level of coaching and therefore quite straightforward to pass. Plus it gave me something to do, and got me out of my parents' house.

Soon after, I landed my first coaching gig, from an unlikely source I might add. I'd known of Dan Housego for a few years. I'd played against him in 2012, when I scored 87 against his Gloucestershire team at the Ageas Bowl. We then bumped into each other on a couple of occasions in 2015, when we were both trialling for different teams. Like me, Dan had been released from his county, Gloucestershire. We met again in March 2015, when he was trialling for Glamorgan and me for Essex. Our teams were playing each other in a pre-season friendly, and we chatted along the boundary while the game was going on, as neither of us had been selected. Then later that summer when I arrived at Somerset, Dan was also there, having another trial.

On both those occasions, Dan told me about the coaching academy he'd set up, and he asked me if I'd be interested in getting involved. But on both occasions, I was still trying to nail down my playing career, so I didn't really give the offer much thought. Similar to my chats with Nick Denning.

But by October 2015, I knew I needed to do something – anything. I was sick of moping around Mum and Dad's house, and coaching seemed to be the thing my mind was on most. So I gave Dan a call and, within days, I was coaching his keepers, as he'd asked me to do years earlier.

The fog was finally lifting. And even better was to come when, in November 2015, I met a girl called Hannah in a bar near Reading. When I first saw Hannah, my jaw just hit the floor. It was a proper Jim Carrey in *The Mask* moment. She was gorgeous, with stunning, bright blue eyes, an amazing smile and an absolutely smoking body. What more could a man ask for? We got chatting and I really fell for her pretty much instantly. She had a great sense of humour – quite geeky but in a cute way. I hadn't laughed that much in ages.

We started dating pretty much straight after that night, and our relationship quickly blossomed. Soon it was Christmas, and I was the happiest I'd been in ages, something I didn't think possible just a few months earlier when Somerset had released me. Instead we had a brilliant Christmas. Hannah and I spent lots of time together and I was just buzzing about what the future might hold. And it was nice because Hannah never knew me as a player, so she didn't know about all the pain and disappointment I'd been through. Obviously I've told her since, but our relationship was fresh, it didn't have the burden or the baggage of those dark times.

The positivity continued into the new year. In January 2016, I was put forward for the position of player coach at Wokingham by a guy called Sam Bracey, who manages the Elite International Cricket Academy at Hampshire. Wokingham had asked Hampshire to recommend some coaches and Sam put me in touch. Unbeknown to us at the time, both Dan and I went for the role, although we only found out later on in the process. And it was a proper process. We had to interview for it, and as we progressed through the process it became apparent that it was a job for more than one person, so they ended up asking us both to do it.

Not long after that, in the spring of 2016, I got in touch with Iain Brunnschweiler, who had been our strength and conditioning coach when I was at Hampshire and was also, by then, working for the ECB. I asked Iain if there were any opportunities he could put my way, and he told me to come along to Loughborough to work with the under-19s. Talk about full-circle! I did a few sessions with the 19s but it didn't last long term, which was fine. It was a great experience to work at Loughborough again, this time as a coach. And I had a feeling I'd be back again, before too long…

By the summer of 2016 things had built up quite nicely. I was coaching kids at schools and clubs around Yateley, as well as coaching – and playing – at Wokingham with Dan. I was enjoying my coaching and I wanted to progress further, so enrolled on the ECB Performance Coach Course (Level 3).

I started working on that course in the second half of the year, while keeping all my coaching roles going at the same time. It was hard work, but I felt like my coaching style was evolving and improving all the time. The Level 3 would hopefully open doors for me within the professional game. And it worked, because in early 2017 Sussex and Hampshire both got in touch, wanting me to do some work with their academy keepers, which was a fantastic opportunity to land.

At Hampshire I was working with the girls in the Southern Vipers' academy. It was strange to be going back to the Ageas Bowl in a work capacity after everything that had happened, but I've got to say that everyone I saw there, all the coaches, the staff and of course all the players, were good as gold to me as soon as they saw me back. It was like coming home, and I was delighted to be back there working with some of the talent coming through the academy programme, like I'd done a decade earlier.

Mark Robinson, who by then was the Head Coach of the England Women's team, came along to one of the Vipers sessions, to see how some of the girls were getting along. I'd known Mark from when I was playing for England under-19s, when he was our head coach for the World Cup in New Zealand.

We caught up after that training session, and chatted about what we'd both been doing since last we'd seen each other, which in my case was quite a lot. I told him about my fledgling coaching career and he asked me what level of coaching qualifications I was working on. He encouraged me to keep working on it, to keep expanding my skillset so that I could offer more as a coach. Ironic really, as that's what I should have done as a player, too.

It was a great chat. One of those you walk away from with a spring in your step. Especially when you're just starting out in a new line of work, as I was. He told me that I was very much on his radar, to keep getting as much coaching experience as I could, and that he would keep me in mind should anything come up with the England Women's team that he was in charge of, which was a fantastic boost for me.

Like in all lines of work, if you know plenty of people in cricket, chances are someone will be able to help you out at some stage. The work I did at Sussex was an example of that. I got that gig through Carl Hopkinson, the Academy Director at Sussex, who like, Robbo, I'd known from my playing days with England under-19s as well. Hoppo was the fielding coach back then, working under Mark Robinson for our World Cup campaign.

When I went down to Hove, I again saw Robbo at one of my sessions. He lived in the area, and on that occasion he said he'd just popped along to have a look, but perhaps he was checking my coaching out.

Not long after that second meeting, in February 2017, Robbo called me up and asked me to come up to Loughborough to run a few sessions for the England keepers. So back I went to Loughborough, this time to coach Sarah Taylor and Amy Jones, England's finest female wicketkeepers, for an hour a week. What an absolute honour. While I was there, Robbo would also ask me to help him out with some other drills for the wider team. He had definitely taken me under his wing by that stage, which I was very thankful for.

I was flat out, and loving my work. And clearly doing something right as the calls kept coming in. Around that time Trevor Griffiths, Head Coach of Kia Super League side Western Storm, got in touch to ask me to join his backroom team. Trevor had been asking around at Taunton, where the Storm play, for people who might be suitable for his coaching team, and I was recommended. I told you the coaches thought a lot of me at Somerset!

Trevor and I arranged to meet at a service station halfway between Exeter – where the Western Storm trained – and Hampshire, to discuss what he was after. We had a good chat and by the end of lunch he'd asked me to join as Assistant Coach and Batting Coach. So within a month I'd added two fantastic opportunities to my coaching portfolio, allowing me to work with some top international players – some of the best in the world.

Then, before the start of the 2017 county season I got another call from Hampshire, this time to come and work with Hampshire's new first-choice keeper, Lewis McManus. He was keen to have a catch-up and a chat about a few things ahead of the new season, a fresh pair of eyes on him before what was going to be a big season for him. I could empathise with him, he was in a very similar situation to the one I'd found myself in five years earlier. Lewis had replaced Adam Wheater behind the stumps towards the end of the previous season, a bit like I'd done to Skeg in 2011. Wheats had since returned to Essex in the close season, meaning Lewis was Hampshire's first-choice gloveman going into 2017.

He wanted to understand how I'd handled being the main man at such a young age, and also how I'd coped taking over from a more senior guy behind the stumps. Working with England under-19s, up at Loughborough, and now this – history really was repeating itself.

* * *

Organisation is one massive difference between playing and coaching cricket. When I was a player I'd be told where to go, when and with whom, pretty much every day of the season. Now I was coaching I had to arrange my own schedule, and with all these different sessions going on, ensuring I wasn't double-booked on any given day was absolutely massive. I walk around with an enormous, A4-sized diary in my bag, so that whenever someone wants me to do anything with them, I first check in my diary to make sure I can do it. It took a lot of discipline to get to that stage of organisation, but it's absolutely vital now I'm so busy.

Towards the end of March 2017 my Western Storm duties first kicked in. We had three weekend camps with a development squad of about 15 players from the south-west region. We put the girls through their paces, getting to know their games and their temperaments before, at the end of the third weekend, we selected eight players to take into our final Western Storm squad. Those eight would then be joined by six international players, who would come into the squad following the Women's World Cup in July, ready for the start of the Kia Super League, which began in early August.

After the Western Storm trials, I was back up to Loughborough to get England wicketkeepers Sarah Taylor and Amy Jones ready for a two-week fair-weather training camp in Dubai. And with the Women's World Cup, which was in England that year, also just a couple of months away, Robbo wanted me to get Sarah and Amy as sharp as possible ahead of what was going to be a huge tournament for us on home soil.

The fact I was there as a keeping coach was obviously ideal for me. I had a lot to say on technique and posture, most of which I've mentioned in my wicketkeeping masterclass chapter earlier. But I also had plenty to say on the mental side of the game too.

Robbo asked me to get involved in some other drills, which was great. I took the whole squad for fielding drills, which was something new for me. And I also ran some batting drills, which I really enjoyed. I had a lot to say from a batting perspective. I may not have lit the world up with my own batting, but the struggles I'd been through had made me learn more about myself and about the art of batting, and that was definitely something I could pass down as a coach now.

Working with the England girls was great; all the stuff I'd done up to that point had been a good experience, but working at this elite level really pushed my coaching ability forward, and that gave me huge confidence in my methods. Plus I loved the fact I was coaching women. They were all great girls and they really welcomed me into the group straight away. They all wanted to learn, and were really interested in hearing about my experiences. It was great to see how much of an impact I was having on them. They really took everything I said on board and it was a pleasure to be involved with the group. When you're coaching blokes, you need to win over their trust a bit more. But the women respected the level I'd played at and were just fantastic to coach.

With the World Cup in England that year, Robbo was keen to take the girls to Lord's, where the World Cup final would be held. He wanted the girls to visualise themselves there at the final. "This is where we start, and this is where we want to end," Robbo said to them at the ground.

Being back at Lord's conjured up mixed emotions for me. After all, this was where that career-defining moment in the CB40 final had played out five years earlier. I took a moment to sit, on my own, in the members' area. I looked out at the lush green turf, recalling the last time I'd been there. Even then, with the ground empty and silent apart from the hushed chatter of the girls walking around the pitch, there was an aura, a barely audible buzz about the place. It was magical. Time stood still for a moment, restarted only by the conflicting thoughts colliding around in my brain. On the one hand I was proud of what I'd achieved at this place half a decade ago. On the other I was gutted I wasn't still playing.

We left Lord's, and soon enough I was back focusing on the job at hand. The past was the past, and although I did still have those moments where I really missed my old life playing, I was also excited by the successful start to coaching I'd made.

I worked with Sarah and Amy every week through May. It was all high-volume stuff, working a lot with the ramp, the plastic orange wedge I'd trained with myself years earlier. (I told you it was a good piece of kit!)

Then we played some warm-up matches, the first of which was against the West Indies at Loughborough on 7 June. Those warm-ups all went really well, and everyone in the group – the players, the coaches and all the support staff – felt like we were in a really good place going into the tournament.

Throughout the build-up, Robbo was at pains to stress to the players that we were on a journey that didn't end at the conclusion of the tournament ahead of us. So while we were all thinking about the World Cup, Robbo would re-emphasise that the series of games ahead of us were simply part of a longer journey, and that defeat at any stage wouldn't actually be the end for this team, even if it was for us in the tournament.

That was a message Robbo had delivered from the day he walked into the job, all the way through the various series the team had played, including this World Cup on home soil, massive though it was. It was said so often that eventually, the players bought into it and if you spoke to any one of them, they'd tell you that exact same thing.

There's no doubt the girls went into that tournament with less pressure on them, and Robbo deserves tremendous credit for altering the mindset, and relieving some of that pressure.

And with that relaxed but assured mindset, we headed into our first World Cup game, against India at Derby on 24 June 2017. Our preparation had been meticulous; the fair-weather training in Dubai, the months of sessions at Loughborough, the visualisation exercise Lord's and Robbo's inspiring words. Now, in Derby, we were ready to put all that work into practice. The girls were all in a good place, they all seemed pretty chilled before the game. There were no injury concerns, and all Robbo's messages seemed to have been taken on board.

However, when they took to the field, that calmness and positivity evaporated before our eyes. Instead of cool, calm and collected, the occasion got to the girls – massively – and they were convincingly beaten by a strong India side.

India were good, but we were so bad. The result was totally unexpected, and so out of character with how the team had performed in practice, and in the warm-up matches a couple of weeks earlier. Instead, here at Derby, they looked nervous, and just didn't play how we all knew they could.

After the game Robbo was really calm. He told the girls that the occasion had simply got the better of them, to forget it, that there was a long way still to go in the competition and that they were going to put it right. The format of the competition was one group of eight teams, with teams playing each other once. The top four would then qualify for a semi-final, meaning we still had another six games left to put things right.

In a way, it was a good reality check having cruised through those warm-up games. Had we breezed through that opening game against India, we might have become complacent and not properly kicked into top gear. It's always better to have a shocker in the first group game than in the knockout stages. Sometimes these things just happen. Remember the one I put down at Lord's in the CB40 final in 2012? That moment had kicked me into gear that day. Maybe this defeat would do the same to the girls.

We certainly hoped so. And when we arrived in Leicester for our second game against Pakistan just three days later, the girls seemed focused, with a determination to put things right in that game. And they did, winning comfortably, a result that we hoped would kick-start our entire campaign.

In the changing room afterwards, the girls were buzzing again. To be honest, though, they had been all the way through. And that wasn't just down to the cricket, although obviously that helped. Robbo had also arranged for the girls to spend the whole tournament "on tour", so they would stay in a team hotel all tournament rather than going home between matches, and would travel to games and training sessions together on a team bus. Even if we had a game near to a player's home town, they'd stay with the group. It was another masterstroke from Robbo, because it kept everyone in the bubble together. They were like a family, having fun together, eating and drinking together, relaxing together, enjoying each other's successes, but there to support each other should things go wrong.

That support network was absolutely vital. At the start of the competition, Anya Shrubsole wasn't in a great place mentally. Her game just wasn't quite there and she lacked a little bit of confidence as a result. Being in and around the group all the time would have been a great support for her, and as it would turn out, that support would prove vital come the end of the tournament.

I wasn't staying in the hotel with the squad. As I was part of the wider back-up team, I stayed at home and hooked up with them for games and training sessions. Those sessions were pretty light on the whole, just keeping Sarah and Amy ticking over throughout the tournament. They wanted to work on a couple of specifics at different points, but it was more about keeping them sharp, but also keeping them relaxed before each game. As I'd found when I was a player, you can't re-engineer technical aspects of your game when you're in the middle of a big competition, so my role was to keep the girls sharp, but not overdo them.

I can honestly say that the whole environment Robbo created around the squad was absolutely perfect, and the girls totally embraced it and were having the time of their lives. It reminded me of my career, travelling around with my mates, staying in really nice hotels, looking and feeling very professional, and being really well looked after by the hotel staff, the drivers, pretty much everyone you came into contact with.

We thrashed Sri Lanka and South Africa in our next two games, but our fifth, against Australia, would be a lot tougher. If we beat the Aussies, we'd qualify for the semi-finals with two games to spare, so we were keen to get the job done at Bristol. But obviously the Aussies had other ideas, and were desperate themselves to beat us and halt our progress in the competition.

The game was hard fought, but somehow we managed to scrape a win. It was one of those games where perhaps we didn't deserve to win. The dot ball percentages and the powerplay comparisons were all against us. We batted first and we kept losing wickets, meaning we didn't get a total we thought was big enough.

But equally it was one of those games where neither team really pulled away from the other. In the end they needed four off the last ball to win, and we managed to restrict them to a single. It was a great win, and we were into the semi-finals.

Away from the cricket, and the training, the girls were really good at getting out and about and exploring their surroundings, wherever they were staying. We moved around the country, staying in hotels close to our next game, and each time we arrived at a new hotel the girls would get out and have a look around the new town. Again, Robbo was a driving force behind that. He was big on keeping the group relaxed between games, and the girls bought into that completely.

We demolished the West Indies and New Zealand in our last two group games meaning we qualified as group leaders, setting up a rematch with South Africa in the semi-final at Bristol.

In the group game Tammy Beaumont and Sarah Taylor had scored big hundreds to secure a 68-run victory against the Saffers. And in the semi-final it was Sarah once again who excelled, with both the bat and gloves this time. She top-scored with the bat as we chased down South Africa's total of 218-6, while with the gloves she pulled off a stunning leg-side take and stumping that any keeper in the world would've been proud of.

I was delighted for Sarah. She is world class, a multi-dimensional cricketer, and a genuine all-rounder. If Gilchrist is the archetypal modern-day wicketkeeper in men's cricket, then Sarah is his equivalent in the women's game. In fact Gilly described her as the "greatest of all time" on Twitter not so long ago – high praise indeed. She is a serious, serious player. In 2015 she went to Australia to play men's Grade cricket, the first woman ever to do so. That's how good she is.

From a keeping perspective she is exceptional. She makes things happen when she stands up to the stumps. She creates chances out of nothing, like that phenomenal leg-side stumping in the semi-final – a high-pressure situation, but her glove work was immaculate. She had no right to take that, let alone effect the stumping. But that's the beauty of keeping up to the stumps in limited-overs cricket, something Sarah is extremely good at.

And me being me, a specialist wicketkeeper if ever there was one, seeing Sarah's level with the gloves is perhaps another reminder that, if you can find a truly multi-dimensional cricketer where the strengths of their games in both disciplines are that high, well, that's a massive feather in the cap of multi-dimensionals over specialists. Put simply, having someone as good as Sarah in your team is like having two players for the price of one.

And the crazy thing is I think she could get even better. It's fair to say, and she'd say this herself, that she hasn't always worked as hard on her keeping as she could have done. So from a coaching perspective it's quite exciting to see how far she could go with her glovework in the future, because there's capacity there for her to get even better. She's an exceptional talent and it was a pleasure to coach her. It still is.

Chapter 15
Glory days are here again

The relief of making it to the World Cup Final at Lord's was massive. We'd done what we'd set out to do, and we couldn't wait to go back to the Home of Cricket where we'd face India, the team we'd lost to in our first game of the tournament.

But before the final itself, we had a few days in London to try to relax. One day, the girls went out on the Boris bikes to go sight-seeing, which was great because the last thing us coaches wanted them to do was to loiter around the team hotel, building up lots of nervous energy. I should know, that's what we did at Hampshire before Finals Day in 2011, and that definitely didn't do us any favours! The girls going out was a great way of keeping everything calm, which was especially important given we had a World Cup Final at Lord's to look forward to.

The days leading up to the final seemed to go on for ages, but eventually Sunday 23 July 2017 came around, and we were off to Lord's for the biggest game of the girls' lives. It was another surreal day returning to NW8, given everything that had happened there for me. I definitely felt torn to be back there; I was loving being a coach, but equally there was still a part of me that wanted to be playing. Also, because I was only really coaching Sarah and Amy, I wasn't as involved as much as I would be with the Western Storm during the Kia Super League a few weeks later, so I was a little more removed from the action as a result.

I didn't sit with the players and Robbo on the Lord's balcony during the game, which is a lot smaller than it looks on TV and therefore couldn't accommodate all of the backroom staff. Instead I watched in one of the corporate boxes along with Alex Davies, the men's wicketkeeper from Lancashire, who was dating Alex Hartley, one of the bowlers in the England women's team.

When we arrived at Lord's, there was a real energy and sense of excitement around the group. Just being at Lord's will do that to you. The grand staircase with its warren of adjoining corridors. The Long Room, with its high ceilings and museum-like displays of artwork. The changing rooms, with the green leather seats. The stands surrounding the pitch, which bristle with energy as soon as the fans start pouring in.

We were all excited, even us coaches. And there was a confidence oozing through the camp that we *would* do it. The girls had worked so hard to get there, and there was a lot of excitement for what lay ahead in the final as a result. Robbo was really good at keeping them all level-headed though. He was constantly talking about how the final was just another game in that journey he'd talked about all tournament. It was a great approach, to keep contextualising each match as "just another game". We knew this was massive, but by constantly bringing it back to just being this one match in the team's journey, it meant the girls really relaxed, and approached the final with more confidence as a result.

Even now, if you speak to any of the players in the England group, they will always say that the up-coming game, be it an Ashes series, or a World Cup Final as in this case, was just another match. It's good to win, but it's not the be-all and end-all. Robbo had instilled that viewpoint from day one, when he took the job on, and now it's ingrained in all the players. It's a great way of taking the pressure off and, you'd have to say looking back at the tournament as a whole, that it worked massively.

At Lord's that Sunday, the ground full – it was magical. The weather was dry, warm and sunny some of the time, but not constantly. It was perfect weather for cricket, at the perfect place. It seemed to take an age for the cricket to actually get going, but when it did, we knew right away we were in a contest. We were batting first, and India bowled really well, taking wickets at regular intervals. But our guys didn't panic. We pulled together as a group and posted a competitive score of 228-7. The girls felt like they were in the game when they went out to bowl. Although on the face of it, with a total like that, it was always going to be tight.

Still, India made us work hard for it – as you'd expect in a World Cup Final. At one stage they needed just 47 runs to win from eight overs, with seven wickets still in hand. You'd have to say they were favourites at that stage. But our bowlers this time stayed calm and kept plugging away. Then Shrubsole got their danger-woman Raut out LBW for 86, and we were back in business.

From that point, we always looked assured in the field. Always looked like we believed we'd do it. It reminded me of that great Hampshire side I'd played in five years earlier. We just always seemed to grind out the win. We just knew how to get over the line, no matter what challenges we encountered in games. And that's exactly what England did on that amazing day at Lord's, in front of a packed house of 28,000 spectators, and an unprecedented TV audience of over 100 million people watching worldwide. Astonishing.

By the time we got to the penultimate over, India needed 11 off 12 but they were gone. They were eight wickets down and they just looked beaten. Shrubsole bowled that final over, and it was simply her day, no doubt. She'd struggled in the first part of the tournament, but she came good when it mattered. That's the nature of professional sport sometimes. At the start of that tournament she was really emotional because her game was off. Yet in the final she smoked it, and now her name is synonymous with that match. Professional sport can be a fickle thing.

In that final over, Anya took a wicket with the first ball, putting us on the edge of victory with India nine down. Then two balls later Jenny Gunn dropped an absolute sitter at mid-on. It was testament to the belief and courage of the team that we didn't let that become the "Jenny Gunn dropped the World Cup" moment. Next ball, Shrubsole bowled a decent yorker right in the blockhole, and it was game over. We'd won the World Cup!

Over in the corporate boxes, I was overwhelmed by emotion. I was so chuffed for the girls, I was shouting and screaming and clapping my hands until they were burning. But I have to admit that part of me was also gutted, that it wasn't me out there still playing. That feeling of winning a final in front of a crowd like that, as a cricketer, as a sportsperson, there's nothing better. And I couldn't help feeling like I was missing out.

Katherine Brunt's family, who were in the box next to Alex and I, were crying their eyes out at what Katherine – and all the girls – had achieved. They'd been there all the way through Katherine's cricket journey, playing to empty crowds when no one seemed interested in women's cricket. Compare that to now, winning the World Cup in front of a packed Lord's with over 100 million watching around the world, what a journey they'd been on. And what a moment this was for England women's cricket.

Watching the celebrations from up in the stands was like an out-of-body experience for me. But there it was, unfolding before us on the fabled hallowed turf of Lord's. The girls went wild, some running around the place, arms aloft, others sinking to their knees in tears. Others cuddling in groups, the look of utter joy and complete disbelief at what they'd just achieved, etched all over their joyous, sweaty faces.

Then the initial euphoria died down. Players did their interviews, before the group was invited to take to the hastily assembled stage on the pitch. The trophy was presented, then hoisted into the air by Heather Knight, our skipper. Then it builds again. The players sprayed each other with champagne, each passing the trophy round the group so that everyone could enjoy their moment with it. Then the cameramen took their photos, and the players took selfies which fans would later see plastered over various social media channels.

And before you know it the crowd empties, the players finish their lap of honour and head back to the changing room, which is where Alex and I headed to meet up with them all. When we got there the celebrations were in full flow. It's at that point where, I think, players sit down and really take in what's been achieved. Anya was quite emotional, she'd come back from a bad start in the tournament to play a huge role in us winning, taking six wickets on the day to finish Player of the Match. She was moved by the sheer relief of nailing it when it mattered, at the very highest level.

Then there were speeches. England's Director of Women's Cricket, Clare Connor, had arrived in the room, and looked as happy as anyone. As a former player, Clare knew the enormity of that moment, having been through so much in her own playing career. Clare talked about what a huge achievement this was, how it would impact the women's game massively in the country, if not the world with those record viewing figures.

We were at the ground for a long while. The girls sang, they chanted, they did their drinking fines. They soaked it all up and enjoyed every moment. Eventually we moved into a hospitality room where media, ex-players – basically anyone who could blag their way in – was there. It was a free bar, so everyone was filling their boots. And their glasses.

Eventually the girls went back to the hotel with the intention of hitting the town after, but most of them didn't make it out again. These occasions are such massive moments in your life, the adrenaline is pumping all day, and once the initial euphoria of winning and the first few celebratory drinks go down, you realise that actually, you're really, really fucked – mentally, physically and emotionally. And it's time for bed. Those nights are rarely the big sessions you'd imagine.

As the girls headed back to the hotel, I went to the train station to make my way home. It had been a fantastic tournament to be involved in. It was amazing to be involved in an elite cricket environment like that, with people like Robbo who I'd known for so long. I was humbled to have been accepted by the girls, and to have played a small part in such a huge success. I felt privileged, and a couple of days later I sent Clare Connor an email thanking her for the opportunity of being involved in what was a huge moment in the history of women's cricket.

It was the highlight of my coaching career so far, no doubt. I'd put so much work into the players during the tournament, particularly Sarah and Amy. And for that effort to contribute in some small way to us winning the World Cup, was just a brilliant feeling. I'd seen at first hand how much this meant to the girls. They'd worked so hard, as had Robbo and all the coaching staff. It was a fantastic effort all-round, and it was great that it captured the imagination of everyone, with Lord's full to the brim, and people in their millions watching on their TV sets around the world.

But still, as I sat on my train back to Yateley, the top button on my white shirt undone, my suit jacket discarded on the baggage rack above my seat, I reflected on a rollercoaster of a day filled with mixed emotions. I can't tell you how much I missed being a player that day. Just to have had the chance to be out there one more time, experiencing such a high while playing with my mates. Those were the dreamland moments, for any professional sportsperson. But at the same time I also thought, wow, if I can get this kind of a high from coaching, without the pressure of actually playing, then this could be the next best thing. To feel that complete elation when we won, I just didn't expect it, and it was as good a feeling as if I'd actually been playing myself. Well, almost.

You can somehow be more taken away with emotion as a coach than when you're playing. When you're playing you're so wrapped up in the moment, you almost don't appreciate what you've actually achieved. As a coach you can take it all in much more, you're watching the game as a whole and although you've coached the players in advance you can't affect the game once they've gone out there.

That game was a turning point for me. It was the moment I realised I could get the same – or very similar – buzz from the game by coaching, as I did when I was playing. Also, I felt I could be a better coach than I was a player, drawing on my experiences – the disappointments, as well as the highlights – when working with players. As my train travelled through the Hampshire countryside towards Yateley station, I realised that my career was heading in a different direction now. I was finally done with playing.

* * *

If the World Cup was a big moment in my professional career, something just as huge was about to happen in my private life. Just after the World Cup final, I moved out of Mum and Dad's and into a place in Fleet with Hannah. We'd been dating for about two and a half years by then and things were going really well, so moving in together was the next logical step. My coaching career was going well, and Hannah had just started her career as a pharmacist following years of studying and training, meaning we were both in a decent position financially to take the step.

Of course as a man of nearly 27, it was nice to finally move out of Mum and Dad's. Again. As much as I love them both dearly, I hope that will be the last time they ever have to bail me out!

Everything always comes at once, doesn't it? No sooner had I moved into our new place, things with the Western Storm were kicking off, too. In fact, just two days after the World Cup Final I was back to work with the Storm, getting ready for the Kia Super League, the women's T20 franchise competition.

In that first week at the end of July, we worked exclusively with the domestic players, as the international girls had been given a break following their World Cup exertions. Our head coach, Trevor Griffin, was really enthusiastic about our chances that year. We'd lost in the final to our arch-rivals the Southern Vipers the year before, and Trevor was desperate to go one better in 2017.

As assistant coach, I led a lot of the team coaching sessions with the Storm. And part of my role was to be the batting coach, an interesting juxtaposition given my travails with the bat during my playing career.

But I learned so much about batting during my playing days, that actually it's made me a better coach in that respect. One thing that really sticks out for me, that I didn't do enough of when I batted, was thinking more about the game. Thinking about the game actually makes batting easier. When I was playing, I was naïve in thinking that if I didn't think about my batting, it would be easier. But actually, thinking about the technical and tactical aspects of the game, that awareness and appreciation of the wider context of what you're doing and why you're doing it, really helps you perform better with the bat.

To illustrate the point, I refer you back to the innings I played against Gloucestershire in 2012, when I was on 87 and Hampshire were just a few overs away from saving a game we'd looked certain to lose. That innings I'd batted instinctively, in the moment. I played my natural game, even in those dying moments when a draw suddenly looked odds-on, after hours of us dangling on the precipice. In my mind I wasn't thinking about anything. Not about the context of the game, not about wanting to get through to my hundred. Nothing. I just wanting that feeling of batting well to continue.

What I've found through my coaching is that if I'd actually been a bit more methodical about that innings, if I'd have thought, "I'm 13 away from a hundred here, and we're six overs away from drawing the game, this is what I need to do to achieve both objectives," I would have stood a far greater chance of achieving both goals. Instead I was almost too relaxed, to the point of almost being ignorant about the state of the game, and my own career in terms of my stats, as well as the chance of adding another hundred alongside my name in the stats book.

Reflecting on those moments definitely helps me as a coach now. Some batters I've worked with, they play like I used to. They play instinctively, they don't think about their technique, or what they're doing when it's going well – they just let it roll. The problem with that approach is that when things don't go so well, they find it harder to pinpoint the weakness, or the problem. Because they never think about their game, about what's working when it goes well, which means they can't analyse their technique when things are going badly. As a result, it takes longer for them to get back to their best.

At Western Storm, we worked really hard in the week before the international girls arrived. We wanted to get the domestic girls up to speed before the international girls came into the group, so that when they joined us, they'd be really impressed by the level the others were performing at.

There was a bit more to it than that. Trevor and I had discussed in advance the idea that the international players on each team would essentially cancel each other out. There was some real talent in the tournament, and while some may play better than others in specific games, generally you'd expect their levels to be consistently very high. So when we played Lancashire Thunder, for example, we'd expect our keeper, Rachel Priest, to more or less match Sarah Taylor. Obviously one of those players could have a blinder and the other a shocker on the day, but generally their performance levels would be similar.

The difference between the teams therefore was going to be the performance of the non-international girls. So we put a huge amount of effort, not just that week, but in the sessions earlier in the summer, trying to get the levels of the domestic girls as high as possible. We worked tirelessly, on their batting and bowling, getting them all into really good shape ahead of the tournament.

Another thing we were adamant about was wanting to be the best fielding team in the competition. From my own experience with Hampshire, I knew that if we could be immaculate in the field, it would make a massive difference in most games. So we did a lot of high-intensity fielding drills in that first week, firing the ball at the stumps from various angles, retrieving balls on the run and throwing them in to the keeper, sweeping on the boundary, throws from deep, catching practice – everything you can think of. Anything we could do to get the girls up to speed, drawing on all my experience from my coaching qualifications, but also my time at Hampshire in particular.

Then the following week, the international girls joined us. Each team was allowed three overseas players and three England internationals. Our England players were World Cup-winners Heather Knight, Anya Shrubsole and Fran Wilson, with our overseas being West Indies all-rounder Stafanie Taylor and New Zealand pair, keeper-batter Rachel Priest and bowler Holly Huddleston.

This was the second season of the Super League, and other than Holly – who was a new signing for 2017 – it was Trevor's second time working with these guys, and he rated them all highly. When I got the chance to work with them in that week before the tournament started, I could see why. As with the England women's team, they were all a coach's dream to work with; open to new ideas, hard-working, keen to progress and desperate to do well for the team. The whole squad was brilliant, it was a great group.

With all that positivity flying about, we headed into our first game against our bitter rivals, the Southern Vipers, on Thursday 10 August, feeling buoyant. As we sat in the coach on the way to Southampton for the game, I remember feeling really confident about what we could achieve in the competition. When we got to the Ageas Bowl, I grabbed a quick coffee with Woody, and I told him, "Mate, we've got something special here – I think we could win the competition!"

But just like the England women had done in their first World Cup game just a few weeks earlier, we got absolutely trounced in our competition opener! We batted first and were all out for 70. The Vipers' star player, Suzie Bates, knocked off an undefeated 47 in no time and they won by nine wickets, with 11 overs to spare. It was a demolition job, and utterly humiliating. After the game I got a text from Woody, simply saying, "Up the Vipers!" Cheers for that, mate!

That game was my first experience as a coach where I felt helpless, completely unable to affect proceedings on the pitch. I'd been involved with England but that was more of a backroom role. Here, I was

Trevor's right-hand man. I'd led most of the training, and this was not what we trained at all. Instead, it was a shocking performance. Truly shocking.

Obviously we knew at halfway we were extremely unlikely to pull this one back. So as the Vipers batted their way to victory at the Ageas Bowl, Trevor and I discussed how we were going to deal with this result from a coaching perspective. Trevor suggested we just let the result sink in after the game, and not have a complete rant at the players. It was a horror-story performance and, from the players' perspective, they knew they'd had a shocker. They didn't need us standing up in front of them, shouting and screaming. There was no benefit in us berating them. What would it actually achieve?

And that's where coaching experience is so important. Because I was ready to let it rip! We'd worked so hard in the weeks leading up to that first match; on the way to the ground just a few hours earlier we'd been thinking of winning the competition, not losing in humiliating fashion like this.

But that's the thing about coaching, you have to pick your moments. What might work for you as a coach; the satisfaction of giving the group a bollocking, might not have been the right solution for the group. A coach's job is to pick the right moment, challenge the players in the right way, and at the right time. We knew this result was an aberration, so did the players. By keeping quiet, almost giving the players the silent treatment if you like, the players would know that what they'd delivered was unacceptable. I mean, they knew that anyway. But us shouting at them would make them get annoyed with us. By staying quiet we would keep them annoyed with themselves.

At the end of the match, we slipped onto our bus and left the Ageas Bowl as quickly and as quietly as possible. On the bus there was a stunned silence. No one said much at all, and when we got back to our training base in Exeter, everyone just headed to their cars and drove home.

The 48 hours that ensued were odd. Frustrating. Each of us individually playing around what had happened in our minds. I wanted to get together as a group and discuss the game, get it all out in the open and then move on. But with another game on Saturday at home to Loughborough Lightning, we had to focus on our preparation for that, and almost put the Vipers calamity to one side.

When Saturday morning came, we all met at the café in the County Ground at Taunton, where the game would later be played. We all exchanged pleasantries and then sat down to eat. The players were all a bit sheepish, and clearly the Vipers game was the great big elephant in the room. But no one brought it up.

It was a difficult one. We had a game to prepare for, so we wanted to focus all our energy on that. Bringing up that shocking performance from two days earlier might have killed the mood, before what was now a crucial game against Loughborough. We left the café and headed to the changing room back at the ground, where finally after quite a tense and drawn out morning, we did actually discuss the Vipers match.

Now, women's changing rooms with male coaches around.... It must be awkward, you might be thinking. To be honest, I've never really thought about it. It's only when writing this book that I've paused to think it might be worth explaining. Trevor, Jon Pitts and I, and the other male members of the backroom team, are obviously present in the changing rooms at all times with the girls.

We hold team talks in there as we would do in a blokes' changing room, but I guess there is a slightly different vibe in a women's changing room. Speaking for myself, I am aware of the girls changing, and obviously give them some space. But to be fair they're always in sports bras and they're all pretty comfortable with us being around anyway, so it's not really an issue. Women's changing rooms are slightly different to the balls-out nature of men's changing rooms, so there are never any real issues.

Anyway, on this particular occasion, there was a bit of tension around the room. The girls were all sitting, listening intently to Trevor, who'd stood up in the middle of the room to give his view on the game in Southampton. Then, totally out of nowhere, Trevor just keeled over. It was like someone had turned him off, he just slumped to the floor.

It was a shocking moment. Eventually he came to, and thankfully, he was fine. He was a bit dazed, but OK. It turned out that Trevor had taken the defeat to Vipers a lot worse than he'd let on. He told us after his fall how he'd hardly slept since, hadn't eaten and his body basically shut down at that point.

Trevor was definitely giving his all to the Western Storm. He'd put so much thought into everything. He'd brought me in, hoping I could get a little more out of the team than the year before. Pittsy was another interesting recruitment. He was there as a performance coach, a psychologist. It was a brave decision by Trevor to get Jon in to do that. Aside from our internationals, the rest of our squad were all amateur cricketers. When they weren't with us, they were normally playing club cricket on a Saturday, and doing other jobs in the week.

They were unlikely to have had any dealings with a sports psychologist before, so it really was an innovate move from Trevor.

Pittsy was great for the team, and he did some fantastic work with lots of the girls. Claire Nicholas was one. Claire was an amateur off-spinner, who had been thrust into a squad with World Cup-winners Anya Shrubsole and Heather Knight. Pittsy worked with Claire to help her learn to relax in this elite environment, so that she could perform to her potential and feel like an equal surrounded by these superstars, which she most certainly was.

Our Kiwi, Rachel Priest, was another player who Jon helped. Rachel came to us from the World Cup distraught after her New Zealand side had totally underperformed. Pittsy did a lot of work with her early on in the Super League, to try to give her a confidence boost – or "pump up her tyres", as we used to call it – to get her into a positive frame of mind for the Super League.

After Trevor's collapse, I didn't really know what to do. He was OK, but without wishing to sound unsympathetic, we had a game to prepare for. In the end me and Jon put on a warm-up session out on the pitch for the players. We pulled together, the girls were great, and we had a brilliant session. It's funny, because you plan the perfect preparation for the players before a match, and something like that happens and it all goes out of the window. We'd lost our first game, so we needed a performance that day. Then that happens. Disaster.

But despite what happened that morning, when the game started the girls were brilliant. They went out against a strong Loughborough Lightning team and got us the victory we needed. Our campaign was up and running. Maybe we could win it after all…

The group stages were nip and tuck all the way through. The Super League is made up of six teams, and each team plays each other once. In our final group game we beat Sarah Taylor's Lancashire Thunder side to book our place at Finals Day. Another Finals Day – they seem to follow me around! Not that I'm complaining, of course.

Finals Day in 2017 was at the small, picturesque ground at Hove, with benches and deckchairs dotted around the boundary on one side of the ground, which is barely a 10-minute walk from the beach.

The format of Finals Day is slightly different to the men's version. Here, the top three teams from the group stages qualify, with second and third competing in a semi-final, for the right to play the group winner in the final.

We'd finished third in the group, meaning we'd need to beat Surrey Stars in the play-off to set up a final with holders the Southern Vipers, whom we'd lost to in the previous year's final. And we were going to have to right a couple of wrongs from our group matches this year if we were to win, having lost to both Surrey and the Vipers in our group games.

As a result, we went to Hove as massive underdogs, something we reminded the girls about in the build-up to, and on Finals Day itself. In those scenarios I think a coach can really earn his or her salt. Although we'd set out our stall at the start of the competition to win it, we were now in the situation where the pressure was on the other teams. They'd both beaten us in the tournament already, so they'd be expecting to beat us here. Maybe a little complacency would set in, which was certainly something we'd be hoping to take advantage of.

As we'd done throughout the competition, we put a lot of focus on fielding practice, both leading up to Hove, and on Finals Day itself. We wanted to be really tight in the field, while we hoped that our domestic girls would be better than their opposite numbers. It was such a huge occasion for those guys, playing at a full, compact ground with the TV cameras present. This in the immediate aftermath of the women's World Cup, where interest in women's cricket had grown exponentially, so this was a massive occasion.

But we needn't have worried, because in that semi-final, the domestic girls were phenomenal, to a woman. Jon Pitts has to take some credit there, because he'd done some fantastic work with them all. For one, off-spinner Claire Nicholas was phenomenal all day, opening up the bowling for us with her darty off-spin. We called Claire, "CT", because her maiden name was Thomas, and the nickname CT had stuck, even when she subsequently got married and her name changed to Nicholas.

Before the semi-final, Trevor and I had had a chat with our skipper, Heather Knight. We thought we should bowl CT through at the start of the innings. Heather had been reluctant to do so earlier in the tournament, pulling her out of the attack after one or two overs and saving her for later on. But Trevor and I felt we needed to go shit or bust against Surrey. We had to get wickets up top, get off to a decent start and put Surrey under pressure early doors, in the hope that the rest of the match would take care of itself. It was an aggressive move, but such is elite sport. Sometimes you've got to back your team to deliver the goods.

And against Surrey, the plan worked perfectly. We bowled brilliantly, and we took them completely by surprise. As we'd suggested, Heather bowled CT through from the start, which worked a treat as her four overs went for just 14, while she also picked up the key wicket of Tammy Beaumont. And on top of our bowling, our intensity in the field was exceptional too, another part of the masterplan we'd flagged at the start of the competition.

We managed to contain Surrey to 100-7, which was a very gettable total. Our response wasn't shy of a few little wobbles, but eventually we managed to get over the line. Stafanie Taylor got us there with a brilliant 37 off 45 balls. She was a bit of a Neil McKenzie type of character for us. She'd block for a bit and we'd be thinking "What is she doing?" But ultimately she'd get us over the line, and that match was another big performance from the brilliant West Indian.

As a coaching unit we'd already discussed what we'd do if we got through to the final. It would be a quick turnaround, so we gave the girls 15 minutes to get a bit of food down them, and then we were back on the pitch warming up for the next game. We wanted to recreate the same process which had worked so well all competition. We went through the same warm-up routine, the same drills, everything was meticulously planned. As I looked around the group, I had a feeling, a confidence, that we were going to win the final.

Vipers batted first and we definitely looked a little fatigued in the field. Understandably so after that semi-final. But all the way through, even when the Vipers were going well, I had this overwhelming sense that we were going to chase whatever total they set us. I don't know where that confidence came from, because although we'd won the semi, we'd made a bit of a meal of chasing 100. But still, I believed.

Vipers ended their innings on 145-5, which was a decent total and as with high-tension matches like this, runs on the board always puts pressure on the chasing team, which was obviously us in this scenario. Suzie Bates and Dani Wyatt had got starts for the Vipers, 20s or 30s, but no more. And that was the message to our girls at half time. One of our experienced girls would need to go out there and convert a start into a big one.

And it was Rachel Priest who took it upon herself to do just that. She came in at the top of the order and took the Vipers down. She didn't like the Vipers anyway, and wanted to win it for us so badly. In one over, Priesty took Linsey Smith apart, smashing 26 off her. The Vipers were visibly shaken by that over, and that was our moment.

Eventually Priesty fell for 72, becoming the leading run-scorer in the tournament with a sensational knock. But there was still a little bit of work to do. We were 94-3 at that stage, and still needed another 52 runs to win.

Stafanie Taylor was joined at the wicket by Sophie Luff, another of our non-international players, and the pair saw us home, both finishing on 30 not out. Stafanie won it with a six, handing us the trophy in style, with two overs to spare. Cue the inevitable scenes of the girls running onto the pitch to join Stafanie and Sophie. There was hugging, screaming and shouting filling the early evening air at Hove – we'd done it, we were the champions!

On a personal note and in contrast to the World Cup Final which had been an overwhelming experience, that moment at Hove was pure joy. I was so pleased for all the girls, and I was so chuffed that the coaching drills and techniques we'd implemented, which I'd been at the heart of this time, had come off. It was so satisfying to think that some of the methods I'd instilled had ultimately helped us win that trophy.

As Trevor, the other coaches and I headed onto the pitch to celebrate with the team, this wasn't a crazy dash around, a wild moment of unadulterated joy. This was a sense of a job well done, of course. But for me, personally, this was the start of the future for me.

This was what I wanted to do going forwards; working with players, with teams, coaching them using my beliefs and methods, developed while playing at Hampshire in that great, successful one-day team of the early 2010s. I wanted to help players achieve their potential, exceed their potential, something I never did.

I couldn't stop smiling all night. I'd watch the girls going through their moments of euphoria. I'd said to them to enjoy it, like Macca, Jimmy, Katich and Dimi had said to me back at the Rose Bowl, at the SWALEC and at Lord's. They probably took about as much notice of me as I did of those guys, but I had to try.

Cricket, professional sport – like real life – it goes round in circles. Now it's my time to watch the next generation of players coming through and have their moments of pure joy. As I watched the girls from the side of the pitch at Hove I just knew, finally, that I was done with the dream of playing again. I'd done my bit. I'd devoted myself to wicketkeeping. Had I come up short? Well the success I'd achieved would suggest otherwise, even though I was young when I last played a game of county cricket.

As for the future of wicketkeeping? Sarah Taylor wasn't at Finals Day that day, but having worked with her earlier in the summer, I knew that she was it. She is a multi-dimensional keeper with glovework as good as a specialist, and with batting better than most of her peers. She's the future. Jos Buttler was right, the keeping of the best multi-dimensional wicketkeepers in the world has improved massively, and I'd include Jos in that bracket. Their keeping is so good now, that when you add it to their batting, you have almost two players in your team for the price of one. They're exceptional.

I'd given playing my all. But now, on a late summer's evening on the south coast, I was finally happy, ready, to wave my playing days goodbye for good. It was time to focus 100% on my new career as a coach. Time to look forward to a life living with Hannah, and who knows what else to come in the future.

Standing on the Hove outfield on a dark, and now somewhat chilly evening in Hove, I watched on with pride as the players went through the presentation; receiving their medals, Heather being given the trophy and then hoisting it high into the air, champagne flying, then players scattering around the ground with some doing interviews, others going to see their families and friends. Their smiles were as wide as the beaches just a short walk away from us.

It was strange. I'd done what they were doing so many times myself in the past, it was like I was watching myself years earlier, going through these amazing experiences as a player. Like an out of body experience.

But this is me now. A coach, on the outside looking in, as opposed to a player inside the cricket bubble itself.

Later we headed back to the changing room where I sat, opened a beer and grinned. It was a smile of satisfaction. A smile of hope, that the future could be this good, or even better still. A smile of pure joy, that while my own playing career was definitely done, I'd finally found a way to be at peace with that decision.

I may not have kept up with the modern, multi-dimensional demands of wicketkeeping. But in coaching, just maybe, I have found something I can really kick on with and be good at.

Epilogue

It's been a long, and at times painful journey to this point in my career. But I'm finally at peace with my decision to leave my playing days behind; I love being a coach, and I'm buzzing to see what comes next – both on the cricket pitch, and away from it.

It was such a tough call to stop playing. In many respects it was taken out of my hands having been released by two counties; I could have ploughed on, playing club and minor county cricket alongside a part-time job, desperately hoping for a short-term county contract to come my way. But I would have been reliant on county keepers suffering injuries or loss of form and, frankly, I felt I deserved more than that.

I played to a really high standard, won competitions and played starring roles in those successes. I worked hard, stayed focused and lived my dream; it just felt brutal in its brevity. Eventually I had to take the hint; it just wasn't going to happen for me. Ultimately, in the winter of 2015, that's what I did.

I'll always hold the view that my batting was good enough for first-class cricket. Maybe breaking into the first team at such a young age did come too soon, and knocked my confidence with the bat. My keeping was ready, but my batting clearly wasn't when I made my debut at 19.

Then again, what do you say to your coach? "Sorry gaffer, I'm just not ready to play in the first team yet" – you'd be laughed out of the changing room.

Maybe my coaches should have spotted that mental fragility in me, rather than pressing ahead with making me the first-team keeper at just 21 years of age. You don't have to be Sir Alex Ferguson to know that, when blooding young players into a first team, it's important to ease them in gently. You don't want to rush things, it's about allowing the player time to adapt, mentally as well as physically, to the new environment. The new demands.

I didn't get that kind of support from Chalks – or any of my coaches for that matter – when I broke into Hampshire's first team. Not in an emotional sense at least. Instead I was thrown the gloves because my keeping was ready, in the hope that my batting would catch up. Too much was left to chance. Hampshire should have asked Nic Pothas to stay at the club. That would have given me more time to bed into the role, while giving the club a credible backup option in case I was struggling. It would also have suited Nic as an aspiring coach.

Alas, it didn't work out for me. But the fact is, it doesn't for a lot of young players. I may feel hard done by because I got into the first team and did well, for a period of time at least. Or so I thought. But the vast majority of players don't get anywhere near the first team. I was one of the lucky ones.

And that's the point. For anyone passionate about getting into professional sport, it's imperative that you keep assessing and improving your game. Your contribution to your team is ultimately what makes or breaks your career, and it's up to you to push yourself as far as you can, to give yourself the best chance pf progressing in your chosen field.

I did discuss my batting with Chalks at a chance meeting at the Ageas Bowl not so long ago. I was there to work with Lewis McManus in the summer of 2017, and ran into Chalks in the Atrium. We had a coffee and a chat, and I thought I'd ask him directly what he thought I could have done differently to overcome my batting frailties. It was a candid conversation, and Chalks spoke a lot about those mental barriers that clearly existed for me. It was the kind of conversation I craved during my playing career; it could have benefited us both, had it happened while I was still on the playing staff.

That said, telling the guy picking the side that you're not feeling too confident about your game is difficult. Maybe it shouldn't be. An open and honest dialogue between player and coach should work for both parties – and the team, which is the most important thing of course. Certainly in my coaching career now I encourage honest dialogue between my players and I, and I think the players value that. There's an appreciation that there will always be a natural limit on what a player feels they can say to a head coach or director of cricket, because at the end of the day they're the ones picking the team each week. To have an openness builds a trust and a respect between the team and the coaches which helps everyone move forwards.

I also spoke to my academy coach at Hampshire, and now the batting coach at the Ageas Bowl, Tony Middleton. I wanted to know what Tony thought I could have done differently to cement my place in the first team. His answer was unequivocal, and totally unexpected. "I felt you fulfilled your potential," Tony said. He told me he felt I never quite scored the runs I maybe should have done – even as a youngster. He thought my batting was always a little below the curve, and never quite made the grade. "It is bloody difficult to establish a career and sustain it," he concluded. He was always unswervingly honest, was Tony.

Tony's words were brutal, but I respected his candour. Obviously I didn't agree with him. I felt my batting *was* good enough, but wasn't given time to develop, and I wasn't given the emotional support that could have helped me reach the levels required. I guess we'll always have contrary viewpoints on that one. I felt I'd proven myself capable of batting in first-class cricket, my hundred at Headingley proof of the (Yorkshire) pudding. I accept that I wasn't consistent, but then the moment I had a downturn, Adam Wheater was brought in to replace me. It's hard to sustain your level when you're discarded in such brutal fashion.

I also sat down with Lewis McManus, Wheater's successor behind the stumps at Hampshire. I wasn't anywhere near as switched on as Lewis is when I was his age. Lewis is mature, as a bloke but also in a cricketing sense, which I think ultimately I lacked when I was starting out. He told me how much it had helped him playing alongside me in the seconds several years earlier. He referenced a match in which we racked up a big partnership, both of us scoring big hundreds. He said how much he'd learned from batting with me in that innings, how to bat long and build a partnership. It's nice to think I was able to help him, as guys like Simon Katich did with me years earlier.

Lewis also talked about my professionalism, how I always trained really hard and prepared well for each match. Obviously I was still playing at that stage, but that attention to detail is definitely something I've taken with me into my coaching. The better you train and prepare, the better you play – it's as simple as that. That's something I always impress on my players now.

While my playing career may have been cut short, I'm proud of the way I conducted myself on and off the field during my time as a professional cricketer. Doing the right things is a discipline and it's extremely important to build that into your approach – that's definitely something I would encourage any young cricketer reading this book to take from my story.

Now, a couple of years on from hanging up my bat and gloves, I'm delighted with where my life is at, both personally and professionally. Hannah and I are still living together in Fleet, and I'm still really enjoying my coaching work with the Western Storm and England women. I'm even working with the keepers down at Hampshire on a regular basis now too – life moves in some mysterious ways!

My journey through cricket is not unique. I'm not the only one to endure a disappointing end to their playing career, and I definitely won't be the last. Reading my story, there may be moments when you may feel I was hard done by, but that is professional sport – only the strongest survive. I'm not sitting here typing away with a massive chip on my shoulder. In fact, I'm one of the lucky ones. I've experienced massive highs, played professional sport for a number of years, represented my country at under-19s level. It was hard to be rejected, but what I achieved was still massive, and something I'm hugely proud of.

As a wicketkeeper, I am just one example of how the game has changed so fundamentally in such a short period of time. We've talked about the advent of one-day cricket, and the impact Adam Gilchrist has had on the wicketkeeping position more generally. I'm not the only specialist keeper whose career has been adversely impacted by teams looking for more multi-dimensional equivalents. James Foster is another fantastic keeper, yet he managed just seven Tests for England – 20 years earlier and he might have had 100 caps.

Sharing my story with you, and discussing my career playing alongside the likes of Joe Root, Sam Billings and Jos Buttler, to mention just a few, has been a massive privilege. Hearing Joe Root tell me that he's frustrated that I'm not still playing first-class cricket is a moment I'll never forget. Nor will I forget the tiny voice inside my head saying to me, "Damn, should I give it another go?" as I drove away from our Bristol meeting.

Those conversations were absolutely fascinating. They allowed me to get inside the minds of some of the best cricketers in the world. It made me realise how all of them, ultimately, just had that little bit more nous about the game, in terms of what was required from them, than perhaps I did. They'd seen the need to contribute more to the teams they were trying to establish themselves in. And that, ultimately, has been the difference.

In Sam's case, he knew he needed to contribute more with the bat, while with Jos it was bringing his glovework up to the required level. Hearing those guys talking about how they themselves identified the need to offer more to their respective teams was, for me, the most important thing to take away from this whole book. It was the realisation that I'd been too focused on my keeping, when perhaps I should have considered how I could give more to the team than I was already doing. Maybe then I could have nailed down my spot in that Hampshire side.

Teams are still looking for multi-dimensional cricketers – if anything that trend is growing. Look at how many all-rounders make up the middle order of England's Test side now. Every player down to number nine can bat and bowl, that's just the way modern cricket is. It gives a captain more options on the field, while it's more cost-effective for counties too, as they don't need as many players on the payroll.

And as Jos Buttler said, the gap between a player's perceived weaker skillset compared to their strongest is shrinking; if Sam Curran is coming in to bat for England at number eight or nine, they still have a player who is more than capable of scoring runs with the bat at the crease. The risk of a tail being blown away just isn't there in the modern game now. If anything, the strength of a team's lower order goes a long way to deciding the outcome of a game of cricket – particularly in Tests.

I have fabulous memories of playing cricket; trophy-winning moments, the likes of which most players can only dream of. Winning at Lord's with that final-ball dismissal – I'll never forget that moment.

But now I'm happy, and comfortable with where I'm at in the game. I'm really excited about my coaching career. I've experienced that buzz of winning as a coach, and that makes me excited to build on that and experience more of those moments in the future.

Of course it's different, and there are many aspects to coaching that I actually prefer to playing. I enjoy not being under that intense pressure and scrutiny that comes with playing. The mental aspect in sport is colossal, and it takes all you have to remain calm and strong at times. Plus, coaching a player, and seeing a difference the next time they play, is utterly rewarding. Whether it's working with the brilliant Sarah Taylor with England, or the young keepers in Hampshire's academy, talking them through something, "Could you try this next time?", and then seeing that demonstrated in a match down the line, is just such an amazing feeling.

Plus I'm still involved in the game I love, so for that alone I am really thankful. When the season is in full flow, I'm out there doing what I love doing; I'm outside, at cricket matches, watching the game and talking about it all the time, but without all that pressure of playing. I'm in the cricket bubble, but I'm able to come out of it as and when I choose.

I'm really delighted with how my coaching skills are developing. I feel like I have a natural flair for it, I can relate to the players because I've been where they are. I've struggled as a player, and have learned from the difficulties I went through at Hampshire and Somerset. That has definitely helped me as a coach. I'm more empathetic than I might have been, had everything gone to plan for me as a player. Particularly as a batting coach. I can really relate to players suffering mental challenges with their batting, and that allows me to give them advice to help them through it – the advice I never received.

I'm grateful for the feeling that I get directly rewarded for my efforts as a coach, whereas when I was playing that wasn't always the case. When I was playing, I'd put in all the work and then get a good nut first ball and I was out. As a batter you fail more than you succeed, and dealing with that mentally is so tough. As a coach, I put in the hard work and I tend to see the results.

I'm in control of my own life now. My itinerary, the things filling up my diary, are arranged by me. As a player, everything was arranged for me. I'd be told where to go, and when, and I'd just have to turn up and do my thing. It can be chaotic, especially as a county cricketer, constantly travelling between games, or training for different matches. One day you're preparing for a Championship game at Hove, a few days later it's a one-dayer in Durham.

Who knows where my latest career path will take me? I've experienced unbelievable highs already, and I'm only just getting started. I want to coach at the highest level, and in cricket you don't get any higher than the England team.

If I were to give young players reading my story some advice I would say, follow your dreams, work hard, and enjoy every moment of it. I would also say, if you really are serious about making it to the top of your chosen profession, constantly re-evaluate yourself. Look at what you can improve on, and work hard to put those things right. In a cricketing sense, if you feel you can add more strings to your bow, by developing your skills in the areas of the game you're not so good at, then do that. The more ways you can benefit a team, the better the chance you have of being selected – and retaining your place in the side. Ultimately cricket is a results business, and you need to be able to contribute to the cause, or you'll be out.

Remember, enjoying what you do is the most important thing. There's so much pressure on kids to make it in sport now. Natural talent comes into it, as does hard work, but ultimately you have to truly love your sport, otherwise the passion to perform and improve will eventually wain, as distractions emerge through your teenage years.

Playing sport, at any level, is the best thing in the world, and it's also one of the hardest. I've been blessed to do it professionally for a number of years, and I'll be forever thankful. I may not be keeping up anymore, but now I'm looking forward to teaching my methods and beliefs about the game I love to all the talented keepers coming through the ranks across the country.

What a blessing.

See you at the boundary's edge.

Michael

Printed in Great Britain
by Amazon